Environmental Justice in South Africa

Environmental Justice in
South Africa

edited by

David A. McDonald

Ohio University Press
Athens

University of Cape Town Press
Cape Town

Ohio University Press
Scott Quadrangle
Athens, Ohio 45701

University of Cape Town Press
P.O. Box 24309
LANSDOWNE
7779
Cape Town, South Africa

Published in the United States of America by Ohio University Press,
Athens, Ohio 45701

Published in South Africa by University of Cape Town Press, Cape Town, 8000

Library of Congress Cataloging-in-Publication Data

Environmental justice in South Africa / edited by David A. McDonald.
        p. cm.
    Includes bibliographical references and index.
    ISBN 0-8214-1415-1 (alk. paper)—ISBN 0-8214-1416-X (pbk. : alk. paper)
        1. Environmental justice—South Africa. I. McDonald, David A. (David
    Alexander)

GE240.S6 E58 2001
363.7'056'0968—dc21

                                                          2001036344

Contents

Acknowledgments

The genesis of this book dates back several years and I thank all the contributors to this volume for their commitment to seeing the project through. I would also like to thank Gillian Berchowitz of Ohio University Press and Solani Ngobeni of the University of Cape Town Press for their commitment to publishing the material. The comments of an anonymous referee were extremely useful, as was the hard work of Christina Decarie and Meg Freer in bringing the final manuscript together. Chris Albertyn assisted in the early stages of the book and I thank him for his support throughout.

Copyright permission for the short narratives has been given by the Environment and Development Agency (EDA) and the Environmental Justice Networking Forum (EJNF). Victor Munnik (EDA) and Amos Dube (EJNF) assisted with this copyright process. The second and fifth narratives in this volume were originally published in *Land & Rural Digest* (No. 5, March/April 1999 and No. 6, May/June 1999). The rest were originally published in *Voices from the Ground: People, Poverty, and Environment in South Africa,* published by EJNF in 1998 (and edited by Gillian Watkins). EJNF's Senior Journalist, Mpume Nyandu, visited and interviewed communities around the country so that people's experiences of poverty, inequality, and the environment could be told in their own words. By reproducing these stories here it is hoped that these voices will find an even wider audience. In return for this copyright permission, and in an effort to assist with the work of the EDA and the EJNF, all royalties from sales of this book will be donated to these two organizations.

I would also like to thank the many people in the environmental justice movement in South Africa with whom I have had the pleasure and the honor of working over the years. The energy and commitment of these individuals and organizations is extraordinary and gives me hope for a more just and sustainable future in South Africa.

And finally, thanks to Lea, Hannah, and Eli, in whom I see the inspiration for environmental humanism every day.

Note on Racial Terminology

Although apartheid-era racial classifications are a social construct with no objective significance, the legacies of apartheid and the heavy correlation between race and class in South(ern) Africa are such that racial classifications remain an integral part of political analysis in the region. There are, however, many different versions of racial terminology and a brief explanation of the use of terms in this book is in order. Following the tradition of the democratic movement, "African," "coloured," "Asian," and "white" will be used to describe the four major apartheid racial categories in South Africa, with the most common use of upper- and lowercase letters being adopted. The term "black" is used to refer to Africans, coloureds, and Asians as a whole, in recognition of their common oppression under apartheid.

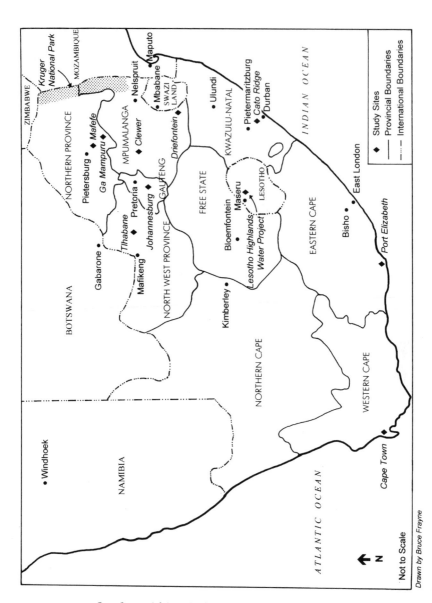

Southern Africa, Indicating Sites of Research

Drawn by Bruce Frayne

Introduction

What Is Environmental Justice?

David A. McDonald

The history of environmental policy in South Africa is a cruel and perverse one. Under colonial and apartheid governments, thousands of black South Africans were forcibly removed from their ancestral lands to make way for game parks, and billions of rands were spent on preserving wildlife and protecting wild flowers while people in "townships" and "homelands"[1] lived without adequate food, shelter, and clean water. Whites-only policies in national parks meant that black South Africans could not enjoy the country's rich natural heritage, and draconian poaching laws kept the rural poor from desperately needed resources (Beinart and Coates 1995; Carruthers 1995). In short, flora and fauna were often considered more important than the majority of the country's population.

As a result, black South Africans (and anti-apartheid activists in general) paid little attention to environmental debates during the apartheid era. At best, the *environment* was seen to be a white, suburban issue of little relevance to the anti-apartheid struggle. At worst, environmental policy was seen as an explicit tool of racially based oppression.

With the easing of apartheid legislation in the late 1980s and the

1

unbanning of anti-apartheid political parties and activists in the early 1990s, all of this changed. The liberalization of South African politics created discursive and institutional space for a rethinking of environmental issues, and a vibrant debate on the meaning, causes, and effects of environmental decay began in earnest. Perhaps the most fundamental of these developments was the simplest: a broadening of the definition of ecology. Once the *environment* was redefined to include the working and living space of black South Africans it quickly became apparent that environmental initiatives were akin to other post-apartheid, democratic objectives. A wide range of trade unions, nongovernmental organizations, civic associations, and academics quickly adopted the new environmental discourse and within a few short years began to challenge the environmental practices and policies of the past (Cock and Koch 1991; Ramphele and McDowell 1991).

Central to this new discourse was the concept of environmental justice—a language that found its first concrete expression in 1992 at a conference organized by Earthlife Africa, entitled "What Does It Mean to Be Green in the New South Africa?" (Hallowes 1993). The conference brought together leading South African environmentalists and academics with their counterparts from around the world in an attempt to map out a future for the environmental justice movement in South Africa. One of the outcomes of the conference was the creation of the Environmental Justice Networking Forum (EJNF), a nationwide umbrella organization designed to coordinate the activities of environmental activists and organizations interested in social and environmental justice. The network rapidly expanded to include 150 member organizations by 1995 and well over 600 member organizations by 2000.

With the election of the African National Congress (ANC) in 1994, the environmental justice movement had an ally in government as well. Noting that "poverty and environmental degradation have been closely linked" in South Africa, the ANC made it clear that social, economic, and political relations were also part of the environmental equation and that environmental inequalities and injustices would be addressed as an integral part of the party's post-apartheid reconstruction and development mandate (ANC 1994, 38). Indeed, the new South African Constitution, finalized in 1996, includes a Bill of Rights that grants all South Africans the right to an "environment that is not harmful to their health and well-being" and the right to "ecologically sustainable development" (section 24).

Environmental Justice in South Africa provides an overview of this relatively new environmental justice movement in South Africa: its history in the 1990s; where it stands today; and where it might (or should) be headed in the future. In the same way that the edited collections of *Going Green* (Cock and Koch 1991) and *Restoring the Land* (Ramphele and McDowell 1991) captured the changing environmental tenor of the late 1980s and early 1990s, this book attempts to outline the key theoretical and practical issues facing the environmental justice movement in South Africa ten years on. How have things changed? What has remained the same? What are the most (and least) effective strategies for environmental activism and how do we conceptualize environmental justice in South Africa in the twenty-first century?

We begin here with a brief discussion of the meaning of environmental justice and then move on to discuss the organization and purpose of the book in more detail.

Defining Environmental Justice

At its core, environmental justice is about incorporating environmental issues into the broader intellectual and institutional framework of human rights and democratic accountability (Wenz 1988; Bullard 1990; Capek 1993; Bryant 1995; Cutter 1995; Goldman 1996; Harvey 1996; Heiman 1996; Dobson 1998; Schlosberg 1999; Bowen and Haynes 2000). The term necessarily encompasses the widest possible definition of what is considered "environmental" and is unrepentantly anthropocentric in its orientation—placing people, rather than flora and fauna, at the center of a complex web of social, economic, political, and environmental relationships. Most important, it concerns itself primarily with the environmental *in*justices of these relationships, and the ways and means of rectifying these wrongs and/or avoiding them in the future. Locating a toxic waste site next to a poor, black community simply because it is poor and black, for example, is an environmental injustice that violates basic human rights and democratic accountability and demands remediation and prevention.

At this most basic level, it is easy to see why the environmental justice movement in South Africa has been able to attract a significant following. Forcibly removing people from their ancestral land, without any consultation or compensation, to make way for a game park is wrong by most moral standards. Spending millions of rands on municipal services for one group of people and not providing the most basic necessities to others is simply undemocratic. Environmental inequities of this sort are so manifestly unjust that it makes sense to speak of an environmental justice movement to address them.

The following definition of environmental justice from the quarterly newsletter of the South African Environmental Justice Networking Forum captures these basic philosophical tenets and exemplifies the focus on human and democratic rights that is so central to environmental justice movements and literature worldwide:

> Environmental justice is about social transformation directed towards meeting basic human needs and enhancing our quality of life—economic quality, health care, housing, human rights, environmental protection, and democracy. In linking environmental and social justice issues the environmental justice approach seeks to challenge the abuse of power which results in poor people having to suffer the effects of environmental damage caused by the greed of others. This includes workers and communities exposed to dangerous chemical pollution, and rural communities without firewood, grazing and water. In recognizing that environmental damage has the greatest impact upon poor people, EJNF seeks to ensure the right of those most affected to participate at all levels of environmental decision-making. (EJNF 1997)

Beyond these core principles, however, there is much that fragments the environmental justice movement. One reason is that the movement lacks a coherent theoretical framework. There are wide differences of opinion, for example, on the relative importance of race, class, and gender, and there are major splits on the potential for reform in a market economy. Even the efficacy of judicial procedure (i.e., whether the courts are an effective means for addressing and preventing environmental injustices) is a matter of debate.

This diversity of opinion is not surprising. As the survey literature on environmental theory makes clear, there are simply too many underlying methodological and ideological differences in environmental thought to allow for any neat conceptualization of environmental justice (Pepper 1993; Merchant 1994). Ecofeminism, ecosocialism, deep ecology, ecological economics, and social ecology all have a claim of sorts to being concerned about *environmental justice* insofar as they pay attention to how environmental resources and their by-products are distributed (within and across generations) and the inequitable power relations that lead to environmental injustices. Even the World Bank can claim to be concerned about environmental justice (although it does not use the term), given its emphasis on poverty alleviation—particularly for women and children—and the improvement of basic infrastructure like sewerage and sanitation (World Bank 1992, 1994). In other words, the environmental justice literature—defined here by its concern with environmental inequalities and democratic accountability—is far from homogenous and is in fact riven with deep ideological splits on foundational questions such as race, class, and gender.

This lack of coherency is not necessarily a problem. On the contrary, the diversity lends itself to a wide range of social circumstances and ideological positions, drawing people and organizations into an ecological movement they might not otherwise have connected to. This has certainly been the case in South Africa, where trade unions, civic organizations, democratic activists, and environmentalists of many stripes have joined a loosely aligned environmental justice movement. Membership in the Environmental Justice Networking Forum has included such diverse interests as the Transport and General Workers Union, the Trust for Christian Outreach, the Wilderness Leadership School, and the Help End Marijuana Prohibition in South Africa Society. Together these organizations have contributed to the building of an important new movement in the country and have placed the central concerns of environmental equity and democratic accountability firmly on the South African environmental policy agenda.

But ideological tensions are not far from the surface. An environmental justice movement as diverse as this in its political orientation and demographic composition is bound to have deep splits. Moreover, with the end of formal apartheid has come a whole new set of highly contentious environmental questions: Should South Africa trade with China? What are the implications of signing the Kyoto Accord? Are market-based land reforms appropriate? Should municipal services be privatized? The adoption by the national government in 1996 of a fiscally conservative approach to reconstruction and development through the Growth Employment and Redistribution (GEAR) policy has been particularly divisive of the democratic movement in the country, and these divisions are beginning to surface in the environmental justice movement as well. Funding and organizational issues are also a factor here, with historically white, suburban environmental groups accounting for the lion's share of financial resources and organizational capacity, while most township-based environmental groups struggle to make ends meet, often breaking up after a few years of effort.

Can these institutional and ideological tensions continue to exist under the banner of environmental justice in South Africa? Is it still possible to reap the benefits of a broad coalition of interests with core beliefs in the environmental rights and dignity of human beings? What are the best ways forward in this regard? What might the environmental justice movement in South Africa look like in another ten years? These are difficult questions to which there are no easy answers. Nor does this book pretend to have the answers. What it does provide is a historical and theoretical account of the environmental justice movement and an overview of what environmental justice has meant in practice since the early 1990s. Not every environmental justice issue in the country is covered—there is no dedicated discussion of land reform, for example—but the book does include many of the key environmental justice concerns in the country and raises conceptual issues that cut across all environmental justice activities.

Structure of the Book

Drawing on the ideas and experience of leading environmental activists and academics in the country, the book is loosely divided into three parts: theory, practice, and narrative. The first four chapters cover key theoretical debates on issues of environmental justice and provide a historical account of the environmental justice movement in South Africa, its links to the American environmental justice movement, and its relationship to the anti-apartheid democratic movement more generally. The remaining chapters are case studies of particular environmental justice issues in practice, from efforts to reform the national parks to the legislative options available to environmental activists.

Interspersed between these chapters are brief accounts of environmental justice struggles in the country. From the survival strategies of people who make a living from a waste dump to the tragedies of asbestosis and mercury poisoning, these nine stories offer powerful examples of the extent and depth of environmental injustices that continue in South Africa to this day. The stories are also a reminder of the ability of individuals, organizations, and communities to challenge their situations and serve as a beacon of hope for a more environmentally just future. Observations by Archbishop Njongonkulu Ndungane on the significance of the environmental justice movement in South Africa, which follow this introduction, set the stage for these vignettes.

Chapter 1 looks at the roots of environmental racism and its relationship to the rise of environmental justice in South Africa. Environmental racism, argues Farieda Khan, is a powerful conceptual rallying point for environmental activists seeking to address racial inequalities in South Africa, but also appears, more controversially, to affect the way that environmental groups themselves operate. With the largest and best-funded environmental groups in the country dominated by white, middle-class activists, Khan asks why an equally effective black environmental group has not emerged after a decade of environmental justice activism.

Marginalization is the central theme of the chapter by David Hallowes and Mark Butler who consider the effects of neoliberal policy reforms and globalization on the ability of poor communities in South Africa to address their own environmental situations and suggest ways of conceptualizing and strategizing these matters.

Chapter 3 is a long-overdue discussion of gender and environmental justice in South Africa. Drawing on a diverse range of ecofeminist and environmental justice literature, Belinda Dodson argues that there is fertile common ground between these two broadly defined schools of environmental thought, and asserts that a recognition of this commonality would lead to a more theoretically coherent and practically useful approach to women and ecology in South Africa.

Greg Ruiters's critique in chapter 4 of environmental justice theories is perhaps the most challenging to the environmental justice movement in South Africa, arguing as it does that too much attention has been paid to race and the process of positive law and not enough to the importance of place and the politics of production. Ruiters goes on to propose a "transitional" view of environmental justice that takes cognizance of both the site-specific and universal aspects of environmental inequalities.

Chapter 5 is an analysis of the South African National Parks by Jacklyn Cock and David Fig. As noted earlier in this introduction, the national parks system was the epitome of racist conservation in South Africa under the colonial and apartheid regimes. The parks system is now struggling to overcome its institutional and ideological past, and this chapter provides a critical analysis of the evolution of this process and of its successes and failures in the 1990s.

Chapter 6 is an environmental analysis of the largest single industry in South Africa—mining. As the engines of economic growth for over a century, mining companies operated with virtual environmental impunity, producing a legacy of solid waste and water contamination that will take another century to remedy. No one has been more directly affected by this environmental fallout than mine workers and the communities that live adjacent to the mining sites and dumps. Thabo Madihlaba takes us inside one such community—Clewer—in the mining heart of South Africa to see just how much (and how little) has changed. New environmental legislation has provided the framework for environmental redress by poor communities, but mining firms, it would appear, are still solidly in the driver's seat when it comes to environmental reforms.

Chapter 7 provides a comprehensive overview of the constitutional and legislative reforms enacted since 1994 in relation to the environment and offers a litmus test of the environmental "justice" system. The oft-quoted constitutional right of all South Africans to an "an environment that is not harmful to their health or well-being" is only one of many constitutional and legislative reforms introduced by the African National Congress (ANC) that offer a formidable array of judicial tools to challenge environmental injustices. Most of these legal tools, argues Jan Glazewski, have yet to be tested in a court of law, but their potential is impressive and they could lead to the formalization of an otherwise abstract set of environmental "rights."

We return, in chapter 8, to another case study of environmental injustice with a look at the South Durban Community Environmental Alliance's struggle to stop the extension of a toxic waste site in South Durban. Bobby Peek describes the solidarity building that led the community alliance to fight the waste site as well as the evasive tactics employed by the company (and to a lesser extent the Department of Water Affairs and Forestry) to enable them to continue with the dumping. South Durban is situated in one of the most intensely industrialized and polluted areas of South Africa, and this case study helps shed light on the future of community resistance to environmental problems for the country as a whole.

Patrick Bond takes us outside South Africa in chapter 9 for an analysis of the Lesotho Highlands Water Project (LHWP). More than twenty-five years in the making, the LHWP is one of the largest infrastructure projects in the world, and, at 185 meters, Katse dam is the highest in Africa. Dams are always socially and environmentally controversial, and the World Bank–supported Lesotho project is no different in this respect, with villages displaced by rising waters and striking workers shot by Lesotho police. But the project is also controversial because of its impact on South Africa. Intended to provide water to Gauteng, the thirsty industrial and domestic heartland of the country, the first flows of water have in fact not even been needed (and may not be needed for more than a decade) and would appear to have had the environmentally unjust consequence of raising the price of water for those who can least afford it. In revealing these injustices, Bond provides a critical insight into the politics of water use and conservation in the region.

The role of trade unions in the environmental justice movement is the subject of chapter 10. Peter Lukey looks at the efforts of organized labor in the past ten years to address environmental health and safety for its membership and paints a mixed picture of success and failure. He argues that the age-old tension of "jobs versus the environment" is the main conceptual stumbling block to a more proactive and effective environmental justice stance by unions, and offers a possible short-term solution to this conundrum. As one of the most powerful nongovernmental voices in South Africa, trade unions have a critical role to play in environmental justice, and their positions on these issues are central to the future of the movement as a whole.

In the final chapter of the book, David McDonald looks at the growing trend to privatize municipal services in South Africa and the impact this is having on the urban poor. The lack of basic services like sewerage and sanitation for millions of urban South Africans is arguably the most pressing environmental justice problem in the country today. The government has made impressive strides in providing these services, but the needs are overwhelming and the state has been turning to the private sector to assist with this task. Although this privatization is only in the early stages of development, there is cause for alarm at the short- and long-term environmental justice implications of having the private sector provide these services. McDonald highlights the most problematic areas.

Intended first and foremost for a South African audience of environmental activists, academics, and decision makers, the book should also resonate with international readers interested in the growing field of environmental justice. South Africa is, in many ways, a microcosm of the world, with a wealthy minority of people overconsuming, and an impoverished majority underconsuming, both contributing to environmental degradation. These inequalities symbolize the kinds of disparities that exist between the "haves" and the "have-nots" on an international scale and help shed light on the globalization and standardization of environmental injustices worldwide. The similarities between environmental racism in South Africa and the southern United States, for example, and the parallels between the privatization of municipal services in Cape Town and Buenos Aires, are powerful reminders of the need to move beyond the particular geographic and issue-specific elements of many environmental justice struggles and to see these events as part of a global shift in the production of environmental "goods" and "bads."

In the end, there are no neat conclusions to be drawn from the book. The environmental justice movement in South Africa has come a long way in a short time, but there are tensions simmering below the surface. The future of environmental justice in the country is thus both exhilarating and challenging, and the material in this book will help map out its various possibilities.

Note

1. Township refers to urban areas of formal and informal housing that were designated "blacks only" during the apartheid era. Homeland refers to rural

areas designated as "blacks only" under apartheid, some of which were declared "independent states" by the apartheid regime but were not recognized by the international community.

References

ANC (African National Congress). 1994. *The Reconstruction and Development Programme*. Johannesburg: Umyanyano Publications.

Beinart, W., and P. Coates. 1995. *Environment and History: The Taming of Nature in the USA and South Africa*. London: Routledge.

Bowen, W. M., and K. E. Haynes. 2000. "The Debate over Environmental Justice." *Social Science Quarterly* 81 (3).

Bryant, B. 1995. *Environmental Justice : Issues, Policies, and Solutions*. Washington, D.C.: Island Press.

Bullard, R. D. 1990. *Dumping in Dixie: Race, Class and Environmental Quality*. Boulder, Colo.: Westview Press.

Capek, S. 1993. "The 'Environmental Justice' Frame: A Conceptual Discussion and an Application." *Social Problems* 40 (1): 5–24.

Carruthers, J. 1995. *The Kruger National Park: A Social and Political History*. Scottsville: University of Natal Press.

Cock, J., and E. Koch, eds. 1991. *Going Green: People, Politics and the Environment in South Africa*. Cape Town: Oxford University Press.

Cutter, S. 1995. "Race, Class and Environmental Justice." *Progress in Human Geography* 19 (1): 111–22.

Dobson, A. 1998. *Justice and the Environment: Conceptions of Environmental Sustainability and Theories of Distributive Justice*. New York : Oxford University Press.

EJNF (Environmental Justice Networking Forum). 1997. *Environmental Justice Networker*, Autumn.

Goldman, B. 1996. "What Is the Future of Environmental Justice?" *Antipode* 28 (2): 122–41.

Hallowes, D., ed. 1993. *Hidden Faces: Environment, Development, Justice: South Africa and the Global Context*. Scottsville: Earthlife Africa.

Harvey, D. 1996. *Justice, Nature and the Geography of Difference*. Oxford: Blackwell Publishers.

Heiman, M. 1996. "Race, Waste and Class: New Perspectives on Environmental Justice" (editorial introduction to special issue on environmental justice). *Antipode* 28 (2): 111–21.

Merchant, C., ed. 1994. *Ecology*. Key Concepts in Critical Theory. Atlantic Highlands, N.J.: Humanities Press.

Pepper, D. 1993. *Ecosocialism: From Deep Ecology to Social Justice*. London: Routledge.

Ramphele, M. and C. McDowell, eds. 1991. *Restoring the Land: Environment and Change in Post-Apartheid South Africa.* London: The Panos Institute.

Schlosberg, D. 1999. *Environmental Justice and the New Pluralism: The Challenge of Difference for Environmentalism.* Oxford: Oxford University Press.

Taylor, D. E. 1989. "Blacks and the Environment: Toward an Explanation of the Concern and Action Gap between Blacks and Whites." *Environment and Behavior* 21.

Wenz, P. S. 1988. *Environmental Justice.* Albany: State University of New York Press.

World Bank. 1992. *World Development Report 1992: Development and the Environment.* New York: Oxford University Press.

———. 1994. *World Development Report 1994: Development and the Environment.* New York: Oxford University Press.

Environmental Justice, Peace, and Prosperity

Archbishop Njongonkulu Ndungane

South Africa is a land of stunning beauty and scenic wonder, with contrasts ranging from arid semi-desert areas to lush green forests; from flat plains to towering mountains. Socially and economically it is likewise a country of extreme contrasts, ranging from the affluence of multimillion-rand mansions to the extreme poverty of people living in tin shacks or under plastic, with no employment or resources of their own.

The greatest challenge to South Africa is to eradicate poverty and develop its people while ensuring that the natural environment is not destroyed in the process. There must be development for this generation, but not at the price of destroying the natural environment for the next generation. The natural wonders of our country, including the magnificent variety of fauna and flora, as well as our water resources, our topsoil, our grazing lands, our clean air, must be preserved and protected for future generations.

The present political pressure for jobs and development at any cost could have serious consequences for future generations. The impact of human activity on the environment must be taken into account. We have ample examples from the apartheid era of damage done both to people and to the environment through the "homeland" policy. Millions of people were forced to eke out an existence on land that could not carry the number of people consigned to these remote areas. Erosion, deforestation, and poverty are the heritage. In

13

the cities, toxic waste, fouled water, and polluted air are commonplace. They impact directly on our health, and generally affect the poorest.

There are ever increasing demands for development, but these demands are infinite while the resources of the world are finite. We have to establish more justice between people, a more equitable distribution of the finite resources of the world, and a more sustainable use of them. We have to learn that we are part of nature and not apart from it. We cannot go on exploiting, polluting, or destroying it regardless of the consequences.

The demands of humans can be rapacious. We must ensure development is sustainable for the future. The environment cannot speak out for itself; it cannot toyitoyi [a militant dance expressing defiance and solidarity]. Just as the poor sometimes need others to speak up for them, so too does the environment.

The lesson we need to learn urgently is that if we do not treat the environment with integrity, we ourselves will pay the consequences of fouled air and water, increasing deserts, rising sea levels, denuded marine resources, and a world vastly impoverished in species diversity. Our children will ask how we could have allowed this to happen.

The protection and preservation of the natural environment has to become a priority to save the poor from becoming poorer. I hope we pay heed to the serious issues facing us in our country and world because when injustice prevails the consequences affect both people and the environment. Environmental justice is integral to peace and prosperity.

Chapter 1

The Roots of Environmental Racism and the Rise of Environmental Justice in the 1990s

Farieda Khan

U ntil fairly recently, the dominant environmental ideology in South Africa was characterized by a wildlife-centered, preservationist approach which appealed mainly to the affluent, educated, and largely white minority. In the past, the agenda of the mainstream environmental movement reflected predominantly the interests and concerns of that minority, alienating most black South Africans, many of whom were hostile to what was perceived as an elitist concern peripheral to their struggle for survival (Khan 1990b). In recent years, however, it began to be increasingly acknowledged that, in order to win broad-based acceptance for conservation objectives, the environmental sector had to take cognizance of the basic needs of human beings, and to accept that the right of human beings to a clean, safe, and healthy environment was a legitimate environmental goal (Cock and Koch 1991; Ramphele and McDowell 1991; Hallowes 1993; Lukey 1995).

Nevertheless, despite the fact that the South African environmental movement has moved dramatically away from its former uncaring, elitist image and has made enormous strides in reaching a far broader spectrum of society than it has done in the past, the issues of race and environmental racism persist. This is hardly surprising, given the fact that South Africa's long and bitter history of racism and racial conflict, dating back to the earliest days of white settlement in the mid-seventeenth century, still resonates in the present, often coloring the attitudes of historically marginalized communities to environmental issues and influencing their environmental perceptions (Khan 1990c). The cumulative effect of racially discriminatory laws and punitive conservation regulations has been the gradual but relentless alienation of blacks from the environmental sphere, and the growth of hostility to conservation issues as defined by the mainstream (Khan 1990a). Issues of race, justice, and the environment continue to be intertwined, as a recent "conservation versus development" controversy in Cape Town so vividly illustrated. Faced with an offer to donate money for low-cost housing on condition that the donor was allowed to develop land he owned on a pristine part of Table Mountain, many mainstream environmental organizations angrily rejected his offer as a "cynical bribe" that would destroy land which should be conserved (*Cape Times,* 2 October 1998), while most squatters were in favor of any plan that would end Cape Town's acute housing crisis (*Cape Times,* 2 October 1998). The following comment on this issue by a spokesman for a civic association representing mainly blacks neatly encapsulates the "poor versus privileged" divide that continues to plague the environmental sector:

> We have to recognize there is a housing backlog and other needs in the province. . . . There has been too much emphasis on the environmental needs in white areas, and an example is that so much money is pumped into Table Mountain and the reserves around it. How come no-one worries about the sandstorms, flooding and other physical problems on the Cape Flats? Why can't we use our natural resources to alleviate the problems? (*Cape Times,* 1 October 1998).

This chapter examines the roots of environmental racism in South Africa and attempts to show how its legacy persists in the midst of the very fundamental changes currently taking place in the environmental sphere. After an overview of key historical periods in the conservation movement in South Africa, the rise of environmental justice discourses and actions in the 1990s is examined and their efficacy evaluated.

The Roots of Environmental Racism

Colonial Conservation

Trends in the establishment of the mainstream environmental movement in South Africa during the latter part of the nineteenth century closely followed those of the United States of America (USA) where members of the well-educated, affluent upper and middle classes established wildlife protection and landscape preservation organizations open only to whites (Dowie 1996, 2). Similarly in South Africa, membership of the various game protection associations such as the Western Districts Game Protection Association and the Transvaal Game Protection Association (TGPA), shared a membership profile of "affluent gentlemen" (Pringle 1983, 63) drawn from the political, professional, and social elite, as did that of another early conservation organization, the Mountain Club (Burman 1966, 15–16). Although none of these organizations had a specific racial bar to membership, there was no question of admitting blacks, since persons of color were generally excluded from social interaction at the upper- and middle-class level during this period (Bickford-Smith 1990). Hence the early conservation movement was, like its counterpart in the USA, protecting nature for the privileged. Because the agendas of the organizations within this movement were dictated by their narrow class and racial support bases, they neglected, and were often hostile to, the interests of blacks. This was clearly demonstrated by the fact that these early game protection associations attempted to protect hunting as a sport by preventing Africans from subsistence hunting (Carruthers 1995, 31).

During this period the foundations were also laid for a system of protected natural areas, which would develop during the twentieth century into a system of national parks and provincial game and nature reserves. From the start, however, the establishment of protected natural areas went hand in hand with the forcible eviction of African residents from those areas, and their exclusion from subsistence hunting on their traditional lands (Carruthers 1995, 43–45). One reason for this was that Africans were perceived as environmentally destructive competitors (Carruthers 1988, 219). The fact that this perception was rooted more in racial bias and greed than in reality did not prevent the acceptance of a concept of the ideal protected natural area as one which was uninhabited, which catered to mobile, affluent visitors, and from which the indigenous people were excluded, except to serve in menial roles.

As Anderson and Grove (1987, 4–5) have pointed out, the conservation ideology forged in Africa at the time incorporated the Eurocentric focus of colonial society, along with its tendency to idealize and preserve the natural environment. White privilege, power, and possession, as extensions of the colonial political paradigm, formed the foundations of this ideology, as did the perception of blacks as environmentally destructive. European impressions of Africa and Africans as "uncivilized" and of themselves as the fount of progress and civilization, were incorporated into a conservation ideology that reflected the social attitudes of white cultural superiority and the concept of the subordinate status of blacks within society. This ideology took root in South Africa as it did elsewhere in Africa and its characteristics were bequeathed to the mainstream conservation organizations that became active during the twentieth century, strongly influencing their actions and direction until late into the century.

The Segregation Era, 1910–1947

The political union of South Africa in 1910 ended all hopes of a gradual move toward democratization in the country. An exclusively white franchise was accepted (Johns 1972, 61), and in the ensuing decades the country moved toward white hegemony in the economic and political spheres by means of legislation which furthered the pattern of land dispossession and the political marginalization of blacks. These laws not only caused widespread hardship, they perpetuated the physical estrangement of Africans from the land that had begun during the process of colonization.

Outside the political arena, this sense of estrangement from the environment deepened as blacks were deliberately excluded from enjoying the accommodation provided in protected natural areas. This discrimination was particularly evident in the national parks, where blacks were seldom tolerated as visitors, despite the fact that the National Parks Act stated that the parks had been established for the benefit of the South African public (Statutes of the Union of South Africa 1926, 846). In practice, blacks, particularly Africans, were not welcome, and the only provisions for the (segregated) accommodation of blacks were made grudgingly when, in 1932, a rudimentary (and little known) tented camp for Africans was established in the Kruger National Park (Carruthers 1995, 99), and in 1937 huts were erected for Indian South Africans at Skukuza (Joubert nd, 92–93). Not only were blacks faced with obstacles in visiting national parks because of the difficulty of securing accommodation, they were also actively discouraged by the portrayal of Africans "homogenously in the role of poachers and whites in the role of conservationists" (Carruthers 1995, 99).

During this period black exclusion from the mainstream environmental movement was especially evident. It was an era in which conservation was rigidly interpreted to mean the protection of wildlife, and Africans were perceived as environmentally destructive. It is therefore hardly surprising that a separate black environmental organization, the Native Farmers Association (NFA), was established in 1918, and that its concerns, unlike those of white conservation organizations, revolved around issues which were perceived to be of greater relevance to its black constituency: access to land and soil conservation (Khan 1994b).

Another reason for black exclusion from the mainstream environmental movement lay in the blatant racism of the soil conservation movement that emerged to dominate the environmental scene during the 1930s (Khan 1997). From its establishment in 1943 the dominant organization, the National Veld Trust (NVT), ensured that its membership was open only to "South African persons of European descent" (*Veld Trust News* 1944). However, it was not only the nongovernmental sector that targeted its resources and literature exclusively at the white public. The government's approach to soil conservation also betrayed a racial bias. The conservation and education services provided by the Division of Soil Conservation and Extension in the Department of Agriculture were aimed solely at the white farmer, while the conservation activities of the Land Service Movement, which was controlled by the Department of Agriculture, was open only to white youth (Khan 1997, 442–43).

The exclusion of blacks from participation in the environmental sector was exacerbated by the use of conservation rhetoric as a political tactic by the white government. An early example of this political ma-neuvering is the NFA's efforts to intervene during a land dispute be-tween the government and the Fingo people. Despite the fact that the Fingo community had been granted the disputed land in 1853, the gov-ernment began granting title to whites and in about 1908 the Depart-ment of Forests began encroaching on their remaining land and levying heavy grazing charges (Khan 1994b, 511–12). By 1923 the problem had escalated, but the protests of the people were met with claims that the area was overstocked, that the area was Crown land, and that Fingo cattle were damaging the sponge sources of the Tyumie and Keiskamma rivers, which were drying up as a result. The NFA and the Fingo people were outraged, and took the matter up directly with the government. The newspaper *Imvo,* which was closely allied to the NFA, highlighted the case in its pages, rejecting the Government's claim that it was acting in the interests of conservation (*Imvo* 1923, 5). The NFA felt that the dis-pute had little to do with conservation, and revolved around the govern-ment's intention of masking with conservation rhetoric its true aim of exploiting the political powerlessness of blacks. Despite the efforts of the NFA and the affected people, the grazing land was lost.

The Apartheid Era, 1948–1989

The victory of the National Party in 1948 was not only the victory of the ideology of racial separatism but also marked the beginning of a period of extreme politicization of environmental conservation and the institu-tionalization of environmental racism. Under apartheid, a body of laws was passed which further disempowered blacks and rendered them even more vulnerable to discriminatory action (Horrell 1978). By making genu-ine participation by blacks in the decision making mechanisms of society impossible, these laws ensured a negligible level of black involvement in environmental decision making. In a system designed to racially catego-rize and divide all citizens and crush all dissent, it was inevitable that blacks would become progressively more marginalized economically and politically with negative consequences for conservation.

This marginalization came about in several ways. First, the govern-ment's "homelands" policy, aimed at moving Africans to ethnically divided rural areas, played a major role in perpetuating the spiritual and physical estrangement of blacks from the land. Despite the reality of urbanization, the government embarked on a policy which confined Africans to small rural areas, where overpopulation, poverty, and a lack of basic services inevitably led to widespread environmental degradation (Timberlake 1986, 152–61; Durning 1990, 7–14). This policy ensured that Africans were treated as foreign migrants in the land of their birth.

Second, apartheid institutionalized black poverty through a battery of laws and regulations which placed enormous obstacles in the way of black socioeconomic advancement. Not only were severe restrictions placed on the activities of African traders (Horrell 1978, 255–56), a wide range of jobs was effectively reserved for specific racial groups, with higher paid and more skilled jobs frequently reserved for whites (Horrell 1978, 263; Giliomee and Schlemmer 1989, 79–80). In addition, blacks routinely received lower rates of pay than whites and unequal benefits for undertaking the same or similar work. With the majority of blacks trapped in a cycle of poverty and a continual battle to survive, few had the means, the inclination, or the leisure to engage in conservation activities.

Third, a racially differentiated and inferior education system was introduced through the implementation of the Bantu Education Act (47 of 1953), which applied to Africans (Horrell 1968). While separate education systems introduced for Indians and coloureds at a later date were also inferior to that of whites (Horrell 1978, 329, 341), "Bantu Education" was specifically designed to educate Africans for a subordinate role in society (Pelzer 1966, 83), and resulted in a deterioration in the already very poor standard of education available to them. The retarding effect of "Bantu Education" on the development of African children also had consequences for the environmental sector since the resultant widespread illiteracy and semi-literacy presented a major obstacle to the development of an aware, informed public, able and willing to participate in environmental decision making.

Fourth, a range of legislative restrictions on freedom of movement rendered blacks unable to explore and become familiar with the broader environment. It was not only laws restricting freedom of movement which limited black opportunities to experience their environment; the application of other apartheid laws such as the Group Areas Act and the Separate Amenities Act also contributed in no small measure. The Group

Areas Act (41 of 1950) provided for the establishment of separate residential areas to which members of the various population groups were restricted. The townships to which Africans, Indians, and coloureds were confined were bleak, hostile environments, frequently lacking community facilities, cultural amenities, or green open space which could be used for social activities. Moreover, the areas in which blacks were forced to live were often devoid of any natural or scenic attractions, since environmentally desirable urban areas were usually reserved for whites (McCarthy and Smit 1983). African townships in particular, having been created on the premise that their inhabitants were temporary residents who would one day return to their "homelands" (Beavon 1982), were monotonous, dormitory-like environments. And since all blacks lacked meaningful political power they were powerless to prevent the location of noxious facilities such as sewage plants, polluting industries, and landfills in close proximity to black residential areas.

The Reservation of Separate Amenities Act (49 of 1953) provided that any public premises could be reserved for the exclusive use of a particular race, and that such action could not be ruled invalid on the grounds that the separate facilities were not substantially equal (Horrell 1978, 113). The Act was used by state departments and provincial and local authorities to provide a grossly unfair and unequal distribution of natural and recreational amenities (Hugo 1974; Cornell 1978). The same applied to the provision of accommodation at nature and game reserves, as well as national parks. The use of racially discriminatory laws by national and regional conservation authorities made it difficult for blacks to gain access to nature and game reserves, hiking trails, picnic and camping sites (Khan 1990a, 58). The exclusion of blacks from these amenities has undoubtedly had a detrimental effect on the environmental attitudes and perceptions of the affected communities, and should be considered a major factor contributing to a lack of interest in or hostility on the part of blacks to the whole concept of conservation.

The cumulative effect of the battery of discriminatory laws enacted during the apartheid regime was to further alienate blacks from mainstream environmentalism. This was reflected in the membership of major conservation organizations such as the Wildlife Society, the Botanical Society, and the Mountain Club of South Africa, which remained predominantly white during most of this period (Schweizer 1983, 46; Odendaal

1993, 100). To a significant extent, apartheid measures restricting the freedom of movement of blacks, as well as a host of laws which sought to prescribe or prevent social interaction between blacks and whites (Horrell
1978, 124), made it extremely difficult for any conservation organization
to organize conferences, meetings, exhibitions, or any other form of activity which included social interaction between blacks and whites. There is
also little doubt that these laws were in some measure responsible for
stunting the growth of the environmental movement as a whole, and en-
trenching its narrow white support base.

These legislative constraints notwithstanding, mainstream environmental organizations must shoulder a large part of the responsibility for
the racial polarization of environmentalism in South Africa. It should be
remembered that at no time during the apartheid era did the government
"directly or indirectly restrict the membership or activities of private voluntary organizations," with the exception of trade unions and political
bodies (Schweizer 1983, 44). In addition, while it is true that a plethora of
socially restrictive apartheid legislation existed, where organizations were
prepared to meet certain conditions (such as applying for permits), it *was*
possible to overcome these restrictions, and for "mixed" gatherings to
take place (Centre for Intergroup Studies 1977, 4).

In many instances environmental NGOs voluntarily implemented
the government's racial policies. Their motivation was either to pander to
the conservative political opinions of their membership, or an attempt to
prevent the loss of continued financial support from the government
(Horrell 1978, 147). Two examples of the establishment of racially separate conservation organizations on the initiative of mainstream NGOs
will illustrate this point. The African National Soil Conservation Association (ANSCA) was established by the NVT in 1953 as a means of taking the
soil conservation message to Africans, without antagonizing the government (on whom it was dependent for financial support) or its members,
many of whom were white farmers with extreme right-wing views (Khan
1997). Unlike the NVT, ANSCA had to struggle to survive. It eventually
collapsed because of insufficient funds, as well as its refusal to bow to the
government's demand that it conform to the government's racial policies
by forming eight separate, tribally based organizations. A second example
was that of the African Wildlife Society, an NGO for Africans established
by members of the Wildlife Society in 1963 (Khan 1992b, 65–70). While

these members were doubtless sincere in their desire to extend their organization's message beyond its narrow membership base, it is also true that the Wildlife Society's constitution contained no racial bar to membership. Given the politically conservative nature of the membership at that time (Khan 1992b, 69–70) it was simply a case of not having the support necessary to admit African members.

The racist attitudes of many whites involved in mainstream conservation was particularly obvious in matters involving the enlargement of protected natural areas, which affected blacks. For example, during the Lake St Lucia Commission of Inquiry in 1964, there was a "complete disregard for Black opinion," in a situation in which thousands would be made homeless by the enlargement of a conservation area (Frost 1990, 58). Those involved in the Commission, as well as white members of the public who sent in comments, had little hesitation in recommending the forced removal of about 5,000 people. Black alienation from mainstream environmentalism was aggravated by the many other cases where Africans were forcibly removed from their traditional lands in order to promote the aims of conservation—a process that is synonymous with the history of protected natural areas in South Africa. One example is that of the Makuleke people, who were summarily evicted from their land in 1969, and the land incorporated within the Kruger National Park (Carruthers 1995, 98–99, see also chap. 5 of this volume). For black communities reeling under the impact of apartheid laws, struggling to survive in the harsh socioeconomic and political climate created by these laws, and with few opportunities for quality education, leisure time, and recreational enjoyment of the natural environment, environmental issues *as defined by the mainstream environmental movement,* were perforce regarded as issues of extremely low priority (if, indeed, they were thought of at all).

In direct contrast to the official line of conservation *within* South Africa, however, was the state-sanctioned slaughter of wildlife, particularly that of elephants and rhino, by high-ranking members of the South African Defence Force during the 1970s and 1980s in the neighboring countries of Namibia and Angola (Kumleben Commission of Inquiry 1996, 91–92). During a period when the South African government was widely publicizing its achievements in the field of conservation, many of its military officials used the cover of South Africa's military involvement in the bush war to decimate wildlife in these foreign countries in order to enrich themselves, or in the name of "sport" (Potgieter 1995; Breytenbach 1997).

The Rise of Environmental Justice Issues

The rise of the concept of environmental justice in South Africa and the gradual process of its incorporation into the prevailing conservation ideology coincided with the development of a more socially responsive ideology, and the transformation that was taking place in the political sphere during the 1990s. In this process of integrating environmental justice issues, South Africa was following a path already laid down by the pioneers of the environmental justice movement in the USA. In the 1970s, the mainstream environmental movement in the USA had begun to respond to increasingly vocal criticism of its "environmental elitism," at first defensively, as in the case of the Audubon Club (*Audubon* 1971, 6), and then with a growing realization of the need to broaden its agenda of wilderness and wildlife protection and make conservation issues more relevant to the poor, and to minorities in particular. The Sierra Club, the country's oldest conservation organization, responded by raising these issues in the pages of its journal (*Sierra Club Bulletin* 1972, 2) as well as by inviting critical comment from nonmembers: "to many of our nation's twenty million blacks, the conservation movement has as much appeal as a segregated bus" (Bradley 1972, 21).

By the 1980s, this critical self-awareness among the mainstream environmental movement continued to grow, with organizations such as the Audubon Club acknowledging their shortcomings (*Audubon* 1987, 6), and decrying the lack of diversity in their membership (Jordan and Snow 1992). However, the awareness and concern of some mainstream environmental groups was not sufficient to stem the feelings of alienation experienced by minorities, and the movement continued to be dominated by the affluent, educated, and predominantly white sector of society (Jordan and Snow 1992; Bullard 1994). It was not until the 1980s that a small group of environmentally aware blacks emerged who, by linking environmental and civil rights issues, challenged the dominant perception of conservation as a white middle-class, leisure issue, and provided the catalyst for the emergence of the environmental justice movement (Melosi 1995, 5). Among this group were Rev. Leon White, Rev. Benjamin Chavis, and

Charles Lee, all active in the work of the United Church of Christ's (UCC) Commission on Racial Justice in the 1980s, and pioneers in the field of environmental justice (Bullard 1994, 14–15; Schwab 1994, xx–xxi). It was during this period that blacks "began to treat their struggle for environmental equity as a struggle against institutionalized racism and an extension of the quest for social justice" (Bullard 1994, 29). Indeed, much of the environmental activism of the 1980s arose as a response to what was perceived as a trend in siting toxic and noxious facilities in close proximity to poor people and people of color. The environmental justice movement thus arose as a result of poor communities taking on environmental issues as community, labor, or civil rights causes (Guerro and Head 1990, 11).

One of the earliest environmental justice protest actions in the USA was the large-scale civil disobedience waged by mainly black protesters in Warren Country, North Carolina, in 1982. This demonstration against the dumping of poisonous PCB (polychlorinated biphenyls) waste into a landfill close to their community has been identified as the first to specifically "forge the connections between race, poverty and the environmental consequences of the production of industrial waste" (di Chiro 1995, 303). Another notable landmark of the environmental justice movement was a study, *Toxic Wastes and Race* by the UCC's Commission on Racial Justice in 1987, which found race to be the single most important factor in the location of several toxic waste sites (Bullard 1994, 102). The term "environmental racism" now began to enter the lexicon of environmental justice activists. Environmental racism, as defined by the man who coined it, Rev. Ben Chavis, Director of the Commission, is:

> racial discrimination in environmental policymaking and the enforcement of regulations and laws, the deliberate targeting of people of coloured communities for toxic waste facilities, the official sanctioning of the life-threatening presence of poisons and pollutants in our communities, and a history of excluding people of colour from leadership in the environmental movement. (di Chiro 1995, 304)

This last point was highlighted by a coalition of environmental justice organizations which sent out letters to ten of the most important mainstream environmental organizations in 1990, criticizing their elitist, racially biased hiring practices, and the exclusion of the perspective and concerns of minorities from their environmental agenda (Austin and Schill 1991, 77–79; Gottlieb 1993, 260–62). The growing environmental justice movement found the ideal platform for its ideas when the First National People of Color Environmental Leadership Summit was convened in Washington in 1991, and it was here that the principles of environmental justice were first agreed upon by several hundred delegates from North and South America (di Chiro 1995, 307–9). The summit was important, not only because it brought together people of color in order to reach consensus on a people-centered, holistic, and socially just approach to the environment, but also because it "broadened the environmental justice movement beyond its anti toxics focus to include issues of public health, worker safety, land use, transportation, housing, resource allocation, and community empowerment" (Bullard 1996, 4).

There are close similarities between the history of the environmental movement in the USA during the 1980s and the way the movement was to develop in South Africa during the 1990s. In both countries a history of racial discrimination, institutionalized black poverty, and political powerlessness are central to the environmental discourse. This factor, together with the nature-orientated and preservationist approach of the mainstream environmental movement, made it inevitable that for much of the twentieth century the main focus of blacks in both countries was political liberation, not environmental conservation. In the USA, when environmental issues were couched in a civil rights context and the right to a healthy environment began to be included as an integral part of a basic civil rights program blacks began to become actively involved in the environmental problems affecting their communities. Similarly, in South Africa it was only when the political scene began to undergo radical changes and a major transformation began to take place within the environmental sphere that black South Africans began to grapple with environmental issues in larger numbers than ever before.

The Era of Transition

The roots of the environmental justice movement in South Africa may be traced to the enormous sociopolitical changes that took place during the post-apartheid period of transition (from February 1990 to April 1994), when there was a discernible shift in attitudes toward, and perceptions of, the environment. One of the most important catalysts in bringing this about was the unbanning on 2 February 1990 of extra-parliamentary organizations such as the African National Congress (ANC) and the South African Communist Party (SACP). This not only created the political space for organizations to broaden their horizons beyond anti-apartheid politics but resulted in a more flexible and relaxed political climate that added impetus to the dissolution of the formerly strict boundaries between politics and conservation. Thus, while political organizations such as the ANC, the Azanian Peoples' Organisation (AZAPO), the Pan Africanist Congress (PAC), and others gradually began to accept that environmental issues could form a legitimate part of their agenda (Khan 1992b, 77–80), the traditional notion that equated "conservation" with the protection of wildlife and the preservation of the natural environment began to give way to a more holistic approach embracing economic and political aspects as well as ecological concerns. It began to be increasingly acknowledged that, in order to win broad-based acceptance, environmental issues had to take cognizance of the basic needs of human beings and that the right of human beings to a clean, safe, and healthy environment was a legitimate environmental goal (Cock and Koch 1991; Ramphele and McDowell 1991; Hallowes 1993; Lukey 1995).

During this transitional period, the resurgence in public support of the environmental sector was increasingly characterized by environmental action at a grassroots level. Impoverished communities in both rural and urban areas began engaging in campaigns such as: protests against plans to site a nuclear power station in their area; demonstrations against the proposed construction of a toxic waste recycling plant, and the launch of an anti-pollution, environmental health campaign (*Weekly Mail*, 20 December 1990–10 January 1991). A wide range of community-based organizations in both the rural and the urban areas undertook greening projects, which included the creation of community parks, the cultivation of indigenous plants for use as traditional medicine, and the establishment of food gardens (Khan 1992a). Such projects were practical expressions of the desire of the poor to take constructive action against the environmental poverty of their immediate surroundings, and to enhance the quality of their environment.

Another significant indicator of the desire to bring about environmental justice was the move by labor organizations into the environmental arena, formerly perceived as being outside their traditional sphere of action. Trade unions began to accept that industrial health and occupational safety were legitimate environmental issues and therefore of concern to them in their commitment to creating working areas that were safe both for workers and for the surrounding communities (Chemical Workers Industrial Union 1991; Crompton and Erwin 1991; Miller 1993; Morokeng 1993; Lukey 1995 and chap. 10 of this volume). Trade unions, especially in the mining, fishing, and chemical industries, have taken a particular interest in the environment and have become actively involved in informing workers of their right to a safe and healthy working environment (Khan 1994a; Magane et al. 1997).

The environmental sector was further energized by the emergence of a small number of more radical organizations that, unlike those in the mainstream, acknowledged the inextricability of conservation and politics, and were willing to adopt a confrontational stance against the authorities (including the government) on behalf of the poor. One of the most important of these new organizations was Earthlife Africa, which had been established in 1988, and which had grown quickly, drawing upon the membership of existing anti-apartheid and activist organizations. Unlike the mainstream sector with its nature-oriented bias, Earthlife concentrated on "brown agenda" issues—those environmental issues which were relevant to the creation of a safe and healthy environment for all, but especially for the poor. A defining characteristic of Earthlife's highly politicized approach was its willingness to form alliances with trade unions and international environmental NGOs in order to effect change. For example, in 1990, Earthlife spearheaded action against the multinational company, Thor Chemicals, which had poisoned the drinking water of a rural community living close to its plant in KwaZulu-Natal with mercury waste. Earthlife formed an alliance with the Chemical Workers Industrial Union, as well as an NGO, Greenpeace International, which conducted tests on soil and water samples taken from around the plant (Butler 1997, 199). After national and international protests, Thor Chemicals was forced to suspend its operations, albeit temporarily (CWIU 1991). Another example of Earthlife's approach in forming cross-sectoral as well as international alliances was its protest action undertaken in

Durban in 1992, together with the Transport and General Workers' Union, against the docking of a ship bound for France carrying a highly toxic cargo of PCBs. This action, together with protest action at each of the ship's ports of call, was coordinated by Greenpeace (Harris 1993, 89).

It is also worth noting that during this transition period impoverished communities served notice that they were no longer prepared to be the victims of the harsh conservation policies and poor environmental decision making so typical of previous years. Thus, in 1989, stock farmers in the Richtersveld region of the Northern Cape refused to accept eviction from their traditional grazing land in order to make way for the creation of a national park (SPP 1990). Instead, the community applied for an interdict (*Weekly Mail*, 21–27 September 1990), and as a result, the National Parks Board was compelled in 1991 to negotiate an agreement to accept the community as a management partner (*Sunday Times Extra,* 21 July 1991). A similar case involved the Riemvasmaak community in the Northern Cape which had been forcibly removed under apartheid laws in 1974 and part of their land occupied by the South African Defence Force (SADF). In 1988 the SADF and the National Parks Board (NPB) had signed an agreement allowing the Parks Board to use some of the SADF land for the preservation of the black rhino and to extend the Augrabies Falls Nature Reserve (SPP nd). However, in 1992, representatives of the Riemvasmakers served notice that they intended to apply for the return of their land.

While the political winds of change were undoubtedly making an impact on the environmental arena this does not mean that there were no conflicts between the poor and the privileged over the issue of the protection of the natural environment and its resources. On the contrary, the era of transition was one of slow and painful progress, with numerous setbacks for the conservation cause, as poor communities, emboldened by political change, began to demand that past injustices be remedied. Many of the resulting protests centered on the loss of traditional land and natural resources to conservation authorities. For example, in 1992, villagers outside a nature reserve kidnapped the managers and locked them up in chalets overnight as part of a protest action in which they demanded compensation for land lost during the reserve's expansion (*Weekly Mail,* 28 August–3 September 1992). In KwaZulu-Natal, from 1990 onwards, squatters started a series of land invasions into the protected forest of Dukuduku (Douglas 1996), while the nature reserves of Dwesa and Cwebe in the Eastern Cape, where locals had fruitlessly demanded access to resources traditionally utilized by them for generations, were invaded in 1992 and again in 1994, and plundered for seafood and timber (*Sunday Times*, 20 November 1994).

In addition to conflicts over land and natural resources, this period also witnessed numerous other environmental conflicts in which poor black communities were at a disadvantage, and which were testimony to the enduring impact of the apartheid era (Cock and Koch 1991; Ramphele and McDowell 1991). Indeed, the era of transition proved to be a difficult period for the implementation of environmental justice, for while the demand for social justice within the environmental sphere could not be rejected, it was frequently accommodated more at the level of theory and principle than in action. Nevertheless, the discourse had irrevocably entered the mainstream.

The Democratic Era: May 1994 to the Present

South Africa's first democratic election in April 1994 not only heralded the dawn of a new political era, it also brought about a political climate in which the concept of environmental justice could flourish. This trend was most noticeable in the unprecedented growth in action taken by environmental NGOs based in the townships and black rural areas. This work built upon the initiatives of earlier organizations such as the National Environmental Awareness Campaign (established in 1976) and the Africa Tree Centre (established in 1980). Community-initiated environmental action has included: the establishment by the Tsoga Environmental Centre in Langa, Cape Town, of a garden for indigenous medicinal plants (*The Argus*, 4 November 1994); the initiation by the Modulaqhowa Environmental Project in Botshabelo, in the Orange Free State, of recycling projects and the provision of assistance to small-scale farmers; the establishment by the Mafefe Environmental Protection Committee (Albertyn 1995) of an environmental education campaign aimed at alerting villagers to the dangers of asbestos; and an initiative to save the Wolfgat Nature Reserve on Cape Town's False Bay coast from degenerating into a desolate wasteland (Wolfgat Nature Reserve 1995).

This period has also seen a move for compensation by some of the many thousands of workers left badly injured or riddled with a fatal disease as a result of being exposed to unhealthy or dangerous working conditions. In the case of mercury poisoning by Thor Chemicals, the prohibition on the company's activities was lifted and permission was granted for it to start operating again. Subsequently, three of Thor's top executives were charged with culpable homicide relating to the death of a former employee, allegedly of mercury poisoning (*Sunday Times*, 5 September 1993). When the criminal case was settled in 1995, the culpable homicide charges were dropped and the company only faced a fine. Civil proceedings on behalf of twenty workers were then brought against Thor in England. The case was finally concluded in April 1997, when agreement on a settlement of R9 million was reached (Butler 1997).

More recently, the issue of vanadium poisoning suffered by several workers at a mine in Mpumalanga has been taken up by a legal rights NGO, the Legal Resources Centre, in an effort to improve conditions and secure compensation (Madihlaba 1998). Another case that has reached the courts is that of British company Cape Plc, which exposed its workers, as well as their families in neighboring settlements, to blue and brown asbestos, and, when it disinvested in 1979, simply left thousands of asbestosis victims to fend for themselves (*Cape Times*, 15 December 1998). These cases, however, represent only a tiny fraction of the workers and communities who were exposed to hazardous conditions by companies who were able to evade their responsibilities as employers because of the conditions that prevailed during the apartheid era. In the case of the asbestos industry, concern for enormous profits came before concern for the health of black workers and members of neighboring communities, thousands of whom died of asbestosis after years of earning a pittance (*Cape Times*, 1 July 1998). A test case in the House of Lords in England opened the way for sick South African asbestos workers and their families to sue Cape Plc in the British courts, and hundreds of them elected to do so (*Sunday Argus*, 7 February 1999).

The environmental agenda of community-based organizations and environmental NGOs targeting the poor revolves mainly around basic needs ("brown" issues) rather than the "green" issues traditionally associated with the environmental movement. This is particularly evident in the growth of the national environmental coalition, the Environmental Justice Networking Forum (EJNF) and the scope of its projects. EJNF has, since its formation in 1993, grown to encompass more than 600 organizations. It has assisted many poor communities faced with a range of problems such as the consequences of being sited in close proximity to a hazardous waste dump *(Environmental Justice Networker* 1996) or working under unsafe and dangerous conditions (Madihlaba 1998). It has also assisted rural communities to make verbal submissions to the "Speak out on Poverty and Environment" hearings *(Environmental Justice Networker* 1998). EJNF has been active in the arena of policy, attempting to influence government to implement the principles of environmental justice through, for example, banning the practice of importing toxic waste *(Mail & Guardian,* 25 July–1 August 1996).

Consensus between the objectives of governmental and nongovernmental conservation agencies, on the one hand, and the aspirations of poor black communities on the other (so often in the past in opposition to each other) is rapidly being reached. This may be seen in the implementation of the new direction and approach of the major national governmental and nongovernmental conservation agencies. For example, the National Botanic Institute (NBI), which is responsible for cultivating, conserving, and popularizing the indigenous flora of South Africa, has for some years now been involved in constructing a dynamic and comprehensive socially responsive national program which would reverse the "eurocentric vision" it was widely perceived to have adopted in the past (Khan 1992b, 92). In addition, the NBI has been developing a garden-based environmental education program firmly rooted in the context of educating citizens for a participatory democracy (Ashwell 1997).

The National Parks Board, renamed South African National Parks (SANP) in 1996, has also undergone radical changes in policy and direction since the appointment of its first gender and racially representative board in 1995. The SANP, formerly an unquestioning arm of the apartheid state, which allowed the demands of that ideology to be subordinated to the aims of conservation, has slowly but inexorably begun to address the problem of the exclusion and alienation of black South Africans (Khan 1992b, 91–92; *Sunday Times,* 27 July 1997). An integral part of this process has been the attention given to resolving the problem of the forced removal of rural communities from their traditional land in order to create protected areas. The communities thus dispossessed had every right to expect redress and the SANP, committed to ensuring the continued protection of its parks, had the responsibility of finding a just solution. Thus in the case of the Kalahari Gemsbok National Park, a large group of San instituted a land claim for their lost ancestral lands, which amount to about half of the Park (*Cape Times,* 26 August 1996) where they hope to have the opportunity finally to put into practice their considerable environmental and tracking skills as part of a proposed ecotourist venture. In December 1998, the SANP agreed in principle to release 55,000 hectares of land to be used by the San and the neighboring Mier farming community as a contractual park (*Cape Times,* 17 December 1998).

The SANP's new approach to neighboring black communities has also been evident in its response to the land claim of the Makuleke people, who were evicted from their traditional land in 1969 when the land was incorporated into the Kruger National Park. The Makuleke have instituted a land claim under the Restitution of Land Rights Act of 1994—not, however, to physically reclaim the land, but to benefit from its natural resources (de Villiers 1998; Moloi 1998). After eighteen months of intense negotiation, it was agreed that the land, the Pafuri area of the Kruger National Park, would be returned to the community on condition that no mining, farming, or permanent residence takes place without the permission of the SANP. The land, which may not be sold without the permission of the SANP (which has the right of first refusal), is being established as a contractual park, on a co-management basis. It is envisaged that ultimately the community will take responsibility for the costs and benefits derived from conservation management and tourism activities.

National Parks authorities are also addressing the issue of community access to ancestral land and the right to use natural resources on a sustainable basis. In the past communities adjacent to nature reserves and national parks were often arbitrarily barred from access to areas traditionally utilized to gather resources such as timber, reeds, seafood, and medicinal plants, a prohibition that led to conflict and the criminalization of traditional activities. Conservation authorities have uniformly rejected the punitive style of old in favor of an approach in which adjacent communities are regarded as "partners" in implementing a more socially responsive solution to conservation issues. The aim is to persuade and educate communities about the benefits of protected natural areas, and to gain their cooperation in a joint conservation venture. This approach is being successfully adopted by all conservation authorities (Howard 1995;

Nussey 1995). One of the SANP's partnership projects, Mayibuye Ndlovu, allows neighboring communities to use the Addo National Park's natural resources (Kerley 1997). The Eastern Cape Nature Conservation Department permits the community on the border of Dwesa Nature Reserve controlled access to the reserve in order to collect natural resources on a sustainable basis (*Mail & Guardian Open Africa Supplement,* January 1995).

The Cape Department of Nature Conservation has also been active in the area of co-management, and is part of a research project that seeks to determine a sustainable fish harvesting industry for a poor fishing community on the Western Cape coast (Sowman et al. 1997). With similar cooperative aims in mind, research on sustainable mussel collection is being undertaken by the KwaZulu-Natal Nature Conservation Service with the cooperation of the people of Sokhulu village (Derwent 1997). Instead of being fined for poaching as in the past, villagers are now allowed to collect mussels in much the same way as their ancestors did, but in specifically designated areas and using low-impact tools (*Mail & Guardian,* 7–13 August 1998). The collection process has been carefully designed to promote sustainable harvesting, and is supervised by a committee on which both villagers and conservationists are represented. At the national level, the Marine Living Resources Act of 1998 was a major step in the process of bringing about equity and ensuring fairer access to marine resources by black communities that had been treated unfairly in the past (RSA 1998).

Given the extent of the exclusion of black South Africans, the residual resentment and anger over forced removals and punitive conservation actions taken in the past, and the extent of the poverty and underdevelopment which still exists, it should be acknowledged that the national and provincial conservation authorities continue to face an enormous task in gaining the trust and support of the majority of South Africans. Nevertheless, with an acceptance at policy level of the need for both social and environmental justice, it is a task that is finally receiving the attention it deserves.

The Department of Water Affairs and Forestry (DWAF), in complete contrast to its previous record, has also emerged as a leading governmental proponent of environmental justice. DWAF's alien vegetation removal program, which incorporates an extensive job creation and training component for poor local communities, provides an outstanding model in this regard. By 1998, the R250 million program had generated 240 projects, which created 40,623 jobs in largely rural areas (*Cape Times*, 20 March 1998). In turn, the "Working for Water" program is underpinned by the department's White Paper on a National Water Policy for South Africa (DWAF 1997), which aims to provide clean drinking water to all South Africans on an equitable and sustainable basis.

But the very real progress in the implementation of environmental justice, the support given to environmental issues by people at a grass-roots level, and the growth in organizations with a far broader agenda than the traditionally narrow focus of conservation bodies, have not been translated into mass support for environmental conservation. In this regard, it is important to note the lack of a national environmental movement that is fully representative of South Africa's population and capable of giving voice to the concerns and perceptions of poor black communities. Even EJNF is not a mass-based organization. Nor has any group yet been able to inspire mass environmental action. The closest any movement has come to such action has been the protests against development in Oudekraal, on the lower slopes of Table Mountain in Cape Town, where Muslim grave sites and shrines are situated. The possibility of development in 1996 gave rise to mass demonstrations in which thousands participated. The protestors, who were mainly Muslim, were joined by others from environmental organizations and other interest groups (*Cape Metro, Sunday Times*, 17 November 1996). At first, these protests seemed to signal the beginning of mass support for conservation and social justice objectives, and these favorable signs were bolstered by the formation of the Environment and Mazaar Action Committee (EMAC), a coalition representing the concerns of the environmental sector and the Muslim community (*Cape Times*, 13 September 1996). However, while the huge swell of support for EMAC's objectives revealed the extent of the potential community support that could be harnessed by the broader environmental movement, thus far this potential remains largely untapped. The EMAC initiative eventually lost its momentum and now appears to have run its course. No statements have emerged from EMAC since 1997 and most of the action taken against any proposed development in the area has come from new groups such as "Save the Mountain Campaign" and "Models for the Mountain," as well as from other established environmental organizations. To date, no other demonstration of mass support for a conservation issue has materialized in the country.

The South African environmental movement comprises a diversity of bodies, but few can claim to fairly represent the views and concerns of black communities, and fewer still to have significant black support. Notwithstanding the establishment of many new township-based NGOs in recent years (EJNF's membership attests to this), there is a long way to go before it can be said that a strong indigenous environmental movement that reflects the concerns of the majority of South Africans has been established. Instead, a myriad under-resourced, understaffed, and financially embattled NGOs with a predominantly black membership are engaged in a continual struggle to survive. These small bodies, many without a proper office or adequately paid staff, lurch from one cash crisis to the next. Lacking such essentials as the skills to write good funding proposals, useful contacts among donor organizations, a proven track record, and the resources and experience to implement projects, these township-based NGOs often founder and collapse or become far too dependent on mainstream NGOs, effectively functioning as the latter's "outreach" projects, and losing their autonomy completely.

Despite the lip service paid by many mainstream as well as radical NGOs to the politically correct strategies of "community-driven projects" and "community empowerment," the often unequal power relations between mainly white NGOs and mainly black NGOs persist. While the situation is undoubtedly changing, it would be true to say that the skills, expertise, and resources are still largely concentrated in the hands of mainstream NGOs, whose staff and membership base are still largely derived from the white sector of society—a situation which simply reflects that of South Africa as a whole. Given this context, it is clear that before historically disadvantaged communities can effectively speak and act for themselves, a strong indigenous environmental movement needs to be nurtured. More specifically, particular problem areas have to be addressed: lack of power; lack of organizational autonomy; and unequal access to skills, resources, information, and funding.

The absence of mass support for traditionally defined environmental issues has been demonstrated by several environmental controversies since 1994 in which the generally polarized environmental perceptions of the privileged and the poor have remained largely unchanged. This fact became painfully obvious during two ecological disasters—floods in the coloured and African areas of the Cape Flats, and an oil spill in Table Bay—which hit Cape Town simultaneously in 1994. Commenting on the impact of these disasters on human beings and penguins respectively, a newspaper with a predominantly black readership editorialized:

> We've got a long, long way to go before we get our priorities straight in the new South Africa . . . the flood disaster this week was preceded by the ecological disaster that threatens our coastline and penguins. Then came the floods which left hundreds of human beings homeless and destitute. . . . What do the media and local government focus on? Penguins. Funds are set up, rescue missions get underway and even kitchens are set up for penguins. Yes, we are all concerned about the penguins— for their safety and security. We must do something to ensure their wellbeing. However, what is of equal or greater concern, is the human tragedy. (*South*, 5 July 1994)

Since then, flooding in the Cape Flats has continued to bring untold misery to thousands, with little attention from environmental groups, while an oil spill in 2000 once more generated enormous national and international support for a drive to save the penguins.

This dichotomy in attitudes to the environment was also well illustrated during the controversy generated in 1995 by the proposal to build a steel plant in Saldanha Bay on the Western Cape coast. Ranged against the establishment of the plant on the grounds that it would pose a threat to the adjoining West Coast National Park, and especially the Langebaan lagoon, were bodies such as the National Parks Board and NGOs such as Earthlife Africa and the Wildlife Society. In stark contrast was the almost unanimous support for the proposed development displayed by spokespersons for black communities on the West Coast (*Cape Times*, 2 August 1995). In many ways, the situation was reminiscent of the support given to the "pro-mining option" by adjoining black communities in St Lucia, Natal, during a public participation process conducted two years previously (Mlambo and Mzimela 1993). As in St Lucia, support for the Saldanha project among west coast communities was wholly based on concern about the widespread poverty and unemployment in the area and the hope that the development of the steel plant would generate jobs. This point of view was powerfully conveyed by Ebrahim Dalwai, who addressed the Board of Inquiry into the Saldanha Steel Project on behalf of seven African National Congress branches in Saldanha and surrounding areas:

> We are all environmentalists and love our environment, nature and the sea-life. The West Coast is traditionally known for its fishing industry and we believe it must stay like that. We will do everything in our power to protect and preserve the environment and fishing resources for the future generations as we have been doing all along. We also strongly feel that the go-ahead for the Saldanha Steel Project should not be delayed any longer. . . . We see no need why the proposed site should be moved elsewhere . . . we will ensure that development takes place not at the expense of the environment. (Board of Inquiry 1995, 435–36)

At one stage, Iscor decided to withdraw from the project, a move that would have delayed its implementation. Dalwai's response was: "People are very upset. . . . It was just a couple of privileged people making a noise. . . . They caused the delay" (*Cape Times,* 28 September 1995). While many of the environmentalists were against the *siting* of the development, rather than against the development *per se,* the level of anger and frustration of poor communities on the West Coast exposed the unfortunate fact that the perception of conservationists as being for the protection of the environment and anti-development, regardless of the cost to the poor, existed, and had been reinforced by this conflict.

This hostility to conservation issues because of the perceived priority given to the protection of wild animals and indigenous plants over the interests of people was also clearly demonstrated in two very different instances—the case of the Makuleke people in the Kruger National Park, and that of the Macassar community in the Western Cape. The story of the Makuleke people encapsulates this divide. While mainstream environmental groups such as the Wildlife Society were at loggerheads with a diamond mining company that planned to prospect in the area, the Makuleke people were angered by the fact that, now that they were finally in a position to recover their land, outside interests were dictating its use. Speaking to a journalist on the issue, Makuleke leader Gilbert Nwaila said:

> You should tell these people who like wildlife that they should come and speak to us before they make statements about how our land is used. And when they come, they should remember we suffered greatly when our villages were destroyed and our homes burnt down so that Kruger could be made bigger. . . . Now that we have a chance to get some wealth from that land, we are being told to put even more animals there. It will be very difficult to convince our people that wildlife is better than mining. (*Mail & Guardian,* 18–24 August 1995)

The second instance involves the working-class community of Macassar in the Western Cape, which was badly affected by a fire that broke out at a neighboring chemical plant (AECI) in December 1995. The fire ignited a sulfur stockpile which blanketed Macassar in a choking cloud of sulfur dioxide. Two people died of respiratory complications and about 2,500 people had to be evacuated. A Commission of Inquiry appointed in 1996 found, firstly, that AECI had been negligent in its handling of the sulfur dump and, secondly, that the impact of the fire was extremely disruptive and traumatic for all residents of Macassar, both during the fire and during the chaotic evacuation procedures which followed (Desai Commission of Inquiry 1997, 67–68, 110, 116). In the aftermath of the fire there were widespread feelings of bitterness among Macassar residents (predominantly coloured), arising from a perception that those in authority did not care enough about them to have either protected them from the dangerous material stored on the adjacent site, or to ensure their safe and efficient evacuation and proper medical treatment when disaster struck. For many residents this merely served to add to their existing anger at having been so thoughtlessly sited next to a hazardous facility in the first place (Desai Commission of Inquiry 1997, 123).

Residents of Macassar were further angered by the fact that a subsequent environmental impact assessment of the fire, commissioned by AECI, had excluded the Macassar area (the area most directly affected by the fire), and had focused instead on the surrounding white-owned farms (Desai Commission of Inquiry 1997, 131). Fueling their bitterness was the fact that while compensation was speedily paid out to the farmers, legal complications and a lack of financial resources has led to a considerably longer wait for the Macassar community. Commenting on this prompt payout, Macassar resident Toyhira Davids echoed the sentiments of many when she stated in her testimony that, "I think the life of a human being is worth a lot more than that of plants" (Desai Commission of Inquiry 1997, Transcript of Public Hearings, 5 November 1996). However, the lengthy process of drawing up legal documents on behalf of 4,000 Macassar residents was finalized in 1998, and residents are seeking damages from the company concerned (*Cape Times,* 15 December 1998; *Cape Argus,* 17 August 1999).

One of the most shocking indicators of the distance South Africa has yet to travel in order to achieve environmental justice was the submissions to the "Poverty, Inequality and Environment Hearings" conducted in May 1998. During these hearings, at which a commission heard submissions from poor communities all over the country, it became clear that the litany of environmental problems which beset the poor, and which are largely the result of apartheid's inequitable, racially based planning, is a long one (*Environmental Justice Networker* 1998). Appalling accounts of the misery resulting from being forced to live without hope in conditions of environmental degradation worsened by poverty and unemployment were delivered verbally or in the form of written submissions. These accounts underlined the fact that the major causes of death in South Africa are related to environmental factors such as inadequate sanitation, inefficient (or no) solid waste removal systems, lack of access to clean drinking water, and the siting of polluting industries in close proximity to areas housing the poor (*Environmental Justice Networker* 1998, 4).

Conclusion

There can be little argument that there has been fundamental political progress in South Africa since 1990 and significant progress in the delivery of services such as housing, electricity, and access to clean drinking water since the first democratic elections in 1994 (GCIS 1999). However, it is

also true that an acute socioeconomic backlog still exists, which is mani-
fested in widespread poverty and homelessness, together with high levels
of illiteracy and unemployment (SAIRR 1997; Statistics South Africa
1998). It is a sad reality that South Africa is still a country in which, because they have nowhere else to go, squatters fight for the right to live on
the banks of a polluted river that periodically comes down in flood. It is
still a country in which unemployed, desperately poor people, because
they have no other alternative, scavenge for food on waste dumps despite
the dangers of food poisoning (Khan 1996). It is still a country in which
development and conservation are viewed by many historically disadvantaged communities as two diametrically opposed options because a history of black alienation from environmental issues, together with a legacy
of underdevelopment, has made this almost inevitable.

Given this context, it is clear that South Africa's deep-rooted legacy
of environmental racism and injustice needs to be addressed urgently,
and that radical development interventions are required in order to resolve the problems of unemployment, homelessness, and poverty. As
the "Poverty, Inequality and Environment" hearings have made abun-
dantly clear, the issue of poverty alleviation remains a crucial element in
any environmental program. Unless this issue is faced head on, and a
concerted effort is made to balance the needs of the environment with
that of the poor, poverty will continue to force the poor into unsustainable living patterns and to perpetuate environmental injustice. This has
been recognized by Archbishop Njongonkulu Ndungane, who has stated
that "The greatest challenge to South Africa is to eradicate poverty and
develop its people while ensuring that the natural environment is not
destroyed in the process. . . . The protection and preservation of the natural environment has to become a priority to save the poor from becoming poorer. I hope we pay heed to the serious issues facing us in our
country . . . because when injustice prevails, the consequences affect
both people and the environment. Environmental justice is integral to
peace and prosperity" (quoted in EJNF 1998b, 1 and in this volume).

The process of facing this challenge has already begun. The decade
of the 1990s was one in which the pervasive problem of environmental
racism was finally confronted, and a dynamic start was made in incorporating the concept of environmental justice into the prevailing conservation ideology. It should, however, also be noted that the acceptance and

implementation of environmental justice has not been a smooth process, nor has it been without conflict, given the persistent legacy of a conservation ideology which rates the survival of endangered indigenous fauna and flora above that of the poor. The persistence of this legacy may clearly be seen in the following responses to animal rights issues. The first is from the representative of a poor rural community, who stated, "I strongly caution the animal rights groups that they do not colonise our minds. Gone are those days. It would be better if you aim your ideals towards the balancing of animal rights and human rights" (Makuleke 1997). The second statement is extracted from a newspaper editorial which gave voice to the feelings of many people when it criticized the moral priorities of a society in which far more publicity, public sympathy, and support followed an exposé of the abuse of young elephants than ever greeted the many instances of torture and murder of human beings, most of them poor and black: "Those facing the brutality of everyday existence find it difficult to feel strongly about animal suffering. . . . The animal rights lobby might gain even more widespread support for their cause if they were at least as active in voicing their protest against cruelty to people" (*Sunday Argus* 10 July 1999).

Nevertheless, despite the inevitable failures, setbacks, and obstacles that continue to face the environmental movement in this country, the process of incorporating environmental justice objectives into the prevailing conservation ideology is irrevocable. The course has been set, and there can be no going back to pandering to narrow sectional interests in the environmental sphere.

References

Albertyn, C. 1995. "Mafefe: The Asbestos Dumps of Death in Northern Province." *Environmental Justice Networker* 16.

Anderson, D., and R. Grove, eds. 1987. *Conservation in Africa: People, Policies and Practice*. Cambridge, England: Cambridge University Press.

Ashwell, A. 1997. "Growing People for Green Environments." *Veld and Flora* 83.

Audubon. 1971. "The Audubon View." *Audubon,* November.

———. 1987. "Saving the World." *Audubon,* November.

Austin, R., and M. Schill. 1991. "Black, Brown, Poor and Poisoned: Minority

Grassroots Evironmentalism and the Quest for Eco-justice." *Kansas Journal of Law of Public Policy* 1.

Beavon, K. S. O. 1982. "Black Townships in South Africa: Terra Incognita for Urban Geographers." *South African Geographical Journal* 64.

Bickford-Smith, V. 1990. "The Background to Apartheid in Cape Town: The Growth of Racism and Segregation from the Mineral Revolution to the 1930s." Paper presented to the History Workshop, "Structure and experience in the making of apartheid," 6–10 February, at University of the Witwatersrand, Johannesburg.

Board of Inquiry into the Saldanha Steel Project. 1995. Submissions from Interested Parties. 1 August.

Bradley, T. 1972. "Minorities for Conservation." *Sierra Club Bulletin* 57 (4).

Breytenbach, J. 1997. *Eden's Exiles: One Soldier's Fight for Paradise.* Cape Town: Quellerie Publishers.

Bullard, R. 1994. *Dumping in Dixie: Race, Class and Environmental Quality.* Boulder, Colo.: Westview Press.

———. 1996. "Environmental Justice: A New Framework for Action." *Environmental Law News* 5 (1).

Burman, J. 1966. *A Peak to Climb: The Story of South African Mountaineering.* Cape Town: C. Struik.

Butler, M. 1997. "Lessons from Thor Chemicals: The Links Between Health, Safety and Environmental Protection." In L. Bethlehem and M. Goldblatt, eds. *The Bottom Line: Industry and the Environment in South Africa.* Johannesburg: International Development Research Centre.

Carruthers, J. 1988. "Game Protection in the Transvaal, 1846 to 1926." Ph.D. thesis, University of Cape Town.

———. 1995. *The Kruger National Park: A Social and Political History.* Pietermaritzburg: University of Natal Press.

Centre for Intergroup Studies. 1977. "Organisations: A Review of Discrimination and Current Trends in Voluntary and Non-profit Organisations." Bulletin 1, University of Cape Town.

Cock, J., and E. Koch, eds. 1991. *Going Green: People, Politics and the Environment in South Africa.* Cape Town: Oxford University Press.

Cornell, J. 1978. "Facilities." Draft no. 8. Cape Town: Centre for Intergroup Studies.

Crompton, R., and A. Erwin. 1991. "Reds and Greens: Labour and the Environment." In J. Cock and E. Koch, eds. *Going Green: People, Politics and the Environment in South Africa.* Cape Town: Oxford University Press.

CWIU (Chemical Workers Industrial Union). 1991. "The Fight for Health and Safety." In M. Ramphele and C. McDowell, eds. *Restoring the Land: Environment and Change in Post-apartheid South Africa.* London: The Panos Institute.

Derwent, S. 1997. "Sharing the Spoils." *African Wildlife* 51 (2).

Desai Commission of Inquiry into the Sulphur Fire at Somerset West. June 1997.

de Villiers, B. 1998. "Makuleke: Breakthrough in Makuleke Land Claim Negotiations." *Custos,* May.

di Chiro, G. 1995. "Nature as Community: The Convergence of Environmental and Social Justice." In W. Cronon, ed. *Uncommon Ground: Toward Reinventing Nature.* New York: W. W. Norton.

Douglas, R. 1996. "St Lucia: Ecotourism challenged." *Africa, Environment and Wildlife* 4 (6).

Dowie, M. 1996. *Losing Ground: America's Environmentalism at the Close of the Twentieth Century.* Cambridge, Mass.: The MIT Press.

Durning, A. 1990. *Apartheid's Environmental Toll.* Worldwatch Paper 95. Washington, D.C.: Worldwatch Institute.

DWAF (Department of Water Affairs and Forestry). 1997. "White Paper on a National Policy for South Africa." Pretoria: Department of Water Affairs and Forestry.

EJNF (Environmental Justice Networking Forum). 1998a. Environmental Justice Networking Forum, mimeo.

———. 1998b. *Voices from the Ground: People, Poverty, and Environment in South Africa.* Dorpspruit: EJNF.

Environmental Justice Networker. 1996. "Behind the Hazardous Waste 'Crisis' in KwaZulu Natal." Winter.

———. 1998. "Outpouring of Anguish at Poverty Hearings."

Frost, S. 1990. "Lake St Lucia: Public Opinion, Environmental Issues and the Position of the Government, 1964–1966 and 1989–1990: A Case Study in Changing Attitudes to Conservation." B.A. Honours thesis, Department of Historical Studies, University of Natal.

GCIS (Government Communication and Information System). 1999. "Realising our Hopes." Information Brochure. Pretoria: Government Communication and Information System.

Giliomee, H., and L. Schlemmer. 1989. *From Apartheid to Nation-building.* Cape Town: Oxford University Press.

Gottlieb, R. 1993. *Forcing the Spring: The Transformation of the American Environmental Movement.* Washington, D.C.: Island Press.

Guerro, M., and L. Head. 1990. "The Environment: Redefining the Issue." In D. Alston, ed. *We Speak for Ourselves: Social Justice, Race and Environment.* London: The Panos Institute.

Hallowes, D. 1993. *Hidden Faces, Environment, Development, Justice: South Africa and the Global Context.* Natal: Earthlife Africa.

Harris, A. 1993. "Greenpeace, Environmentalism and Labour." In *Hidden Faces, Environment, Development, Justice: South Africa and the Global Context.* Natal: Earthlife Africa.

Horrell, M. 1968. *Bantu Education to 1968.* Johannesburg: South African Institute of Race Relations.

———. 1978. *Laws Affecting Race Relations in South Africa, 1948–1976.* Johannesburg: South African Institute of Race Relations.

Howard, B. 1995. "Conservation for the People." *On Track,* May/June.

Hugo, M. L. 1974. "An Investigation into the Nature and Magnitude of the Demand for Outdoor Recreation Among the Urban Black Communities of South Africa." *The South African Journal of African Affairs* 4 (2).

Imvo. 1923. "The Forest Department." 8 May.

Johns, S. 1972. *Protest and Hope, 1882–1934, Vol. 1.* Washington, D.C.: Hoover Institution Press.

Jordan, C., and D. Snow 1992. "Diversification, Minorities, and the Mainstream Environmental Movement." In *Perspectives for a New Era.* Washington, D.C.: Island Press.

Joubert, S. C. J. nd. "Masterplan for the Management of the Kruger National Park." Vols. I–VI. Kruger National Park, mimeo.

Kerley, G. 1997. "The Winning Game: An Ecotourist Success Story that Almost Never Happened." *African Wildlife* 51 (2).

Khan, F. 1990a. "Contemporary South African Environmental Response: An Historical and Socio-political Evaluation, with Particular Reference to Blacks." M.A. thesis, University of Cape Town.

———. 1990b. "Involvement of the Masses in Environmental Politics." *Veld and Flora* 76 (2).

———. 1990c. "Beyond the White Rhino: Confronting the South African Land Question." *African Wildlife* 44 (6).

———. 1992a. "Targeting Environmental Poverty: The Role of Community-based Greening Projects." *Veld and Flora* 78 (1).

———. 1992b. *Black Environmental History as a Facet of Current South African Environmental Perceptions.* Research Report, University of Cape Town.

———. 1994a. "Environmentalism in a Changing South Africa: Incorporating Development Needs into the Environmental Debate." Paper presented to the Journal of African Studies Conference, September, York University.

———. 1994b. "Rewriting South Africa's Conservation History: The Role of the Native Farmers Association." *Journal of Southern African Studies* 20 (4).

———. 1996. *Waste Picking for Survival: A Report on the Waste Pickers of Frankdale Informal Settlement.* Report No. 02/96/11, Environmental Advisory Unit, University of Cape Town.

———. 1997. "Soil Wars: The Role of the African National Soil Conservation Association in South Africa, 1953–1959." *Environmental History* 2 (4).

Kumleben Commission of Inquiry. 1996. *Commission of Inquiry into the Alleged Smuggling of and Illegal Trade in Ivory and Rhinoceros Horn in South Africa.* Report of the Chairman Mr. Justice M. E. Kumleben, Judge of Appeal. Durban.

Lukey, P. 1995. *Health before Profits: An Access Guide to Trade Unions and Envi-*

ronmental Justice in South Africa. Pietermaritzburg: Environmental Justice Networking Forum and Friedrich Ebert Stiftung.

McCarthy, J. J., and D. P. Smit. 1983. *South African City: Theory in Analysis and Planning.* Cape Town: Juta and Co.

Madihlaba, T. 1998. "Campaign against Injustices Caused by Vantech Continues." *Environmental Justice Networker* 17.

Magane, P., S. Miller, M. Goldblatt, and B. Lel. 1997. "Unions and the Environment." In L. Bethlehem and M. Goldblatt, eds. *The Bottom Line: Industry and the Environment in South Africa.* Johannesburg: International Development Research Centre.

Makuleke, L. 1997. "Rural Communities as Roleplayers and Stakeholders in the South African Wildlife Industries." Presented at a conference held by the Wildlife Utilisation Forum of South Africa, 14 April, Suikerbosrand Nature Reserve.

Melosi, M. 1995. "Equity, Eco-racism and Environmental History." *Environmental History Review* 19 (3).

Miller, S. 1993. "Health, Safety and the Environment." In D. Hallowes, ed. *Hidden Faces, Environment, Development, Justice: South Africa and the Global Context.* Pietermaritzburg: Earthlife Africa.

Mlambo, B., and T. Mzimela. 1993. *St Lucia Rural Communications Programme: Comments on the Environmental Impact Report.* Pretoria: Council for Scientific and Industrial Research.

Moloi, D. 1998. "The Land between Two Rivers." *Land and Rural Digest* 1 (2).

Morokeng, M. 1993. "Statement on the Role of Trade Unions in Environmental Protection and Development." In D. Hallowes, ed. *Hidden Faces, Environment, Development, Justice: South Africa and the Global Context.* Pietermaritzburg: Earthlife Africa.

Nussey, W. 1995. "National Parks Board of South Africa." *Africa, Environment and Wildlife* 3 (4).

Odendaal, L. 1993. "Climbing to Greater Heights: Together." *Tribute,* November.

Pelzer, A. N. 1966. *Verwoerd Speaks: Speeches 1948–1966.* Johannesburg: APB Publishers.

Potgieter, D. 1995. *Contraband: South Africa and the International Trade in Ivory and Rhino Horn.* Cape Town: Quellerie Publishers.

Pringle, J. 1983. *The Conservationists and the Killers: The Story of Game Protection and the Wildlife Society of South Africa.* Cape Town: TV Bulpin and Books of Africa (Pty) Ltd.

Ramphele, M., and C. McDowell. 1991. *Restoring the Land: Environment and Change in Post-apartheid South Africa.* London: The Panos Institute.

RSA (Republic of South Africa). 1998. "Marine Living Resources Act, No.18." Vol. 395, No. 18930. Pretoria: Government Printers.

SAIRR (South African Institute of Race Relations). 1997. *South Africa Survey, 1996/1997.* Johannesburg: South African Institute of Race Relations.

Schwab, J. 1994. *Deeper Shades of Green: The Rise of Blue-collar and Minority Environmentalism in America*. San Francisco: Sierra Club Books.

Schweizer, C. D. 1983. *Environmental and Related Interest Groups in South Africa*. MSc Research Report, University of Cape Town.

Sierra Club Bulletin. 1972. "Editorial." 57 (2).

Sowman, M., M. Bergh, G. Maharaj, and K. Salo. 1997. "An Analysis of Emerging Co-management Arrangements for the Olifants River Harder Fishery, South Africa." In *Fisheries Co-management in Africa: Proceedings from a Regional Workshop on Fisheries Co-management Research*. Denmark: Institute for Fisheries Management and Coastal Community Development.

SPP (Surplus People Project). nd. "SPP Factsheet: Riemvasmaak." Information Brochure, Surplus People Project.

————. 1990. "Dossier: Richtersveld Nasionale Park." Information Package, Surplus People Project, 10 November.

Statistics South Africa. 1998. *Census in Brief: The People of South Africa Population Census, 1996*. Report no. 1.

Statutes of the Union of South Africa. 1926. National Parks Act.

Timberlake, L. 1986. *Africa in Crisis: The Causes, the Cures of Environmental Bankruptcy*. Philadelphia: New Society Publishers.

Veld Trust News. 1944. Membership Form. 1 (1).

Wolfgat Nature Reserve Interim Management Committee. 1995. "Community Involvement in Wolfgat Nature Reserve." *Veld and Flora* 81 (3).

People Are Living Here

Mpume Nyandu

I t's just gone 11:30 in the scorching heat of a Thursday morning. A tractor with trailer drives into the heart of the Tlhabane dump site. People emerge from all corners of the dump—men and women, young and old—and hurry in the direction of the tractor. They wait impatiently as the trailer is tilted, and a pile of Chibuku beer cartons is heaved off. Then they pounce. Each person grabs as many Chibuku beer cartons as they can. This local brewery is just one of the many industries that dump expired products on this illegal site. Ten-year-old Joyce is also here to grab a few cartons of beer for her dad.

The expired products serve as food for the scavenging community and discarded cans, bottles, and cardboard are a source of income. The stench of rotting food and human waste hangs in the air, and in the middle of it all is a stinking puddle from which the goats drink.

Joyce and her parents often come to the dump to scavenge. Both her parents are unemployed but they manage to send her to a nearby school. On this particular day Joyce is not at school because "my teacher is writing exams." When asked what she thinks about coming to the dump to collect beer cartons, she says, "I don't think it's a good thing to do. I only come here because my father sends me."

Joyce and her parents live in a nearby settlement called Lefaragatlha. Most of the people at the dump site come from Tlhabane township, about twenty kilometers from Rustenberg in the North West province. The Tlhabane dump site dates back to the times of Lucas Mangope, one-time dictator of what used to be the "homeland"of Bophuthatswana. It started up informally as there was no reliable refuse collection system for the township's residents. There was no objection from the Bophuthatswana government so the dump site just grew.

Now it covers an area of approximately four hectares. It is not fenced and is less than two hundred meters from the township, posing a serious health hazard to township residents. Chief Chemist at the Rustenberg Municipality, Johan St Arnaud, admits that the site does not meet the requirements of a legal dump site and says there are plans to close it down.

More than twenty people have made the dump their home. Unemployment, followed by failure to pay rent, and then eviction, brought them here. Piet, aged 41, who has been living there for ten years, says, "When I lost my job in 1987, I was evicted from the place I rented because I could not pay rent anymore. We have driver's licenses here but we can't drive anything except the cans we collect." Piet and his fellow residents make between R20 and R27 per week collecting cans and bottles. They use the money to buy things they cannot pick up from the dump like sugar, salt, tea, toiletries, and so on. They collect water from a nearby hostel.

According to the dump residents various people and organizations have promised to help them, but nothing has come of these pledges so far. "You are not the first people to come here," they said. They dream of a better life, but Walter (19) says "it's always difficult to get consensus here because we all come from different parts of the North West."

If the site is closed what will happen to the people who are living there? St. Arnaud of the Rustenburg Municipality says that one of the ideas being explored is to turn the site into a mini recycling site, properly fenced, where different types of waste will be deposited into specific bins: "Maybe the people living in the dump can be employed to work with or for the recycling individuals or companies they are already selling cans and bottles to." Other rubbish will be disposed of by the municipality. "There is already a system of refuse collection in place on which the municipality has spent millions of rands but the problem at the moment is that residents have not been paying for the service," he says.

In the meantime, the residents of Tlhabane township will have to put up with the dump for a little longer.

Chapter 2

Power, Poverty, and Marginalized Environments

A Conceptual Framework

David Hallowes and Mark Butler

This chapter explores the interrelationship between power, poverty, and environment in South Africa from an environmental justice perspective. Environmental justice might broadly be described as a rights- or values-based discourse which locates environmental degradation within a sociopolitical context. While environmental justice might be said to have emerged as a more or less distinct discourse on environmental management, for the most part it has been defined and understood through examples of environmental *in*justice rather than a positive statement of the "ideal" of environmental justice. The following is an initial attempt to provide a positive definition:

> Environmental justice obtains where relations between people, within and between groups of people, and between people and their environments[1] are fair and equal, allowing all to define and achieve their aspirations without imposing unfair, excessive or irreparable burdens or externalities on others or their environments, now and in the future.

Even though such a statement relies on a number of underlying sub-definitions and assumptions (e.g., what are "fair and equal" relations, and what conditions could produce or sustain them?), it is rather long and complex. A simpler rendition might be:

> Empowered people in relations of solidarity and equity with each other and in non-degrading and positive relationships with their environments.

Central to these working definitions, and to the idea of environmental justice, is the understanding that *environment* chiefly expresses a set of relations—it is not something "out there." This means that *development* is concerned with understanding how relations are established and maintained, what powers and interests they express and serve, and how they enhance or inhibit the possibilities of "a better life for all" within the various environments where people live. This overcomes the dualism of development and environment that is characteristic of other major environmental management discourses. The "Charter for the Participation of People's Organisations in Environmental Governance in Southern Africa" (written in February 1997) expressed this view: "All people at all times live and work in relationship to their environments because their environments provide the resources by which they can live."

Environmental *in*justice therefore refers principally to the experience of those who are excluded from the benefits of development and/or who carry the burden of its costs and externalities. The agenda for environmental justice emerges, in turn, from a sound understanding of history and an analysis of the conditions of the poor and the marginalized in relation to the way they live, work, and participate in social and institutional life.

A Conceptual Framework

These definitions of environmental justice make it clear that it is not simply achieved through equal and fair distribution of benefits and costs but goes to the heart of how power relations define and re-produce development itself. Thus, one must ask of development: who benefits, who loses, and who *did* it—that is, who are the beneficiaries, who are the subjects, and who are the agents of environmental injustice? The question of who, however, is embedded in multiple relationships that can be made visible through an understanding of how environmental injustice is created.

The most important means, or mechanisms, by which environmental injustice is generated, are externalization of costs, enclosure, and exclusion.

Understanding environmental conditions and issues through a critical appreciation of these mechanisms allows for fresh insight into the evolution of South Africa's environmental history and suggests how its present challenges and future trajectories might be examined. The approach outlined in the following paragraphs marks a departure from previous concepts of the environment in South Africa and also raises uncomfortable questions about current dominant approaches.

Externalization of Costs

To externalize something is to give it "external existence." Conventional economics, markets, and accounting systems tend to externalize a range of costs and benefits because they are not generally given monetary value and accounted for. Social and environmental impacts associated with development are clear examples. When they are not accounted for or valued, these impacts inevitably occur either as free benefits to the producer or as uncompensated costs carried either by the environment or by any body bearing the remediation costs (usually government and ultimately the public), or people disadvantaged by the effects (either through their loss of a resource damaged by pollution, or through their health).

Various techniques have been developed to evaluate in monetary terms such social and environmental externalities.[2] Using these techniques it is possible to try and estimate the "Total Economic Value" of resources.

Shadow pricing can also be derived for otherwise uncompensated costs by ascribing a monetary value to their impacts on people. For example, where a causal link is established between a particular pollutant source and negative health impacts, the costs can be implied in, for example:

- ■ "defensive expenditure": an estimate of what community members might have had to pay to mitigate the effects of the pollutant source. It may also estimate money that might have been spent under better resourced social conditions, but was not spent because of poverty and lack of income;
- ■ productivity loss: the economic value attached to any loss in working productivity as a result of the pollutant source, in particular lost working days, as well as any loss in income caused by the declining quality or productivity of an environmental resource like a river system; and
- ■ "hedonic pricing": Residents in a polluted area also bear the cost of a generally poor environment and the associated loss of amenities and recreational value. In order to estimate the total value of lost environmental quality, one can make use of land value depreciation approaches that would assess the discount in market-based property prices in the surrounding or affected areas as a result of the proximity of the pollutant source.

Costs borne by "the environment" (and usually functioning as a free benefit to a producer) can be valued by surrogate measures, for example:

- ■ The costs of controlling ongoing pollution and cleaning up historical pollution;
- ■ The difference between what is paid for waste disposal and the real costs of safe disposal;
- ■ The costs of retrofitting or replacing the plant;
- ■ The costs of introducing proper health and safety;
- ■ The price difference between environmentally unfriendly and friendly non-labor production inputs;
- ■ The difference in per unit production costs—particularly where environmentally sound production requires more labor.

The loss of natural environments is usually more difficult to calculate because it is often difficult to attribute monetary values to what has been lost or what is intangible. In addition to the techniques discussed above, attempts have been made to value such losses, especially in terms of the "non-use value" of a resource.

Subsidies can be deployed as tools for the externalization of costs.

Subsidies are important, often hidden, mechanisms through which producers gain free benefit, funded by public money, and often at the expense of people and environments. Subsidies and related government measures can also underwrite the risk element of a venture or industry (again with public monies) to secure private profitability for the beneficiary. In South Africa's apartheid history, for example, large sectors of the white farming industry were subsidized to secure political support, encouraging hopelessly inappropriate farming on marginal land subject to periodic drought. Will more recent supportive interventions carried out in the name of industrial development (e.g., Spatial Development Initiatives [SDIs]), or agricultural development (e.g., emergent farmer support) go in the same direction?

Enclosure

Enclosure involves the appropriation of a common resource. It therefore implies the dispossession of those who previously had access to that resource.

The main forms are:

- Conquest (or forced appropriation): Conquest here is used as a metaphor. It involves the state or private interests grabbing a common asset by force, and the state legitimating the new possessor.
- Technological enclosure: This refers to instances where the impact of the use of a powerful technology results in the effective monopolization of a resource. It frequently involves the depletion of the resource so that less powerful technologies are no longer able to access it (e.g., a powerful water pump is installed which subsequently lowers the water table it draws on, thereby reducing the availability of water from village wells).
- Commodification or Monetization: Rights in common resources are generally defined by something analogous to citizenship rather than by money. Where a monetary value is placed on the resource, the poor are excluded. In short, it becomes a commodity, and access is conditional on individual purchasing power in the market. Privatization is an increasingly common means of

commodification. Commodification also tends to undermine ethics and customs that previously regulated the use of a resource. As a commodity, its trade and exchange is more likely to be subject to the rules of the marketplace.

Exclusion

Exclusion may relate both to institutions of markets and of governance—implicitly reflected in the phrase: "the poor and the marginalized." Given the weight of economic forces in shaping broader social institutions and relations, these two aspects of exclusion frequently reinforce each other to describe the multiple weaknesses of the poor—they are denied access to, and control over, both material resources and the social resources, processes, and institutions which define and reinforce their "place." Exclusion denotes the ways in which social institutions define (and limit) access to resources—institutions of patriarchy for example operate at all levels to exclude women from the macro- to micro-level (so poor women are excluded to a greater degree than either the poor in general or women in general).

There are important parallels between the mechanism of exclusion described here and the framework developed by Forsyth et al. (1998) to articulate an "environmental entitlements" approach to understanding poverty-environment links. Adapted from Sen's (1981) work on entitlements in the context of famine, their approach shifts the emphasis from questions of resource availability to those of access, control, and management.

The advantage of using these conceptual tools in assessing environmental (in)justice in South Africa is the task of the remainder of this chapter. We look first at the dominant environment paradigms in the country (past and present) and then demonstrate the need for more critical analytical frameworks.

Challenging Environmental Orthodoxies

In the past the governance of environmental matters in South Africa reflected the racial, gender, and class bias of the colonial and apartheid authorities (see chap. 1). It is equally important however to recognize that the construction of *environment* in South Africa was not—and is not—shaped only by South African peculiarities and racial distortions. It articulates with broader intellectual currents and ideological projects. In the current South African context, while the concept of *environment* is being democratized and de-racialized, its reconstruction is intimately connected with global environmental discourses which, in turn, are intimately connected with developmental discourses. This is the obvious implication of the argument put forward earlier in this chapter that environmental issues are, or express broader developmental concerns that define and/or reflect relations to resources and power.

While acknowledging the dangers of gross oversimplification, one can characterize contemporary dominant environmental/developmental discourses as reflecting at least two key currents (discussed below) both of which function powerfully in the South African context.

"Growth First": Unfettered Economic Development

Some of the basic tenets of neoliberal economic thinking radically subordinate environmental (let alone environmental justice) problems. At the core of this thinking is the assumption that market-based and market-led economic growth, within an international regime of private property, is not merely the only path to development, but also the only effective (and certainly most efficient) mechanism for distributing the benefits of and opportunities for development and for stimulating solutions to all challenges encountered along the way.

Environmental problems are largely disregarded or denied and externalities are placed where they will not be noticed by anyone powerful enough to make a fuss. Indeed, one might argue that this is not so much a discourse of environmental management as a discourse that tends to exclude environmental concepts. Whereas strict neoliberalism became quite globally dominant through the 1980s and early 1990s, few significant sectors would now publicly articulate such a crude version of the orthodoxy which completely denied some degree of market failure in relation to the environmental (and other) consequences of development. Even so, for many the underlying assumptions of the approach remain in place—and the practice (if not the rhetoric) of much development remains firmly embedded in this approach.

Capitalist neoliberalism was not the only model to prioritize economic development over environmental considerations, although, given the global power of capital, it is arguably the most powerful one to do so. Historically, state-socialist economic development models (e.g., the Soviet-bloc countries) also externalized the environmental implications of the industry- and military-led development path. Furthermore, in the South African context, it is not uncommon to view people's developmental needs as such a priority that environmental constraints cannot be pandered to, except perhaps in the long term.

"Sustainable Economic Development": Ecological Modernization

A second discourse, which can be labeled ecological modernization, was effectively endorsed by governmental negotiators at the United Nations Conference on Environment and Development (UNCED) in 1992. The concept of sustainable development as developed by the Brundtland Commission is central to this discourse. State regulation is recognized, but the role of the state is now to be "supplemented by strong international organizations as well as local governments."

Market mechanisms are given a prominent role in environmental management. There has therefore been a strong focus on costing externalities so that they can be brought into the marketplace. Whereas the early motivation for this was to leverage the internalization of external costs, there is now a growing emphasis on using such costing to provide the basis for trading pollution credits. This trend is most noticeable in climate change negotiations where the ground (or rather the atmosphere) is being prepared for the privatization of rights in "carbon credits." Larry Lohmann (1999, 16) points out that this market is already being rigged in the northern and corporate interest. He sees the consequence as the commodification and enclosure of the atmosphere as well as further dispossession of land to make way for aforestation.

Within this discourse, forms of accumulation are naturalized as "progress," and poverty is constructed as the condition of being without development. In this manner, poverty is seen as isolated from the process of accumulation of wealth that in fact defines development. At the same time, the environment is placed in opposition to development. Access to resources is presented as conditional on modernizing development. Within what is represented as the common project of humanity, the only option is to mitigate the "hazards" of development.

The Articulation of Environment and Poverty

From an environmental justice perspective, by contrast, the marginalization of the majority of Southern Africans from decision making of all kinds lies at the core of unsustainable development. Imperialism initiated a long and continuous process of alienating people from their environments, both economically and psychologically, and of coercing them into a subordinate relation within the modernizing economy.

However, the history of development has created different interests in, and relationships to, the environment. This puts environment at the center of complex and contradictory interests. It places everyone in an ambiguous relationship to the environment because access to resources is predicated on unsustainable development. Although the costs and benefits are unevenly spread, everyone is implicated in the causes and everyone is subject to the consequences. Those who are excluded from defining the terms of development are frequently constrained to replicate the model in their demand for "delivery" (e.g., for jobs, goods, and services).[3]

Furthermore, people must defend their environmental rights from a range of different positions. Workers and rural women do not struggle on the same terrain; they are confronted by different issues and institutions. The environmental interests of poor people are located on many different fronts of development: in the factories and farms; as permanent, casual, or seasonal labor; on the land, in formal or informal settlements; across the gender divide; in the politics of consumption, of technical development, and of media representation. These do not add up to a common front. Rather, the fronts of development are discontinuous and contradictory.

Nor do these fronts encompass static and discrete groups of people. The world of the poor is particularly unsettled and dislocated. Poor households frequently have members located in different places so as to combine the slender opportunities offered by each. As households or their members move, or are forced to move between locations in search of a livelihood, they may be subject to cumulative environmental costs. There are also considerable differences between people within communities, and even within households. Rural people are not all poor; workers are not all equally marginalized within the market economy; and women are mostly subordinated within households.

The environment too is in constant flux, and environmental costs are frequently displaced so that the effects appear to be separated from the cause in time and space. Thus, the effects of commercial farming are not restricted to the impact of chemicals on soil or water. The displacement of people associated with modern agriculture and apartheid land policies produced overcrowding and environmental degradation in African rural areas. Such links, however, are not immediately visible, and their concealment in the dominant development discourse allows poverty to be identified as an independent cause of degradation.

Poverty, then, cannot be viewed simply as the failure to enter the modern economy. Seabrook (1997) points out that people who satisfy their needs outside the market economy are not poor, even if they have no cash income. Yet people who depend on bought goods may be poor even with a relatively substantial income if that income does not cover the cost of the goods that they need.

The history of modernity cannot be undone. Few South Africans are fortunate enough to live well without cash. Nevertheless, the simple equation of poverty with cash incomes legitimizes forms of development which dispossess people of their remaining access to environmental resources and forces them into total reliance on a market economy which will not adequately provide for most of them.

The official cash economy of a country, measured by GNP, is only part of the whole economy. Externalities of the cash economy—costs not included in pricing mechanisms—are imposed on the non-monetized economy. These externalities are composed of unpaid work in homes and fields, caring for the sick and disabled, mutual aid within communities and families, bartering, "sweat equity," and the environment which provides the natural resource base and absorbs the cost of pollution.

It is clear, therefore, that people do relate differently to the environment but that their positioning is determined by the history of development. In what follows, we attempt to locate the environment within that history in South Africa.

Historical "Development" and the Margins of Modernity

Land and Labor

Dispossession is at the root of poverty in South Africa. It starts with land and the colonial need to coerce labor. Land and labor remain key areas of struggle today. From the early nineteenth century, British occupation linked the Cape Colony to the expanding imperial economy (Bundy 1979). Capital, new technologies, and colonists came into the Cape and British manufacturing markets, particularly for wool, creating new demands for both land and labor. Fifty years later the discovery of diamonds rescued the Cape economy from recession and massively expanded markets and a further demand for labor. The process was repeated when the flagging diamond economy was overtaken by the gold boom.

The resultant demand for cheap labor could not be satisfied by market forces as long as people had access to independent resources and livelihoods, and the state intervened to create a labor supply. During the nineteenth century, successive wars on independent African polities were conducted with increased ferocity and the territories that were conquered were administered in a way that imposed a dependency on cash wages. Despite this, Bundy (1997) shows that an emerging African peasantry rapidly adapted to the market and was its principle source of agricultural produce throughout that century. Some peasants acquired freehold land on the market. Many entered into tenancy and sharecropping arrangements with white landowners who could not compete with the Africans' productive capacities because they could not command the requisite labor. Others carried market production, technologies, and social relations into African occupied territories with various implications. These innovations included: replacing the traditional abundance of land with a land shortage; destroying patterns of transhumance (moving between summer and winter grazing); expanding cultivation; privatizing common land; passing control of cultivation from women to men; placing increasing control of land and ownership of stock in the hands of chiefs and wealthier peasants; and eroding systems of reciprocal loans which had enabled those without productive resources to acquire them. The technology complex itself was a tool of dispossession. It exposed people to economic and ecological shocks and precipitated environmental degradation that undermined productivity.

In the 1890s peasant debt multiplied and social conflict escalated. Peasants who failed were forced onto the labor market. The clamor for labor intensified from the 1890s and intensified further after the South African war (1899–1902). Mining interests viewed the peasantry as refugees from wage labor, while white farmers wanting to commercialize production saw them as competitors for both markets and labor. Land legislation became increasingly racial and, after the establishment of the Union of South Africa in 1910, the 1913 Land Act confined Africans to 13 percent of the land, prohibited land acquisition in "white areas," and outlawed tenancy and sharecropping.

The letter of the law was pervasively ignored but it nonetheless helped to shift relations of power on white-owned farms. In time, tenants were reduced to sharecroppers, sharecroppers to labor tenants, and labor tenants to wage laborers. At each step, their command of productive resources was forfeited to the landowners. The pace of the process was uneven. Those, like Kas Maine, who attempted to retain their independence were slowly and inexorably forced towards more marginal farms, and finally to the crowded and stressed African rural or urban locations (see Van Onselen 1996).

Under apartheid, the land policy was enforced with increasing vigor but the process was not only political; technology played a key role. The capitalization of agriculture was deployed as a weapon in the struggle for the land and was supported by state policy. Tractors made landlords independent of the sharecropper's plowing teams and family labor. They also greatly extended the land under the plow, reducing the grazing available for the sharecropper's stock.

While more extensive cultivation initially increased the demand of white farmers for labor (particularly cheap seasonal labor) further mechanization brought the combine harvester which enabled them to shed labor (Williams 1993, 8). The growth in agriculture-based rural economies continues to be accompanied by population decline and the further casualization of labor.

Capitalization has also brought severe direct environmental consequences in land degradation and chemical runoff. Disregard for health and safety has exposed farm workers to toxic chemicals and high risks of mechanical accidents:

> Large commercial farms use huge amounts of pesticides. . . .
> As well as being major polluters of the farm and the natural
> environment, pesticides also pose risks to users. An estimated
> 11 million people are poisoned by pesticides every year in
> Africa. . . . Some poisonings are fatal. . . . South Africa, Tanza-
> nia, and Zimbabwe each report about 200–300 deaths annu-
> ally. (Booth et al. 1994, 236)

Under apartheid, mining and industry were also virtually immune to
effective environmental regulation and workers suffered from the neglect of
health and safety standards. For the majority, access to wages took prece-
dence over labor conditions. This placed them in an ambiguous relationship
to the environment. Lukey (1995, 16) observes that "workers are closely
linked to environmental degradation both as victims or, as labor in dirty industry, directly involved in the generation of toxic pollution." This point is
poignantly confirmed by Josiah Makola who works at a vanadium mine in
Mpumalanga: "Even though I know I am dying, I am just persevering because I was told by the company that I will not be employable anywhere else
when I leave the company. So I think I am going to die here for the sake of
keeping a job so that my child can finish school" (Nyandu 1998, 16).

Although its contribution to the South African economy has recently declined, mining remains central to the economy and is a major
source of environmental degradation:

> Mineral production, unless carried out with scrupulous care,
> is exceedingly damaging to the environment and dangerous
> to the workers involved. . . . For every ton of metal that
> leaves a mining operations mill, about 100 tons of wastes are
> left in a heap topside where they can blow away on the
> winds, run off into rivers, or leach into groundwater. Mining
> wastes account for three fourths of all solid wastes in South
> Africa. (Durning 1990, 15)

The health and safety impacts on miners are also alarming: "Half a
million men descend into the gold mines each morning; on a typical
day, two of them are carried out dead. Since the beginning of the century, some 46,000 workers have died underground" (Durning 1990, 18).

A critical factor in the relatively low price of South African coal is the exploitative wages paid to miners. Cheap coal is the basis for cheap electricity which provides a basis for an energy- and capital-intensive industrial complex with a tendency to displace labor. As Booth et al. (1994, 227) argue:

> Manufacturing and service industries are the primary sources of pollution in southern Africa, producing millions of tons of effluents (poisoned waste water), ten of millions of tons of solid waste (rubbish stored on land), and hundreds of millions of tons of emissions (air pollutants). Major polluters include thermal electric power stations which burn coal or petroleum products, fertilizer factories, textile mills, chemical manufacturing plants, pulp-and-paper plants, slaughterhouses and tanneries.

Shirley Miller (1993, 96) points out that "workers are the first to experience the toxic effects of . . . chemicals, [and as such] they are the guinea pigs of our society." Many companies use subcontracting and short-term contracts to evade responsibility for the consequences. Workers suffering occupational diseases tend not to be re-employed.

Since the 1970s the demand for labor in the economy as a whole has fallen ever further below the level of supply created by the dependency on wages. The decline of gold mining has obviously been a key factor. Beyond that, however, what happened on the farms is now happening in the factories. It can be summed up in the phrase "job-shedding growth."

Not only are jobs being shed, formal sector employment has become increasingly impermanent, using casual workers who are excluded from the forms of security—pensions, medical schemes, regulated dismissal procedures, and so on—which had been developed through worker struggles. There are now suggestions that even the service industry, heralded during the 1980s as the new unregulated job creation sector, is beginning to shed labor.

If we imagine industry as a geographic region, we can see economic growth being accompanied by depopulation of the region except for a small relative elite of permanent workers and bands of temporary laborers.

When the isolation of apartheid ended, South Africa re-entered the global market at an unpropitious moment. Job-shedding growth and the casualization of work are characteristics of globalization. Ownership has been increasingly concentrated and resources controlled on a global scale as new technologies have increased the mobility of capital and enabled the creation of global markets. Southern countries with poorly skilled labor are now "competing for the bottom," cutting wages and environmental protection, to attract and keep investment. Dirty technologies are being relocated from northern to southern countries where labor organization and environmental movements tend to be weaker.

Marginalization in Space

The subordination of rural to metropolitan market economies has been an important element in the development of South Africa's industrial and market economy. The migrant labor system contained the costs of social reproduction within the African "reserve" areas, ensuring cheap labor and inhibiting the development of a potentially dangerous black urban working class.

In 1914 the Royal Commission on Natural Resources, Trade, and Legislation in Certain of His Majesty's Dominions heard just how useful black rural areas were as labor reserves. The reserve was "a sanatorium where [African workers] can recuperate; if they are disabled they remain there. Their own tribal system keeps them under discipline, and if they become criminals there is not the slightest difficulty in bringing them to justice. All this absolutely without expense to the white man" (cited in Bundy 1979, 126).

In the late nineteenth century, rural areas were already picking up the health costs of the mining industry. Tuberculosis spread through the mining compounds into which workers were densely packed and they carried it back to rural homes throughout Southern Africa. Workers suffering from occupational diseases or disablement were similarly sent home, the costs of care and the loss of earnings being imposed on rural households and particularly on rural women.

Migrancy, however, also developed out of the tenacity with which African men clung to a rural resource base, however diminished, so as to retain some measure of independence from the market economy. Beinart (1982, 94ff.) shows that as access to rural resources and agricultural markets became more restricted, Mpondo household heads deployed young men to earn wages with which to pay taxes or provide the means for rural investments. And migrants themselves attempted to use their earnings to buy access to rural resources of land, cattle, and bride wealth.

This resulted in a struggle within households over control of wages, contributing to the fragmentation of familial authority. Migrancy also instigated a revolution in gender relations. In time it became something like a rite of passage for young males. It emphasized the advantages of educating boys before girls, and it gave men access to a broader world of experience while confining women to responsibility without authority in maintaining the rural household economy (Derman 1993, 199).

It also demonstrates the manner in which households were becoming dependent on multiple incomes sourced both in rural and urban areas, and presages the increasing interdependence of rural and urban economies. The prevalence of circular migration in other "developing" nations and its persistence in South Africa (see Mabin 1989, Bank 1995) places a major qualification on the notion that development is accompanied by a simple transition from rural to urban living.

The reservation of a mere 13 percent of land for Africans was, as we have seen, an assault on the capacity of Africans to compete with white farmers for expanding agricultural markets. From within the reserved land, however, the chiefly class was quick to point out that agricultural capitalization itself was a means of dispossession, from which the Land Act provided some refuge. Thus Cingo, a counsellor to the Mpondo paramount, declared: "Is it not a fact that more land than what today belongs to natives has hitherto been steadily dropping from their hands. . . . The prospects therefore of the position 50 years hence at this course. . . is enough to stagger the mind" (cited in Beinart 1982, 123).

Worse, however, was the impact on what were to become "homelands" and "independent states." As the pace of removals from white farms and "black spots" accelerated in the 1960s, the flow of refugees into black rural areas swelled dramatically (Mabin 1989, 6). Notwithstanding the perceptiveness of Cingo's comment, many of the social and environmental costs of the racial division of land were visited on the refugees and on their hosts. Population growth no doubt exacerbated the situation, just as the resultant social conflict, pervasive insecurity, and worsening gender relations exacerbated population growth. In itself, however, population growth is insignificant next to the extraordinary concentration of population and poverty engineered by apartheid.

Rural Margins

African rural areas have at least ten times the population of commercial farming areas (Durning 1990, 13) and suffer chronic erosion. Despite this, agricultural production and resource gathering remain critical to livelihoods in rural and peri-urban areas. Redundancies in the formal urban economy and the growing wealth gap in all population groups are reinforcing poor people's reliance on natural resources. Not only does environmental degradation result from the concentration of poverty, it becomes a cause of further impoverishment.

Ardington and Lund (1996) argue that current quantitative research undervalues rural production and migrant remittances. Cross et al. (1996, 188ff.) distinguish between the extraction economy (collecting water, firewood, traditional medicinal plant material) and the production economy (cultivation, stock keeping). The very poor depend most heavily on the extraction economy. Better off (or less poor) people have greater control over production because they can command both labor and land. Local elites are frequently stock owners.

Urban redundancies can result in intensified production as more labor becomes available in rural areas. In many areas, however, men accustomed to wages have not adapted to subsistence or domestic work. Their presence and the loss of earnings merely increases the pressure on the women's time and labor. At the same time, the insecurities engendered by apartheid have broken down micro-institutions relating to common resource management. In KwaZulu-Natal, user groups no longer defend common resources from outsiders and in many areas the boundaries between different "use domains" have collapsed. For example, cattle are not kept out of cultivated fields.

Experience of apartheid conservationist interventions such as Betterment Planning has made black rural people suspicious of any outside intervention relating to resource use. They resist limitations on stock or access to resources, particularly when neighboring conservation areas and white farms have what appear to them to be unused lands (Cross et al. 1996, 182) from which, in many cases, they were previously removed.

Many rural people still do not have reasonable access to clean water, a resource that links the possibility of intensified cultivation with women's labor time:

> Gardening is undertaken as a hedge against the lean season. As a result, it serves a critical supportive function at particular times of the year. To be sustainable, and to have maximum effect, water availability is critical. . . . The rural poor see land for gardening as a key element of adequate housing. (May 1996, 116)

Food security and women's time are also tied to domestic energy. Environmental pressures for fuel wood reflect the grossly skewed provision of energy under apartheid. The South African Participatory Poverty Assessment found that "women tended to put electricity high up as a priority for lighting (safety) reasons as well as for cooking" (May 1996, 102). The vulnerability of rural women to violence is revealed by the fact that this desire for electricity reflects a need to be freed from collecting firewood and from darkness—the combination of which was/is the context for rape and other violent attacks.

Development, however, brings its own hazards. Service provision can have the effect of further marginalizing the poorest, who cannot afford the costs associated with the service (Cross et al. 1996, 201). Agricultural intensification may increase the use of pesticides as is happening elsewhere in southern Africa (Booth et al. 1994, 236).

The capacity to optimize sustainable livelihoods in these conditions must be supported by integrated development, including agricultural extension, credit arrangements, skills development programs, appropriate technology, and targeted research and development programs. Apartheid has failed spectacularly in this regard too, having bequeathed to the present state an "agricultural extension system [that] does not deliver to the poor and is perceived by them to be useless" (May 1996, 115).

Similarly, nature conservation authorities are seen as policing access to resources rather than facilitating their sustainable use. The history of removals from parks is intensely resented. "Good neighbor" schemes initiated by conservation authorities do provide some access to gatherers but they are small compensation. Rural communities have only been reconciled with conservation where they have been able to take real control, as in some land restitution cases, and are persuaded of the economic potential of tourism.

Urban Margins

Urban influx control under apartheid, and its attendant harassment, low urban wages, and high urban costs, drove many people to secure a rural base however meager. The appearance of unserviced towns (sometimes referred to as rural slums) in allegedly rural areas devastated the environment and people's health. Natural vegetation was rapidly cleared, human waste and garbage accumulated, smoke filled the air, and water sources were contaminated or difficult to access. Some of the unserviced towns were very remote from urban job opportunities. Most, the "peri-urban settlements," were close enough for long distance commuting to be possible, but this imposed on workers heavy transport costs and long hours of traveling. They are now part of the bizarre metropolitan urban form structured by apartheid.

Formal black urban townships were removed to the outer edges of the cities where they received only partial services and suffered massive overcrowding. Much of the growth in informal urban settlements since the early 1990s has resulted from the movement of urban people attempting to escape the crowded conditions imposed by apartheid or to move closer to jobs.

In formal and informal urban settlements, the poor quality of the built environment creates an ongoing health crisis. Without sanitation and waste removal, raw sewage runs in the roads and litter accumulates everywhere. Fecal contamination remains a major source of water pollution, and is associated with a wide range of diseases including diarrheal diseases, cholera, hepatitis, and a range of skin and eye infections. Diseases such as bilharzia and malaria are also exacerbated by environmental degradation. Litter, for example, provides breeding habitats for mosquitoes (Satterthwaite 1993, 89ff.).

The provision of potable water is a priority of the present government. This represents a major advance. Provision has, however, been highly uneven and sometimes unreliable. Many people still rely on contaminated water sources. The privatization of water services in some areas is likely to impose unaffordable costs on poor people, while the push for cost recovery on water services has forced many poor families to use unsafe water sources like stagnant ponds. In fact, it is this push for cost recovery on water which has been blamed for the outbreak of cholera in KwaZulu-Natal in May 2000, with more than 100,000 cases of illness and over 200 deaths by mid-2001.

Reliance on firewood in the proximity of unserviced towns has inevitably led to the cutting down of forest and other tree cover. Women have had to walk further and further to gather wood and carry massive loads. Many suffer spinal injury as a result. Gathered wood and the associated women's labor are pervasively regarded as free goods. The possible replacements—coal, paraffin, or bought wood—cost money that the poor can ill afford.

Burning of solid and liquid fuels in poorly ventilated houses creates a high level of indoor air pollution and contributes to outdoor air pollution. Indoor levels of carbon monoxide have been measured at between ten and twenty-eight times acceptable limits, and in Gauteng townships outdoor pollution levels are amongst the worst in the world (*Sunday Times,* 1 March 1998). The effects on health relate primarily to the respiratory system, including asthma, bronchitis, and lung cancers. "Acute respiratory infections are a leading cause of death in South African children, killing one hundred times more children than in western Europe" (Booth et al. 1994, 241).

While the electrification program has greatly increased access, many people cannot afford to use it. Its distribution is thus uneven both within communities and within households. The costs of converting to electric appliances is high and households that do connect tend to use electricity for low energy consumption items such as televisions and lights. These also reflect male priorities. Housing programs have paid scant attention to energy conservation.

High levels of malnutrition and endemic tuberculosis make the poor particularly vulnerable to infection. Although state health provision in South Africa is cheap, the pressures on the service make for long delays in treatment and access for many is difficult and expensive. Health services represent only a portion of the costs of ill health. Casual workers in the formal sector whose conditions of employment are deregulated, small traders who are self employed, and cultivators and gatherers are all vulnerable to considerable loss as a result of ill health. For many this loss is catastrophic. Peter Ngobese (1994, 97) notes that, "The over-crowding, environmental and health problems associated with these areas has created a social pathology of violence."

Downwind and Downstream

Apartheid's racial planning located black communities "downwind and downstream" (Durning 1990, 17) of polluting industries and poorly man-aged waste landfill sites. Particular forms of degradation are associated with specific industries and are concentrated in particular locations.

Industrial air pollution, for example, is most concentrated in urban areas such as South Durban. In Gauteng it combines with toxic dust blown off mine dumps. Workers often live in these areas and so get a double dose. In unserviced urban settlements, industrial and mining pollution combines with domestic pollution to produce a chemical soup with cumulative impacts on people's health.

But the environment has no strict boundaries. Air pollution from the power stations in the Eastern Highveld affects rural as well as urban areas. Many mines are located in rural areas and their wastes pollute land, air, and water. Asbestos, for example, causes asbestosis, mesothelioma, and lung cancer. South Africa has the highest rate of mesothelioma in the world. Even after mining operations end, asbestos waste sites remain and affect rural villagers in the Northern Cape and Northern Province (Nyandu 1998, 19). Pollutants from urban industries flow downstream through urban and rural areas where people depend on natural water sources. Industrial agriculture's heavy use of fertilizers and pesticides also contaminates air, water, and people.

Toxic wastes from industry are not only disposed of in poorly man-aged but legal sites. An unknown quantity is illegally poured down storm water drains. More is dumped "in the veld" by criminal waste operators, invariably in poor neighborhoods where their activities are unlikely to be questioned. In a number of cases drums which previously contained toxic substances have been used as domestic water containers.

The water resources of the poor have also dried up as a result of the heavy water consumption of formal sector industries. Irrigation agricul-ture, plantation forestry, and mining all have a direct impact on local water sources. The dams that supply them, on the other hand, usually flood good agricultural land. Where black communities have suffered the loss, compensation has been inadequate.

Environment and Catastrophe

South Africa's energy intensive production makes it a significant contributor to global warming and climate change. The local consequences for rainfall are not well understood but it seems reasonably certain that weather patterns will become more erratic and extreme. That means more droughts and floods (see Flavin 1996).

At the same time, watershed degradation means that the consequences of drought and floods will be more extreme than they might be if the "sponges"—wetlands and indigenous forests—were properly conserved. Industrial agriculture bears the greatest responsibility for forest clearance and wetland drainage. Soil compaction and encrustation on commercial farms reduces the absorptive capacity of soils, contributing to flooding. Irrigation farming pumps out water tables and rivers and plantation forestry reduces runoff and lowers the water table, exacerbating drought conditions.

Inappropriate agricultural technologies have increased the vulnerability to drought on commercial farms. About 80,000 farm workers lost their jobs, and consequently their homes, during the drought years of the late 1980s and early 1990s. Farmers, on the other hand, received massive compensation from the state.

Leslie Bank (1995, 32ff.) observes that environmental factors combine with political factors. In 1993, labor legislation, which had previously protected only urban workers, was extended to include farm workers. Farmers reacted by reducing the number of people they employed. The pattern was repeated with the passage of the Security of Tenure Act in 1997. The Act gives workers and their families housing rights that are independent of their jobs. But before the legislation could be passed, thousands more workers were made redundant and evicted with their families from their homes. Evictions are still taking place though they are now illegal.

Those evicted followed in the footsteps of the millions of others who lost their livelihoods in "white" rural areas during the twentieth century. Some found refuge in African rural areas; others moved to informal settlements in the cities or on the outskirts of small rural towns.

In many areas rural production has already been severely undermined by land degradation. During the drought years, food production all but collapsed, water sources dried up, and many local people were forced to migrate. Clearly, climate change will increase the risks of rural production, further undermining a crucial element of the household economy in many rural and peri-urban communities.

Poorly located informal settlements will also face increased risk from floods and mud slides. The urban land market does not value steep land or floodplains so that is the land that poor people have access to. Many informal settlements are already at risk from floods and mud slides and the level of risk will increase.

The poor quality of the built environment in informal settlements makes them vulnerable to a different kind of hazard—fire. Densely packed shacks made of flammable materials are vulnerable to the rapid spread of fire. The problem originates within domestic environments where the dependence on unsafe energy sources is reflected in the observation of residents: "We live in paraffin and burn in it" (Bank 1995, 48). Crowding within the domestic environment greatly increases the risk of accidents of all sorts and the incidence of injury, particularly to children.

Environment and Conflict

Violence too produces environmental shocks. Stress related to poor and crowded domestic and built environments and insecurity contributes to violence within households and neighborhoods. Women and children are the main victims, but psychosocial disorders and diseases also have a major affect on adolescents and young adults. We would suggest that stress and trauma may combine with the effects of malnutrition and chemical pollution to produce a propensity for violence.

Within the pool of poverty and insecurity created by apartheid, competition over diminishing resources is a constant source of conflict. Betterment Planning, which imposed external resource management rules, intensified conflict and frequently triggered violence. During the 1950s and 1960s a number of local rebellions in black rural areas were brutally suppressed by the state, and further violence was contained within communities.

At the international level, environmental resources are increasingly a key cause of conflict. In Africa, international wars have already been fought over control of water resources. The Southern African region is subject to water stress and the potential for international conflict over water is already evident. Modern warfare has serious environmental impacts and undermines people's rights in the environment. The apartheid policy of destabilizing neighbors, particularly Angola and Mozambique, helped devastate peasant production. Landmines remain a constant hazard long after the cessation of hostilities.

As is evident from the earlier sections, conflict and violence is at the root of modern development. Jacklyn Cock (1991, 9) observes: "There are similarities between violence against people and violence against the environment. Both are about maintaining power and maximizing profit."

They use similar technologies within a symbolic economy that values domination, conquest, and control.

Conclusion

If, as is suggested in this chapter, development is, inter alia:

- framed by the social reproduction of power in history;
- pre-eminently concerned with and driven by the accumulation of wealth, and;
- implicated in the phenomena of exclusion, poverty, and environmental degradation,

the pursuit of environmental justice goes beyond mitigating environmental impacts and "balancing" economic growth and environmental protection. Rather it implies that the poverty/environment complex which has resulted from South Africa's history and which defines the real world of the majority of its people can only be satisfactorily transformed through a fundamental reorganization of the relations of power which currently direct the distribution of development's costs and benefits.

The political democratization of South Africa after apartheid has occurred at a global historical juncture that is more hostile than helpful in this task. One might debate whether, and to what extent, South Africa's post-apartheid government should be held responsible for complicity in steering the country's basic developmental path in a broadly market-oriented direction or whether the space for options was simply not there to be taken up. Both perspectives speak volumes about the contemporary power of global capital and the imperative of the struggle for environmental justice.

Acknowledgments

The authors acknowledge all those who contributed to the drafting of this chapter. In particular, we thank two organizations with whom we have had the privilege of working. First, the Environmental Justice Networking Forum which, in 1998, commissioned us to do a background briefing paper on environment and poverty in South Africa for the "Speak out on Poverty" process organized jointly by the South African NGO Coalition (SANGOCO), the South African Human Rights Commission, and the Commission on Gender Equality. Early drafts of that paper formed the basis for much of the work presented here. Second, ground-Work which, in 2000, commissioned a methodology paper on possible approaches to reporting on the "state of environmental justice" in South Africa. This work allowed us to explore some of the more systematic assumptions that underpin an environmental justice perspective and we have drawn on this material in the current chapter.

Notes

1. Natural, cultural, social, political, and economic.
2. These include, for example: contingent valuation methods; dynamic opportunity cost valuation; hedonic pricing; input and output valuation; panel valuation; threshold valuation; travel-cost method.
3. Within the dominant discourse, ambiguity and complexity are used to obscure or conflate responsibility by claiming that everyone is equally part of the problem. Everyone is not. For example, workers in a polluting factory may have an interest in preserving their jobs, but worker struggles to force industry to reveal the health and safety hazards demonstrate that the two sides do not share the same relationship to the environment.

References

Ardington, E., and F. Lund. 1996. "Questioning Rural Livelihoods." In M. Lipton and F. Ellis, eds. *Land, Labour and Livelihoods in Rural South Africa, Vol. 2: KwaZulu-Natal and Northern Province.* Durban: Indicator Press.

Bank, L. 1995. "Poverty in Duncan Village, East London: A Qualitative Perspective." Grahamstown: Institute of Social and Economic Research, Rhodes University, mimeo.

Beinart, W. 1982. *The Political Economy of Pondoland 1860–1930.* Johannesburg: Ravan Press.

Booth, A., J. McCullum, J. Mpinga, and M. Mukute. 1994. *State of the Environment in Southern Africa.* SARDC, IUCN, SADC.

Bundy, C. 1979. *The Rise and Fall of the South African Peasantry.* London: Heinemann.

Butler, M. 1997. *Environmental Information and Governance in South Africa.* Johannesburg: CASE.

Cock, J. 1991. "Going Green at the Grassroots." In J. Cock and E. Koch, eds. *Going Green: People, Politics and the Environment in South Africa.* Cape Town: Oxford University Press.

Cross, C., L. Luckin, T. Mzimela, and C. Clark. 1996. "On the Edge: Poverty, Livelihoods and Natural Resources in Rural KwaZulu-Natal." In M. Lipton and F. Ellis, eds. *Land, Labour and Livelihoods in Rural South Africa, Vol. 2: KwaZulu Natal and Northern Province.* Durban: Indicator Press.

Derman, P. 1993. "Is the Environment Gender Neutral?" In D.Hallowes, ed. *Hidden Faces: Environment, Development, Justice: South Africa and the Global Context.* Pietermaritzburg: Earthlife Africa.

Durning, A. B. 1990. *Apartheid's Environmental Toll.* Worldwatch Paper 95. Washington, D.C.: Worldwatch Institute.

Flavin, C. 1996. "Facing Up to the Risks of Climate Change." In L. Brown, ed. *State of the World 1996.* London: Earthscan.

Forsyth, T., and M. Leach, with I. Scoones. 1998. "Poverty and Environment: Priorities for Research and Policy—An Overview Study." Prepared for the United Nations Development Programme and European Commission, Institute of Development Studies.

Lohmann, L. 1999. *The Dyson Effect; Carbon "Offset" Forestry and the Privatisation of the Atmosphere.* The Corner House Briefing 15.

Lukey, P. 1995. *Health Before Profits: An Access Guide to Trade Unions and Environmental Justice in South Africa.* Pietermaritzburg: Environmental Justice Networking Forum and Friedrich Ebert Stiftung.

Mabin, A. 1989. "Limits to Urban Transition Models in Understanding South African Urbanisation," Paper presented at Department of Community Health, Witwatersrand University, Johannesburg.

May, J. 1996. *Experience and Perceptions of Poverty in South Africa.* Data Research Africa (for the South African Participatory Poverty Assessment).

Miller, S. 1993. "Health, Safety and Environment." In D. Hallowes, ed. *Hidden Faces. Environment, Development, Justice: South Africa and the Global Context.* Pietermaritzburg: Earthlife Africa.

Ngobese, P. 1994. "Sustainable Development Priorities for the New South Africa." *Voices from Africa 5.*

Nyandu, M. 1998. "Workers and Community Suffer for Profit." In G. Watkins, ed. *Voices from the Ground.* Environmental Justice Networking Forum.

Satterthwaite, D. 1993. "The Impact on Health of Urban Environments." *Environment and Urbanization* 5 (2).

Seabrook, J. 1997. "Defining Poverty." *Econews Africa* 6 (14).

Sen, A. K. 1981. *Poverty and Famines: An Essay on Entitlement and Deprivation.* Oxford: Clarendon Press and Oxford University Press.

Van Onselen, C. 1996. *The Seed Is Mine: The Life of Kas Maine, a South African Sharecropper, 1894–1985.* Cape Town: David Philip.

Whyte, A. V., ed. 1995. *Building A New South Africa, Volume 4: Environment, Reconstruction and Development: A Report From the International Mission on Environmental Policy.* Ottawa: International Development Research Centre.

Williams, G. 1993. "Setting the Agenda: A Preliminary Critique of the World Bank's Rural Restructuring Programme for South Africa." Paper presented to Land Redistribution Options, Johannesburg, LAPC.

Dying for a Job

Mpume Nyandu

"**I** have been working at this mine for many years and when I was still healthy they used to call me 'gooie boy [good boy]' and 'gooie onderwyser [good teacher]' because I was teaching other workers. But now that I am ill and have made a lot of money for the company they are saying if I think the mine is killing me I must go home."

Josiah Makola is relating his experience as a worker affected by the chemicals he works with at Vantech, a vanadium mine situated on the border of Mpumalanga Province and Northern Province.

Makola, father of a teenager, has worked at the Vantech mine for about six years. His job is to cook vanadium. This has exposed him directly to the smoke and fumes emanating from the pots. In 1996 he became ill. His constant cough was diagnosed as chemical bronchitis. An independent medical doctor advised him to change jobs as he was putting his health at risk.

But Makola says the mine forced him to continue working in his original position because that is where he had been employed to work. Later the mine doctor confirmed that he was seriously affected by the chemicals.

Makola applied for compensation and alleges that when he received it the management told him the amount was too high for a black person and would set a precedent for other affected workers. The money was allegedly returned to the Workmen's Compensation Fund.

Makola was transferred from a high-risk to a low-risk area for only two weeks, after which he was sent back to his original position. He now pays for his medical expenses from his own pocket. He says: "Even though I know I am dying, I am just persevering because I was told by the company that I will not be employable anywhere else when I leave the company. So I think I am going to die here for the sake of keeping a job so that my child can finish school. The mine is very dangerous—people get affected after working for one year only."

Makola is just one of many workers affected by vanadium exposure at Vantech. Peter Maroga, a former employee of Vantech, also tells of the problems and frustrations he has encountered as a result of working for this mine. Maroga also worked directly with the mined material, pouring it into the cooking pots. He maintains it was almost impossible to avoid inhaling the smoke. After only six months of working at the mine he became ill. On two occasions he was admitted to hospital suffering from asthma. He was later diagnosed by two doctors as suffering from asthma bronchitis caused by vanadium exposure.

The mine changed his job, saying it was too risky for him to work with the chemicals and he was given light duty—work unrelated to mining activities.

Like Makola, he applied for compensation but says that when his money arrived it was sent back to the Workmen's Compensation Fund. The mine is reported to have said the money was too much for Maroga and that it was a mistake to pay him as his illness was not work related.

Maroga is not currently working at the mine but has not officially been retrenched. The mine is currently offering him free treatment for his condition, an offer Maroga interprets as an admission of guilt.

Working at Vantech robbed Maroga of both his good health and his family. When his wife learned that he would be ill indefinitely and that he was to be retrenched as a result, she left him. Maroga now lives with his mother and makes a living by doing part-time work for residents of "white" suburbs.

"The mine says they want to improve the health and safety standards but at the same time they say to keep good health and safety standards is expensive. I think people like myself will benefit very little from the health and safety improvements because we are already affected, so it is better if they just compensate us for the damage they have caused to us," he says.

Maroga agrees and adds that "the whole community is going to die because all the people who worked at the mine before me are affected, even the ones who are still working there now are ill, so those who are still coming to work here are also going to be affected."

Workers and villagers believe the chemical exposure problems do not stop within the Vantech plant. They extend beyond its boundaries, affecting people living in the nearby communities in a variety of ways.

One village affected by Vantech's mining activities is Ga Mampuru, situated about four kilometers away, in the Northern Province. Mine chimneys puff clouds of smoke into the air all day, almost every day. The fumes are carried by the wind, polluting the air in the area. According to Makola the water in the nearby river, used both by people and by livestock, is polluted by vanadium dust, especially during the rainy season. Even the trees surrounding the mine area, he says, are covered with vanadium dust and are dying. As a result, community members suffer from illnesses similar to those common to Vantech mineworkers. "We think people get it from the smoke that is blown into the village from the mine," says Kgakishi Morewane, chairperson of the local Reconstruction and Development Programme (RDP) committee in the area.

Another problem is the effect of blasting activities at the mine on houses in Ga Mampuru. According to people in the community, when blasting takes place, window panes break or crack, and children and animals run in all directions, as though they are possessed. Some houses are so badly damaged that residents have trouble closing their windows. In some cases roofs are falling in. The constant need to repair houses is causing homeowners financial problems.

Morewane says: "We wrote several letters to Vantech complaining about all these problems but the mine never responded. We requested Vantech to come to the community during blasting to have firsthand experience of what is happening and the mine refused." The community has tried to engage the services of the environmental awareness group in Johannesburg which invited Vantech to several meetings both in Nelspruit and in Ga Mampuru but Vantech is reported to have refused to attend.

Chapter 3

Searching for a Common Agenda

Ecofeminism and Environmental Justice

Belinda Dodson

O f all the strands of contemporary environmentalist discourse, those of environmental justice and ecofeminism provide especially useful frameworks for understanding relations between nature and society in South Africa. Indeed, as the country's post-apartheid reconstruction proceeds, not always in predictable or even desirable directions, there is much to be learned from the application of these two paradigms.[1] Yet curiously, neither environmental justice nor ecofeminism enjoys the same level of intellectual currency in South Africa as it does in other geographical contexts, although environmental justice has begun to make some political inroads. By applying ideas from the international literature on environmental justice and ecofeminism to the South African case, this chapter seeks to make both an intellectual and a practical contribution, advancing theoretical debates while at the same time giving impetus to progressive social and environmental transformation.

This dual aim is reflected in the chapter's structure. The first section covers the intellectual ground, outlining the development of environmental justice and ecofeminist thinking; identifying various strands within these bodies of discourse as well as the links and divergences between them; and examining some of the criticisms that have been leveled against these branches of environmentalism. Rather than continuing as separate movements, it is then argued, they should join intellectually and politically to advance what is in effect a common agenda. The second part of the chapter brings these debates "home," applying principles of environmental justice and ecofeminism to an understanding of human-environment relations in South Africa during and after apartheid. The concluding section looks to the future, drawing theoretical lessons from the South African experience to further intellectual debate, while drawing practical lessons from international experience to advance the environmental justice and ecofeminist movements in South Africa.

Environmental Justice: Race, Class, and Gender

From its grassroots origins, environmental justice has moved to the rarefied realms of formal philosophical debate. It is not the intention here to provide a comprehensive overview[2] of theories of environmental justice, which is a far more heterogeneous body of thinking than is commonly assumed, marked by considerable internal debate (not least over questions of definition and terminology) and encountered across a range of academic disciplines as well as in more popular and political discourse. Rather, my aim is to summarize the essential features of environmental justice, particularly as they relate to issues of gender and environment, and to draw out those features most relevant to the South African context.

Many authors, both popular and academic, describe rather than strictly define environmental justice. American geographer Susan Cutter (1995, 113), for example, talks of people being "deprived of their environmental rights," and views environmental justice as "political action and social mobilization that marshals public and private commitment to change . . . merging environmental, social equality and civil rights movements into one potent political force." Sociologist Stella Capek (1993) also locates environmental justice firmly within the framework of human, and especially citizens', rights. Pulido (1996, 142), another American academic and activist, offers a pragmatic, shopping-list description of environmental justice as "a broad set of concerns [that] has focused on the relationship between marginalized groups and environmental issues, including the elitism of mainstream environmentalism, the biased nature of environmental policy, the limited participation of nonwhites in environmental affairs and . . . the disproportionate exposure of nonwhites to pollution." Australians Low and Gleeson (1998a) are rather more ambitious in their attempts at definition. They argue for an extension of environmental justice thinking from the local, distributional definition to a more global, ethical definition, including rights for the environment as well as rights for people. They, however, are the exception. Most definitions of environmental justice are resolutely anthropocentric, extending *social* justice to include the right of all human beings to a clean and healthy environment. Indeed this anthropocentrism is one of the major criticisms of environmental justice by environmentalists of a more bio- or eco-centric persuasion. It is this very characteristic, however, which allows environmental justice to be incorporated into bills of rights and national constitutions, as in the case of South Africa, and which permits it to be linked to other movements for social equality, such as feminism.

Moving from theoretical definition to environmental justice as a social movement, it is clear that its roots lie firmly in the United States (Cutter 1995, Goldman 1996, Low and Gleeson 1998a, b). A seminal work was Bullard's (1990, xiv) *Dumping in Dixie,* in which he explored "the thesis that black communities, because of their economic and political vulnerability, have been routinely targeted for the siting of noxious facilities, locally unwanted land uses, and environmental hazards." Another landmark event was the First National People of Color Environmental Leadership Summit in October 1991 (United Church of Christ 1991). Since then, not only have thousands of local groups emerged in the United States to oppose perceived environmental injustices, but the language and principles of environmental justice have made inroads into that country's federal, state, and local government discourse (Szasz 1994, Goldman 1996). In 1994, then-President Bill Clinton signed an executive order "requiring every federal agency to achieve the principle of environmental justice by addressing and ameliorating the human health or environmental effects of the agency's programs, policies and activities on minority and low-income communities in the US" (Cutter 1995, 111).

Yet despite the apparent success of the United States environmental justice movement, two features in particular combine to restrict its scope and influence: first, it is very much about industrial pollution, toxic waste contamination, and related environmental health issues; and second, its central concern is the question of race, cast in the frame of "ethnic minorities" (Szasz 1994, Goldman 1996). Environmental justice in the United States is essentially about the location of environmentally undesirable facilities in or near black (or, less often, Hispanic) communities. Pulido (1996) is one author who challenges this version of environmental justice and the monolithic racism it implies, urging instead the construction of a more multi-ethnic movement and that greater attention, both academic and political, be paid to other forms of marginality, including gender. The focus on race may have contributed to the movement's early success, allowing it to attach itself to the coattails of America's strongly race-based civil rights tradition. Ultimately, however, it serves not only to limit the transferability of United States–style environmental justice to other social, political, and geographical contexts, but also to impede the future development of the environmental justice movement within that country itself (Goldman 1996). Further criticisms leveled at the U.S. environmental justice movement are that it is local to the extent of parochialism; is biased toward urban rather than rural communities; is anthropo- rather than eco-centric; and neglects class- and gender-based forms of environmental discrimination.

Even the most ardent advocates of environmental justice are alert to these and other weaknesses of the movement as currently constructed (Szasz 1994, Tesh and Williams 1996). Pulido (1994) points out how the movement has favored strategies involving *procedural* justice—making environmental decision making more open and accountable—while failing to address the broader *structural* injustices of material inequality, uneven development, economic restructuring and globalization, all of which have environmental implications. Working as she does across the southern California–Mexico border, Pulido calls for both a conceptual and a spatial expansion of the environmental justice framework, not just across the border but around the globe. Her views are shared by geographer David Harvey (1996, 402), who has taken the environmental justice movement to task for being trapped in a "phase of rhetorical flourishes, media successes and symbolic politics." He sees the movement as having reached a crisis point, faced with a choice between remaining as it is, a series of militant particularist movements, or adopting "a politics of abstraction capable of reaching out across space, across the multiple environmental and social conditions that constitute the geography of difference . . . without abandoning its militant particularist base." The movement should move from "fighting an incinerator here, a toxic waste dump there, a World Bank dam project somewhere else, and commercial logging in yet another place," to trying to confront "the fundamental underlying processes (and their associated power structures, social relations, institutional configurations, discourses and belief systems) that generate environmental and social injustices" (Harvey 1996, 400–401).

Conceptualizing environmental justice in such terms allows the movement to transcend its position as a sort of politically correct NIMBYism, tied to particular places (mostly in the developed world) and particular constructions of race-based identity politics, to become an altogether more powerful force for social and environmental change. In this way gender, class, and other bases for unfair discrimination can more readily be accommodated. Environmental justice becomes not merely the equitable location of the environmental "bads" of modern urban-industrial society, but also the fairer distribution of environmental "goods"; not simply a series of local struggles, but potentially scaled up to embrace national, regional, and even global environmental justice (Jamieson 1994).[3] Justice toward the environment itself can begin to enter the equation, which becomes one of overall reduction and not simply spatial redistribution of environmental harm.

This broadened notion is beginning to gain currency in the literature (Jamieson 1994, Sachs 1995, Low and Gleeson 1998a, b). In the words of Low and Gleeson: "Environmental and ecological justice are ultimately about security for people across the globe, for places, for environments and for the planet." As will be demonstrated below, this vision of environmental justice—what one might term *critical* environmental justice—shares considerable common ground with certain strands of ecofeminism. It is also the version that has the greater relevance for South Africa, both in understanding the environmental injustices of the past and in promoting greater environmental justice for the future.

Ecofeminist Perspectives

Despite their potential overlap, environmental justice and ecofeminism remain strangely separate, both intellectually and in terms of their popular support base. Part of the explanation is simply geographical: women are not spatially "ghetto-ized" in the way ethnic communities frequently are. Thus although women are certainly exposed to particular forms of environmental injustice and deprivation based on their gender roles and identities, both at home and in the workplace, the forms of environmental discrimination against them are less place specific than those based on race or class. Significantly, many people involved in the environmental justice movement, as well as many of the leading environmental justice scholars, are women; but it is almost as if one has to choose either a race or a gender focus in one's personal brand of environmentalism (Taylor 1997). Ecofeminism itself contains a range of competing ideologies, making solidarity even within the movement an elusive goal. Nevertheless, there is considerable scope for strengthening the alliance between environmental justice and ecofeminism to pursue what should be a common agenda of social equity and environmental protection.

Ecofeminist Theories

As with environmental justice, there is a wide variety of scholarly and popular interpretations of ecofeminism's definition and scope, and it is beyond the ambit of this chapter to provide a comprehensive overview.[4] In essence, ecofeminism connects the oppression of women with that of nature, and hence stresses the connections between feminist and environmentalist concerns. In the United States and Europe, it arose primarily out of the 1970s and 1980s movements against nuclear power and nuclear weapons, although its philosophical and political pedigrees date back much further. According to Merchant (1996), ecofeminism can be said to have become a distinctive movement, in both intellectual and political terms, by about 1980. Since then, it has grown to become a major division of both feminism and environmentalism.

Two primary theoretical positions can be distinguished under the ecofeminist umbrella, paralleling those within the broader feminist movement (Plumwood 1993; Pepper 1996; Rose et al. 1997). *Cultural ecofemi-*

nism emphasizes the biological and ideological connections between women and nature, seeing their joint oppression and exploitation as a consequence of a patriarchal social system. "Cultural ecofeminism sees masculinity as formed in terms of separation from and control of both women and . . . nature, and sees the dominance of male views in patriarchy as creating a society obsessed with dominance and control" (Plumwood 1992, 10). Women, in this view, are regarded as having a distinctive and superior relationship with nature. Thus, were patriarchy to be dismantled and women's values allowed to prevail, the society that would emerge would by definition be one in which both women and nature would be less exploited. Many cultural ecofeminists define their ideology in spiritual or religious terms, advocating the (re)establishment of women's bonds with "Mother Earth" or "Gaia."

Social ecofeminists, by contrast, emphasize the social and political (or structural) rather than the personal and spiritual. They reject the biologically deterministic reading of women's "closeness" to nature, and instead view both gender and nature as socially constructed. With Plumwood (1992, 10), they hold that "it is not so much that women themselves are the model for a better relation to nature . . . but that the entire development of the dominant culture and its relationship to nature has been affected by male and other forms of dominance, expressed in the dualism of nature and reason." From a social ecofeminist standpoint, such dualisms should not be celebrated, as in cultural ecofeminism, but radically overturned (Plumwood 1997; Spretnak 1997). Certainly the adoption of a social feminist stance allows a less reductionist reading of environmental problems and admits other forms of oppression—class, race, and species—into the debate. Karen Warren (1997, 1), one of the leading contemporary ecofeminist scholars, explicitly emphasizes this de-essentializing of the movement when she defines ecofeminism as "the position that there are important connections between how one treats women, people of color, and the underclass on one hand and how one treats the nonhuman natural world on the other." She thus demonstrates the potential for interweaving ecofeminism and environmental justice, both in theory and in practice.

Caroline Merchant (1996) and David Pepper (1996) both construct a finer categorization of the ideologies of ecofeminism, and indeed it may be that the social/cultural division has become too crude a device through which to understand the contemporary ecofeminist movement. Merchant adds liberal and social*ist* ecofeminism as further versions of ecofeminist thinking. By liberal ecofeminism, she means the brand of ecofeminist thought that parallels mainstream environmentalism, but with gender added in:

> For liberal eco-feminists ... environmental problems result from the overly rapid development of natural resources and the failure to regulate pesticides and other environmental pollutants. ... Better science, conservation, and laws are therefore the proper approaches to solving environmental problems. Given equal educational opportunities to become scientists, natural resource managers, regulators, lawyers, and legislators, women, like men, can contribute to the improvement of the environment, the conservation of natural resources, and the higher quality of human life. (Merchant 1996, 9)

No fostering of women's special relationship with nature, or any radical social transformation, forms part of the liberal ecofeminist agenda, which fits comfortably within the social and political mainstream. Socialist ecofeminists, by contrast, ground their environmentalist and feminist struggles specifically in an understanding of the relations of economic production and social reproduction, calling for the radical re-ordering of those relations as the only basis for meaningful environmental and social change. Rather than being either biologically determined or set simply within the realm of ideas, men's and women's relationships to and views on nature are seen as structured by the gender roles assigned them in particular modes of production and their associated social formations. With roots in socialism as much as in feminism, socialist ecofeminism brings with it an explicitly anti-capitalist political agenda. In essence, it is "a feminist transformation of socialist ecology that makes the category of re-production, rather than production, central to the concept of a just, sustainable world" (Merchant 1996, 15). A new, ecosocialist mode of production, based on need not profit, "would reverse the priorities of capitalism, making production subordinate to reproduction and ecology" (Merchant 1996, 17).

To these various camps might be added postmodern ecofeminists, who downplay all forms of essentialism and determinism, whether biological or materialist, in favor of "situated knowledges that are shaped by many dimensions of identity and difference" (Rocheleau, Thomas-Slayter, and Wangari 1996, 4). Postmodern ecofeminism shuns any single central organizing concept or meta-theory, instead embracing complexity and diversity. In consequence it lacks any unitary political agenda, encompassing an eclectic array of movements and agendas. From a more pragmatic viewpoint, the range of ecofeminist ideologies outlined above is not merely diverse but mutually contradictory and competing. Liberal ecofeminists see the solution to environmental problems as lying in the greater involvement of women in environmental management and decision making within the status quo. Cultural ecofeminists call for an end to patriarchy and its replacement with female values of nurturing and caring for the earth. Socialist ecofeminists see the overthrow of global capitalism as the only real solution to environmental problems. Clearly these are incompatible positions.

Partly as a consequence of these internal contradictions, the ecofeminist movement has come in for considerable criticism. Cecile Jackson (1995, 140–41) takes it to task for being "uninterested in the actually existing conditions of life which are dismissed either with postmodernist arguments about subjectivity, or with reference to the importance of myths in mobilizing and political action."[5] "We need," she writes, "to reassert the value of a historical and materialist analysis, informed by a deconstruction of some unexamined key terms in eco-feminist positions." Jackson is joined in her criticisms by Melissa Leach and Cathy Green (1997). Significantly, all three of these authors develop their critiques of ecofeminism from a base within their own research on gender and environment in countries of the South. Leach and Green criticize the overgeneralized interpretation of women's relationship with nature in ecofeminist accounts, their portrayal of women as a homogeneous category, their neglect of men (except as the other half of a simplistic dichotomy), and their oversimplified view of history, in particular the impact of colonial science and ideology on women and the environment. Ecofeminist histories, in their view, "obscure rather than clarify linkages between changing gender relations, ecologies, and colonial science . . . and they deploy history to suggest policies which could well prove detrimental to women" (Leach and Green 1997, 343). Rejecting ecofeminism's assumption of women's special role as guardians of nature, they argue instead for a *gender* analysis of ecology and politics, both in understanding environmental history and in developing present-day policy on environment and development.

Feminist political ecology attempts to address such criticisms and at the same time to recombine some of ecofeminism's diverse strands (Rocheleau, Thomas-Slayter, and Wangari 1996). Political ecology posits the analysis of power relations as fundamental to any understanding of environmental problems, while appreciating that the determinants of those relations—and thus the solutions to environmental problems—vary in different social, historical, and geographical contexts. *Feminist* political ecology, therefore:

> brings into a single framework a feminist perspective combined with analysis of ecological, economic, and political power relations. It does not simply add gender to class, ethnicity, race, and other social variables as axes of power in investigating the politics of resource access and control and environmental decision-making. The mutual embeddedness of these hierarchies forbids this simplistic approach. Instead, the perspective of feminist political ecology builds on analyses of identity and difference, and of pluralities of meanings in relation to the multiplicity of sites of environmental struggle and change. (Rocheleau, Thomas-Slayter, and Wangari 1996, 287)

Such an approach admits both individual agency and social structure as forces influencing relations between people and the environment; retains the critical insights of materialist ecofeminism without resorting to economic or other forms of determinism; and avoids both the essentializing tendencies of cultural ecofeminism and the uncritical openness of postmodernism. Feminist political ecology is wholly compatible both ideologically and politically with what I have termed "critical environmental justice," and provides an appropriate framework within which to interpret local experiences, including those of South Africa, in the context of wider processes of environmental and economic change.

Ecofeminism in Practice

Despite attempts at intellectual rapprochement (e.g., Rocheleau, Thomas-Slayter, and Wangari 1996; Warren 1997), ecofeminism as a social movement remains weak and fractured. The strength of *cultural* ecofeminism has alienated the movement both from much of the intellectual and political left and from the conservative right. Its support base, certainly in countries of the North, remains predominantly white and middle-class, mirroring the racial and socioeconomic composition of mainstream environmentalism (Taylor 1997). In the United States, women of color have tended to ally themselves with the environmental justice movement rather than with ecofeminism. Native American women too, despite being held up as the "ultimate eco-feminists," tend to reject the label and the "naturalization" of natives that it typically implies (Sturgeon 1997).[6]

If, however, one looks to countries in the South, there are promising signs that ecofeminism is strengthening both theoretically and politically, largely because of its deliberate connection to debates about environment and development, thus providing better models for South Africa to emulate. One of the most influential contributors to ecofeminist discourse has been India's Vandana Shiva (1989, 1991; Mies and Shiva 1994). Her work embodies many of the tensions and contradictions within ecofeminism, incorporating strands of both cultural and social ecofeminism within a broadly materialist framework, yet having a strong grounding in Hindu philosophy. Through patriarchal "maldevelopment," argues Shiva, both nature and Third World women—who are closely linked to nature by their responsibility for the provision of food, fuel, and water for their families—are devalued and destroyed. In her view, women of the South have always borne the brunt of the environmental damage wrought by the forces of colonialism, capitalism, and misguided state socialism. This binds women's issues inextricably to those of environment and development. Her critics accuse her of being anti-modern and anti-science; of essentializing women's traditional relationship to nature as inherently positive (see Agarwal 1992; Jackson 1993, 1994, 1995). Much of the Leach and Green (1997) critique outlined above was directed explicitly at Shiva's ideas. Nevertheless she has become internationally recognized as a champion of the ecofeminist cause, and can certainly be credited with drawing international attention to the "women, environment, development" (WED) triangle.

Indeed the whole WED theme, while remaining problematic on a number of grounds (Leach and Green 1997), has attained remarkable intellectual and popular currency. It was given considerable prominence at the United Nations Conference on Environment and Development (UNCED) in Rio in 1992 where it was explicitly included in both Agenda 21 and the Rio Declaration (Jackson 1994; Merchant 1996), and remains influential in international policy circles. Its high profile in these arenas is matched, perhaps even exceeded, by a high level of grassroots activism and global networking. Links have been established between women in the North and women in the South, as well as between academics, activists, policymakers, and "ordinary women" in countries around the world (Rocheleau, Thomas-Slayter, and Wangari 1996), including South Africa. Any South African ecofeminist movement would thus be able to draw on a strong tradition of activism and scholarship in other countries. Such emulation, however, should not be uncritical and should be tailored to suit South Africa's distinctive social, political, economic, and ecological conditions.

Proponents of ecofeminism in South Africa can also learn from the wider discourse on gender and development. An important shift in this discourse over the past decade or so has been the change from talking about "women in development" to talking about "gender and development," acknowledging that gender is not simply biologically determined but also socially and historically constructed, and that women's oppression is often linked to other forms of oppression that include men. Gender analysis looks at men *and* women, as well as the relations between them as couples, families, households, and communities. In ecofeminism, too, recent years have seen signs of a maturing into a "gender" approach, for example in the literature on feminist political ecology:

> Feminist political ecology offers a new perspective on structures and processes of social change. Through its recognition of threats to equity and diversity, and its promotion of social and environmental justice, it helps to strengthen the balance between men's and women's rights and responsibilities in local communities. It clarifies linkages among gender, envi-

ronment, livelihoods and poverty, in ways that benefit both women and men. In so doing, it addresses the economic and political barriers to environmental sustainability and social justice. (Rocheleau, Thomas-Slayter and Wangari 1996, 306)

As the above quotation suggests, there is considerable scope for both greater intellectual engagement and stronger political links between environmental justice and ecofeminism. Although neither movement subsumes the other, an appreciation by both of the existence of different forms of social discrimination, including race and class as well as gender, can only serve to enhance understanding of the causes and impacts of environmental problems locally and globally. The ecofeminist and environmental justice movements should therefore be viewed not as competing but as complementary, and efforts should be made to build bridges between them (Miller, Hallstein, and Quass 1996; Sturgeon 1997; Taylor 1997). South Africa provides the ideal arena for just such a collaboration.

Overcoming Apartheid's Environmental Injustices

South Africa presents a telling, almost paradigmatic, example of the relationship between the natural environment and social discrimination, especially, though not exclusively, on the basis of race. The impact of apartheid on the environment can be read in the eroded hillsides of the previous black "homelands," the unsanitary and hazard-prone conditions in townships and shack settlements, and the stark racial differences in statistics of morbidity and mortality relating to environmental health. These environmental manifestations of apartheid have been well documented, for example in Durning (1990), Cock and Koch (1991), and Ramphele and McDowell (1991). For each topic these books address—land tenure, population, energy provision, water supply, soil erosion, industrial pollution, worker health and safety, urban environments, nature conservation, environmental law and policy—attention is drawn not simply to the inequitable distribution of environmental resources and hazards, but also to the actual environmental costs of apartheid. As Ramphele writes:

South and Southern Africa experience many of the same environmental problems as the rest of the world. . . . But apartheid has severely increased the damage. It has been a profoundly unnatural system; a system of removal and separation. It has forced large numbers of people into unsuitable environments, putting disproportionate pressure on natural resources and carving deep fissures into valleys and hillsides. It has broken urban areas into fragments: some green, spacious and healthy, others—occupied by the black majority—cramped, unwholesome and degraded. In the wider region, it has wreaked ecological havoc by sponsoring wars and undermining economies. (Ramphele and McDowell 1991, 201)

Interestingly, none of the contributors to these works adopted an explicitly environmental justice or ecofeminist stance, despite the obvious relevance of these ways of thinking to the South African context. In content, however, the works are all about environmental injustice, environmental racism, and environmental inequity, including injustice *to* the environment, and the basis of such injustice in the apartheid political economy. Although gender is not the primary focus of any of them, the particular environmental injustices suffered by South African women are a recurrent theme, from rural women's daily burden of gathering fuel wood and fetching water to urban mothers' concerns over their children's health.

The examples of "apartheid's environmental toll" (Durning 1990) are legion, with women its particular victims. With regard to land tenure, for example, the restriction of the black majority to a meager 13 percent of the land created artificial overpopulation, with disastrous consequences for soil and vegetation. The location of the black "homelands" was not, as is so often argued, in the poorest agricultural areas. Rather, it was the forced overcrowding of black people onto potentially productive agricultural land which created degraded environments. Racial oppression and environmental destruction were thus not merely coincidental but mutually causative and reinforcing. Black women, demographically overrepresented in the "homelands" as a consequence of a male-dominated migrant labor system, bore the brunt of the damage. It was women who were forced to cover ever longer distances to obtain water and fuel wood; women who had to work ever harder on the land to ensure even the most basic household food supply.

A similar argument applies in the case of what Gandar (1991) called "the imbalance of power." White South Africans enjoyed a reliable supply of relatively low-priced electricity. It became a cliché to describe the irony of electricity pylons marching across black areas without supplying power to any of the local residents, who had to rely on wood, candles, gas, paraffin, and animal dung to meet their needs for heating, lighting, and cooking. It was African women, largely responsible for both fuel gathering and food preparation, who suffered the consequences: neck and spinal injuries as a result of carrying heavy loads of wood; lung and eye problems from exposure to smoke; burns from paraffin stoves. Even in urban areas, all but a handful of black households lacked electricity, and the use of coal as an alternative created major environmental pollution and health problems. In power supply as in so many other areas, apartheid South Africa combined First and Third World environmental problems, not merely in juxtaposition but in direct causal relationship through the mechanisms of race- and gender-based discrimination.

Thus if ever one needed a case to demonstrate how a critical environmental justice or (feminist) political ecology approach can contribute to an understanding of environmental problems, apartheid South Africa surely provides it. In a typical paradox, the environment was simultaneously sacrificed in the interests of racial segregation and claimed as justification for the country's race-based socio-spatial rearrangement. Being such poor farmers, went the official argument, blacks would only destroy more land if it were made available to them.[7] Soil conservation was thus put forward as the basis for forced removals, resettlement, and the betterment schemes that met with such resistance in black rural areas (Beinart 1984; Showers 1994).

Logically, urbanization would have relieved some of the environmental pressures on black rural areas, but black South Africans were not permitted simply to move to towns and cities, urban influx control being strictly enforced until the mid-1980s. Only those blacks who provided essential labor in the mines, factories, and homes of "white" South Africa were granted permission to live in urban areas, creating a distorted demographic distribution of urban and rural populations by race, age, and gender that persists to this day. It was mostly black men of working age who migrated, while the rural "homelands" became the preserve of women, children, and the elderly, forced to deal with the day-to-day realities of land shortage, soil erosion, fuel wood depletion, water scarcity, and food insecurity. The largely male urban workforce experienced other sorts of environmental problems: inadequate housing, poor sanitation, industrial pollution, and frequently dangerous working conditions. Race, class, age, and gender thus combined to create particular patterns and experiences of environmental injustice.

There are many further, perhaps less obvious, connections between apartheid and the environment: the "whites-only" membership restrictions of environmental organizations; the state's deliberate strangling of an incipient black environmental movement; racist assumptions and biases in environmental policy; the exclusion of blacks from environmental decision making (Khan 1990a, 1990b, 1992, 1994). Always held up as something of a model for the rest of Africa to follow, the country's game reserves and nature conservation programs have been subjected to an alternative reading to demonstrate how they prioritized "rhinos over people," displacing black people from their land in order to provide a "wilderness experience" for privileged (mostly male) whites (Khan 1990b). "Apartheid did not only separate people, but encouraged thinking and action that separated people from the environment. The word 'environment' became associated with leisure concerns of white elites, evidenced by forced removals of communities to make way for reserves to protect animals and plants" (Albertyn 1994, 1). In addition to discriminating on the basis of race, nature conservation in South Africa has always been very much a male domain, with strong militaristic overtones, giving women at best a marginal role, and black women barely any role at all.

After seven years of democratic, non-racial government, while there has been progress in certain areas, many of the environmental injustices of the apartheid era persist. The most positive developments have been in the areas of water and power supply, with mass electrification and water provision programs in both rural and urban areas leading to immediate environmental and social improvement.[8] This has been especially significant in the lives of black women. The Department of Water Affairs and Forestry has taken the lead in a concerted campaign to achieve "water for all." Among its more innovative strategies have been the implementation of scaled water tariffs based on consumption; the employment of people (many of them rural black women) to clear alien vegetation in order to enhance catchment water yield; and the establishment of community bodies, also involving African women, to take responsibility for post-delivery maintenance of water supply infrastructure. While such interventions leave unchallenged the gender division of labor that makes the provision of household water and energy "women's work," they have freed women from hours of time-consuming and back-breaking physical labor, as well as giving them new skills and opportunities. The social, economic, and health benefits are, of course, also experienced by the male members of communities that have received new water and electricity connections. And although there are environmental costs attached to the increased overall consumption of water and electricity, there are also environmental benefits, as people are no longer forced to overexploit their immediate local environment to meet their basic energy and water needs.

This is an example of the positive environmental impact of the end of apartheid, but there are also many situations where apartheid's legacy is proving rather more intractable. Urban environments, despite improvements in certain areas, present a particular problem. The racially divided cities left behind by apartheid were specifically designed to marginalize and exclude Africans, and were thus fundamentally ill-equipped to cope with the mass influx of poor people from rural areas that followed the lifting of restrictions on freedom of movement. As a result, millions of people now live in shacks on the fringes and in the interstices of cities like Johannesburg, Durban, and Cape Town. These shack settlements are typically located in areas either naturally hazardous, such as on floodplains or steep slopes, or adjacent to environmentally noxious facilities such as factories, power stations, sewage works, waste dumps, highways, and airports. It is not simply that noxious facilities have been deliberately located next to existing black communities, although there are certainly many cases where this has happened, but also that newly urbanized black communities have often had little choice but to settle near existing noxious facilities. To compound the problem, the scale of the influx has completely overwhelmed the capacity of urban authorities to cope. The provision of housing, sanitation, and even the most basic of services lags far behind demand, resulting in the settlements themselves constituting an environmental hazard and health risk, both to their own residents and to neighboring communities.

What has changed since the end of apartheid, then, is not so much the *nature* of environmental injustice nor the identity of its victims, as its geography. Greater population mobility has meant that problems once confined to townships and homelands have been exported to the backyard of what was white South Africa. Previously, the apartheid state's rigid system of social and spatial control meant that negative environmental externalities could remain just that—external—to the white population in whose interests the system operated. The environmental problems produced by poverty could be confined, along with the majority black population, to the townships and homelands. Those who suffered most were those with the least power to protest, such as rural black women.

The complicated socio-spatial dynamics of post-apartheid South Africa create a much more messy picture. The removal of official race-based discrimination has not been able to eliminate the gross socioeconomic inequalities, nor to erase the existence of a large black underclass. Poverty may have replaced race as the primary determinant of social and environmental disadvantage, but as the poor remain largely black, the outcome, in demographic terms, remains largely the same. Gender discrimination has certainly not disappeared, and women remain the primary victims of environmental injustice. Indeed, for many black women the end of apartheid has simply meant exchanging one set of environmental injustices for another, the impoverished rural homeland for the overcrowded urban slum.

Some problems have even been magnified, and new ones added. As Ramphele and McDowell pointed out in 1991 (p. 201), "the formal demise of apartheid . . . leaves the structures largely intact. As long as endemic inequality and poverty persist, people will be forced to go on using their environment in an unsustainable way." Yet if links between poverty, inequality, and the environment provide the clue to understanding South Africa's environmental problems, they also provide the key to their solution. As Ramphele and McDowell (1991, 201) go on to say: "the first principle guiding future action must be that the struggle against abuse of the environment and the struggle against poverty and social injustice are inextricably linked." This is essentially an argument for applying the principles of ecofeminism and environmental justice: for the social upliftment of women, the poor, and other disadvantaged groups as the only meaningful basis for environmentally sound development.

Ecofeminism in Post-apartheid Policy and Practice

An analysis of the emerging environmental policies of the post-apartheid era provides some grounds for optimism. The very advent of democracy, giving equal rights to all South Africans regardless of race or gender, is itself significant. In addition, Section 24 of the Constitution enshrines the fundamental principle of environmental justice by giving citizens the right "to an environment that is not harmful to their health or wellbeing" (Republic of South Africa 1996).

New laws are beginning to give force to these constitutional principles. The National Environmental Management Act (RSA 1998c) embodies environmental justice and ecofeminism in several of its provisions:

- Environmental management must place people and their needs at the forefront of its concern, and serve their physical, psychological, developmental, cultural and social interests equitably.
- Environmental justice must be pursued so that adverse environmental impacts shall not be distributed in such a manner as to unfairly discriminate against any person, particularly vulnerable and disadvantaged persons.
- Equitable access to environmental resources, benefits and services to meet basic human needs and ensure human well-being must be pursued and special measures may be taken to ensure access thereto by categories of persons disadvantaged by unfair discrimination.
- The participation of all interested and affected parties in environmental governance must be promoted, and all people must have the opportunity to develop the understanding, skills and capacity necessary for achieving equitable and effective participation, and participation by vulnerable and disadvantaged persons must be ensured.
- The right of workers to refuse work that is harmful to human health or the environment and to be informed of dangers must be respected and protected.
- Decisions must be taken in an open and transparent manner, and access to information must be provided in accordance with the law.

- The vital role of women and youth in environmental management and development must be recognised and their full participation therein must be promoted.

Women, as well as being included in general provisions concerning environmental justice for people "disadvantaged by unfair discrimination," thus receive special treatment under the law.

Two other Acts which promote environmental justice and the
rights of women are the National Water Act (RSA 1998a) and the National Forests Act (RSA 1998b). The Water Act recognizes "sustainability
and equity" as guiding principles for water resources management, and
lists, inter alia, as its purposes:

- Meeting the basic human needs of present and future genera-
  tions;
- Promoting equitable access to water;
- Redressing the results of past racial and gender discrimination;
- Promoting the efficient, sustainable and beneficial use of water
  in the public interest;
- Facilitating social and economic development.

The Act also provides for the establishment of "suitable institutions" with "appropriate community, racial and gender representation"
(Section 2). There are similar provisions in the Forests Act. Noting that
"the economic, social and environmental benefits of forests have been
distributed unfairly in the past," the Act lists among its purposes to:

- Promote the sustainable management and development of forests for the benefit of all;
- Promote the sustainable use of forests for environmental, economic, educational, recreational, cultural, health and spiritual
  purposes;
- Promote community forestry;
- Promote greater participation in all aspects of forestry and the
  forest products industry by persons disadvantaged by unfair discrimination.

As these legislative provisions demonstrate, a supportive legal
framework is now in place to foster greater environmental and social jus-

tice on the basis of race as well as gender. The fact that gender is explicitly included in the new environmental legislation and is not simply lumped into a general category of unfair discrimination places women in a strong position to demand rights to resources and full participation in environmental decision making and management that affects their lives.

Forces beyond the country's borders are also contributing to a re-linking of gender, environment, and development. South Africa's re-acceptance into the international community has brought the country within the ambit of international social and environmental agreements, as well as subjecting it to the environmental and social conditions imposed by trading partners such as the European Union. Another interesting development has been the initiative taken by large companies such as the British supermarket chain TESCO, whose representatives go directly to the South African farms from which they import their fruit and vegetables to assess both environmental management practices and the working and housing conditions of the agricultural laborers, many of whom are women (Frost 1999). Of course the relationship between capitalism and the environment is still problematic, but there is evidence of a consumer-driven movement toward more ethical trade practices that take issues of environmental and social justice into consideration.

Also promising is the growing involvement of blacks and women in the professional environmental sector, whether in government, the civil service, the private sector, or NGOs—although it can be argued that gender discrimination persists even where racial discrimination has been overcome. Women are prominent in both local action groups and national organizations within the environmental movement, and there is encouraging evidence of black South Africans beginning to take a more active interest in environmental issues. A Green Party, headed by a woman, contested the June 1999 national elections. The media give considerable coverage to environmental issues, often focusing on questions of environmental justice or gender equity. Indeed the South African environmental movement as a whole has undergone a dramatic shift in the past decade, from a "fauna and flora" conservationism to a socially aware political ecology that addresses "brown" as well as "green" issues.

This transformation is nowhere more evident than in the emergence of organizations such as the Environmental Justice Networking Forum, a "loose alliance and network of over 550 South African non-profit organizations united in our desire to bring about environmental justice in the world" (EJNF 1998). EJNF lists among its objectives the promotion of social justice and ecologically sustainable development; non-racism and non-sexism; putting people before profits; democratic and transparent governance; and "acting with and in the interests of the poor, aiming to build their voice" (EJNF 1998). It places blame for the worst of South Africa's environmental problems at the door of both apartheid and capitalism, which allows businesses to exploit both workers and the environment in the pursuit of profit.

EJNF has been involved in a number of ways in promoting the causes of environmental justice and ecofeminism in South Africa, from lobbying at the national level to assisting local communities to identify and achieve their social and environmental needs. It played an active and influential role in the development of the new national environmental policy, holding more than forty discussion workshops with people from more than three hundred organizations representing a broad spectrum of South African civil society (EJNF 1997a). The 1998 Environmental Management Act, which clearly bears an environmental justice stamp, is an indication of EJNF's success. EJNF has also joined the "war against poverty" declared by the government and NGO sectors, seeing this as an important platform from which to redefine the environmental debate in South Africa:

> The idea of environmental justice is a way of thinking about environment and development which links environmental abuse to social injustice. It helps us understand that the unequal power relationships in our society result in the abuse of people and environments. Poor people suffer most from environmental degradation and benefit least from the wealth produced from exploitation of their environments. Women in particular carry significant costs of environmental degradation. (EJNF 1997b, 2; see also Nyandu 1998)

Gender and poverty are thus as much EJNF's concern as race, although the South African context dictates that race will continue to be the most significant social variable in understanding and tackling environmental injustice. Certainly EJNF has not allowed itself to become defined by the narrow "environmental racism" frame of the United States environmental justice movement. Although its ambit is environmental justice in the broadest sense, gender issues have been at the forefront of many of its campaigns, and many EJNF members would certainly label themselves ecofeminists. EJNF has also succeeded in widening its reach to include organizations in other Southern African countries, as well as establishing links with similar bodies around the world. It is to be hoped that the lull in its activity at the time of writing represents a hiatus rather than the beginning of its demise, although the network of organizations it represents will probably persist regardless. Whether or not EJNF survives as an organization, ecofeminism and environmental justice constitute a powerful partnership for the future development of environmentalism in South Africa.

Future Prospects for Ecofeminism in South Africa

After a slow start, environmental justice is rapidly becoming an established part of the South African environmental movement. Ecofeminism, rather than developing separately and in competition, seems to have found a place under the environmental justice umbrella. These "alternative" versions of environmentalism exist alongside more "mainstream" forms, although these too have been forced to change to fit the new social and political climate. What the South African case clearly demonstrates is that the direct causal link between various forms of social discrimination and negative environmental outcomes is fertile ground for the development of an environmental justice perspective. Environmental justice provides a highly appropriate vehicle for environmental concerns in a country where the legacy of social injustice is both extreme and entrenched, and where mainstream environmentalism can seem an elitist indulgence. Certainly there is no shortage of issues for the environmental justice and ecofeminist movements to tackle. The environmental legacy of apartheid will take decades, even centuries, to erase, while the forces of globalization bring new risks and vulnerabilities, not least to women.

In my view, the environmental justice and ecofeminist movements in South Africa will continue to grow in support and significance for as long as they remain a united force for social and environmental change.

There is a danger that South Africa may drift toward the American model, where environmental justice has become equated with environmental racism, and ecofeminism has been branded an elitist white women's movement. Women's environmental needs and concerns are best perceived and addressed within a broader environmental justice framework; environmental justice is incomplete if it prioritizes race (or "blackness") over other forms of discrimination. In building their alliance, proponents of environmental justice and ecofeminism in South Africa must learn, both politically and intellectually, from international experience. Similarly, the South African experience may come to provide a model for the rest of the world and contribute to theoretical developments in critical environmental justice and feminist political ecology. In a remarkably short time, environmental justice has made its way onto the political agenda, giving South Africa some of the most enlightened environmental legislation of any country in the world. It is a long way from policy and legislation to social and environmental justice in practice, but the seeds have been sown and there are keen gardeners, black and white, male and female, to nurture them to fruition.

Notes

1. As Harvey (1996) points out, every sociopolitical project is simultaneously an ecological project and vice versa. Post-apartheid reconstruction thus becomes as much environmental as social, political, or economic.

2. For a more detailed discussion the reader is referred to chapters 1, 2, and 4 of this volume, as well as to Low and Gleeson (1998a and b) and articles by Cutter (1995), Heiman et al. (1996), Jamieson (1994), and Perrolle et al. (1993).

3. The stirrings of such a global movement were evident in the recent anti-globalization protests in Seattle, Washington, and Prague.

4. Plumwood (1993), Merchant (1996), and Warren (1997) are recommended reading for anyone wishing to engage more deeply with ecofeminist thought.

5. Jackson's full critique in *New Left Review* (1995), as well as the responses by Mary Mellor (1996) and Ariel Salleh (1996) and Jackson's subsequent reply (1996), indicate just how heated the debate about ecofeminism has become.

6. This has important implications for South Africa, where the relative weakness of ecofeminism within the local environmental movement may in part be explained by its perceived irrelevance to the majority of the population.

7. This argument is put forward in countless documents in the files of the Departments of Agriculture and Native Affairs.

8. It should be noted, however, that the extent of water and electricity delivery to the rural and urban poor is hotly debated. While the Department of Water Affairs and Forestry claimed, in early 2001, to have delivered water to more than 6.5 million South Africans who did not have it in 1994, critics such as the Rural Development Services Network (RDSN) maintained that as many as 80 percent of these new connections were no longer functioning because of technical failure and lack of operating funds. It is also true that thousands of poor South Africans have had their water and electricity cut off because of non-payment. It is also claimed that cost recovery policies on water are responsible for the outbreak of cholera in KwaZulu-Natal, which, by mid-2001, had infected more than 100,000 people and led to more than 200 deaths. These criticisms notwithstanding, it is clear that efforts to provide water and electricity in particular have had a positive impact on the living conditions of poor South Africans, especially women.

References

Agarwal, B. 1992. "The Gender and Environment Debate: Lessons from India." *Feminist Studies* 18 (1): 119–58.

Albertyn, C. 1994. "Towards Sustainable Reconstruction." *Environmental Justice Networker* 1: 1–2.

Beinart, W. 1984. "Soil Erosion, Conservationism and Ideas about Development: A Southern African Exploration, 1900–1960." *Journal of Southern African Studies* 11 (1): 52–83.

Bullard, R. 1990. *Dumping in Dixie: Race, Class and Environmental Quality*. Boulder, Colo.: Westview Press.

Capek, S. 1993. "The 'Environmental Justice' Frame: A Conceptual Discussion and an Application." *Social Problems* 40 (1): 5–24.

Cock, J., and E. Koch, eds. 1991. *Going Green: People, Politics and the Environment in South Africa*. Cape Town: Oxford University Press.

Cutter, S. 1995. "Race, Class and Environmental Justice." *Progress in Human Geography* 19 (1): 111–22.

Durning, A. 1990. *Apartheid's Environmental Toll*. Worldwatch Paper 95. Washington, D.C.: Worldwatch Institute.

EJNF (Environmental Justice Networking Forum). 1997a. "Government Policy

Paper a Victory for Environmental Justice." *Environmental Justice Networker* 14: 1–3.

———. 1997b. "EJNF Joins Campaign Against Poverty." *Environmental Justice Networker* 15: 1–2.

———. 1998. "Register As a Participant in EJNF." Registration form enclosed in *Environmental Justice Networker.*

Frost, P. 1999. Personal communication (on a farm in Mpumalanga Province, South Africa).

Gandar, M. 1991. "The Imbalance of Power." In M. Ramphele and C. McDowell, eds. *Restoring the Land: Environment and Change in Post-apartheid South Africa.* London: The Panos Institute.

Goldman, B. 1996. "What is the Future of Environmental Justice?" *Antipode* 28 (2): 122–41.

Harvey, D. 1996. *Justice, Nature and the Geography of Difference.* Oxford: Blackwell.

Heiman, M. 1996. "Race, Waste and Class: New Perspectives on Environmental Justice" (Editorial introduction to special issue on environmental justice). *Antipode* 28 (2): 111–21.

Jackson, C. 1993. "Women/nature or Gender/history? A Critique of Ecofeminist 'Development.'" *Journal of Peasant Studies* 20 (3): 380–419.

———. 1994. "Gender Analysis and Environmentalisms." In M. Redclift and T. Benton, eds. *Social Theory and the Global Environment.* London: Routledge.

———. 1995. "Radical Environmental Myths: A Gender Perspective." *New Left Review* 210: 124–41.

———. 1996. "Still Stirred by the Promise of Modernity." *New Left Review* 217: 148–54.

Jamieson, D. 1994. "Global Environmental Justice." In R. Attfield and A. Belsey, eds. *Philosophy and the Natural Environment.* Royal Institute of Philosophy Supplement 36. Cambridge: Cambridge University Press.

Khan, F. 1990a. "Involvement of the Masses in Environmental Politics." *Veld and Flora* 76 (4): 36–38.

———. 1990b. "Beyond the White Rhino: Confronting the South African Land Question." *African Wildlife* 44 (6): 321–24.

———. 1992. "Black Environmental Experience as a Facet of Current South African Environmental Perceptions." Research report submitted to the Human Needs, Resources and the Environment Programme of the South African Centre for Science Development.

———. 1994. "Rewriting South Africa's Conservation History: The Role of the Native Farmers Association." *Journal of Southern African Studies* 20 (4): 499–516.

Leach, M., and C. Green. 1997. "Gender and Environmental History: From Representation of Women and Nature to Gender Analysis of Ecology and Politics." *Environment and History* 3 (3): 343–70.

Low, N., and B. Gleeson. 1998a. "Situating Justice in the Environment: The Case of BHP at the Ok Tedi Copper Mine." *Antipode* 30 (3): 201–26.

———. 1998b. *Justice, Society and Nature*. London: Routledge.

Mellor, M. 1996. "Myths and Realities: A Reply to Cecile Jackson." *New Left Review* 217: 132–37.

Merchant, C. 1996. *Earthcare: Women and the Environment*. London: Routledge.

Mies, M., and V. Shiva. 1994. *Ecofeminism*. London: Zed Books.

Miller, V., M. Hallstein, and S. Quass. 1996. "Feminist Politics and Environmental Justice: Women's Community Activism in West Harlem, New York." In D. Rocheleau, B. Thomas-Slayter, and E. Wangari, eds. *Feminist Political Ecology: Global Issues and Local Experiences*. London: Routledge.

Nyandu, M. 1998. "Outpouring of Anguish at Poverty Hearings." *Environmental Justice Networker* 17: 1–2.

Pepper, D. 1996. *Modern Environmentalism*. London: Routledge.

Perrolle, J. 1993. "Comments From the Special Issue Editor: The Emerging Dialogue on Environmental Justice." *Social Problems* 40 (1): 1–4.

Plumwood, V. 1992. "Feminism and Ecofeminism: Beyond the Dualistic Assumptions of Women, Men and Nature. *The Ecologist* 22 (1): 8–13.

———. 1993. *Feminism and the Mastery of Nature*. London: Routledge.

———. 1997. "Androcentrism and Anthropocentrism: Parallels and Politics." In K. Warren, ed. *Ecofeminism: Women, Culture, Nature*. Bloomington: Indiana University Press.

Pulido, L. 1994. "Restructuring and the Contraction and Expansion of Environmental Rights in the United States." *Environment and Planning A* 26: 915–36.

———. 1996. "A Critical Review of the Methodology of Environmental Racism Research." *Antipode* 28 (2): 142–59.

Ramphele, M., and C. McDowell, eds. 1991. *Restoring the Land: Environment and Change in Post-apartheid South Africa*. London: The Panos Institute.

Rocheleau, D., B. Thomas-Slayter, and E. Wangari, eds. 1996. *Feminist Political Ecology: Global Issues and Local Experiences*. London: Routledge.

Rose, G., V. Kinnaird, M. Morris, and C. Nash. 1997. "Feminist Geographies of Environment, Nature and Landscape." In Women and Geography Study Group, eds. *Feminist Geographies: Explorations in Diversity and Difference*. London: Longman.

RSA (Republic of South Africa). 1996. The Constitution of the Republic of South Africa. Pretoria: Government Printers.

———. 1998a. National Water Act. Pretoria: Government Printers.

———. 1998b. National Forests Act. Pretoria: Government Printers.

———. 1998c. National Environmental Management Act. Pretoria: Government Printers.

Sachs, A. 1995. *Eco-justice: Linking Human Rights and the Environment*. Worldwatch Paper 127. Washington, D.C.: Worldwatch Institute.

Salleh, A. 1996. "An Eco-feminist Bio-ethic and What Post-humanism Really Means." *New Left Review* 217: 138–47.

Shiva, V. 1989. *Staying Alive: Women, Ecology and Development.* London: Zed Books.

———. 1991. *The Violence of the Green Revolution: Third World Agriculture, Ecology and Politics.* London: Zed Books.

Showers, K. 1994. "Early Experiences of Soil Conservation in Southern Africa: Segregated Programs and Rural Resistance." Working Paper 184. Boston: African Studies Center, Boston University.

Spretnak, C. 1997. "Radical Nonduality in Eco-feminist Philosophy." in K. Warren, ed. *Ecofeminism: Women, Culture, Nature.* Bloomington: Indiana University Press.

Sturgeon, N. 1997. "The Nature of Race: Discourses of Race in Ecofeminism." In K. Warren, ed. *Ecofeminism: Women, Culture, Nature.* Bloomington: Indiana University Press.

Szasz, A. 1994. *Ecopopulism: Toxic Waste and the Movement for Environmental Justice.* Minneapolis: University of Minnesota Press.

Taylor, D. 1997. "Women of Color, Environmental Justice, and Ecofeminism." In K.Warren, ed. *Ecofeminism: Women, Culture, Nature.* Bloomington: Indiana University Press.

Tesh, S., and B. Williams. 1996. "Identity Politics, Disinterested Politics and Environmental Justice." *Polity* 18 (3): 285–305.

United Church of Christ. 1991. "Principles of Environmental Justice." Proceedings of the First National Peoples of Color Environmental Leadership Summit, Washington, D.C., October.

Warren, K. ed. 1997. *Ecofeminism: Women, Culture, Nature.* Bloomington: Indiana University Press.

Living on a Wetland

Mpume Nyandu

"The biggest problem we have here in Diepsloot is people coming in and making empty promises," complains resident Violet Rophela. It seems a lot of individuals have given the people of Diepsloot settlement a variety of promises ranging from employment opportunities to helping them start community projects. "Look at these women," continues Violet, "they have been waiting here since early this morning because someone promised to come back today to organize sewing lessons for them. It's after ten now, where is she? Now you see what I mean by empty promises!"

Diepsloot is an informal settlement north of Johannesburg consisting of approximately 3,500 shacks and a population of about 15,000. The settlement is divided into three sections: Diepsloot 1, Diepsloot 2, and Waterfront. People living in Diepsloot 1 and 2 mainly came from the "East Bank" of Alexandra Township (colloquially known as Alex), in eastern Johannesburg. Diepsloot is further away from the richest parts of the city than Alex and there are very limited basic services available to the residents.

According to an official of the Northern Metropolitan Sub-Structure (NMSS) (a part of Johannesburg), the people of Diepsloot were moved from Alex by the Eastern Metropolitan Council because they were occupying land that had been earmarked for a housing project. Some of them lived on the banks of the Jukskei river, which meant that each time there were heavy rains their shacks were washed away.

However, the move from Alex seems to have added to their problems. Gloria Sibiya, a Diepsloot 1 resident, says: "Transport is very expensive here. I had to stop working shortly after moving into this place because it was pointless. The money I earned was only enough for transport to and from work and nothing else." So Gloria and her friend Violet decided to start a crèche in their new community. On rainy days the crèche, which is run from the front of Gloria's shack, closes as there is not enough room indoors for all the children. This poses a problem for working parents, many of whom have nowhere else to leave their children. The only school in Diepsloot has no furniture, no stationery, and no textbooks; and it is privately run. "If you look on my left hand side this is the school I was telling you about," says Violet, pointing towards a structure made of shining corrugated iron and too small to be a school. "Until last week the pupils were sitting like in the rural areas where children used to go to school under a tree."

The only services available to Diepsloot sections 1 and 2 are water, toilets, and a mobile clinic, but it seems the quality and quantity of these services is not satisfactory. "Look what the time is now, it's ten past twelve!" exclaims Gloria. "People this side have not received water and I don't think the water truck is coming back this way."

Three water trucks come once a day at irregular times. Sometimes towards month's end the trucks do not come at all. The residents also complain that the water has mucous-like substances in it, which may mean that the water tanks are not cleaned regularly.

To get water, people have to leave uncovered water containers in the street for the water truck drivers to fill. If a container has a lid the owner does not get water. Some of the water containers remain exposed at the side of the road all day until their owners return to collect them. Residents who have toilets in front of or near their shacks have no choice but to leave their containers next to the toilets.

Toilets are also a major problem. They are out on the streets and are shared by up to fifteen families. If selfish residents lock the toilets in front of their shacks, their neighbors must walk further to find an available toilet. The toilets frequently capsize in heavy rains.

The only clinic available is a mobile clinic that comes on Wednesdays and it is not always able to provide the services people need. As a result they are referred to the nearest clinic, in Witkoppen, about eight or nine kilometers from Diepsloot. It is difficult for many of the residents to get there because of high transport costs. When they do reach the clinic they are often expected to pay about R10 as a levy for the medication they receive.

There is high unemployment in this community. Many people live on disability grants and pensions. The problem again is that they have to travel all the way back to Alex to collect their money every month, which is very costly. For some it is physically impossible to get there. According to Violet, "Just yesterday a person died. He was due to get his disability grant but could not do it because Alex is far, now he's dead, and there's no money for the funeral." Some community members have tried to organize for pensioners and people who receive disability grants to collect them at a more accessible place.

Problems in the Waterfront section are even greater than those in Diepsloot 1 and 2. The section is a wetland, hence its name, and many houses are plagued by damp. The section has no roads, no clean drinking water, no toilets, and no clinic, sharing the already limited services available to residents of Diepsloot 1 and 2. The stream that runs a few meters from the shacks and the small bush near it are used as a toilet and a dumping ground.

Most of the plots or stands in this section are very small, approximately 2.5 square meters. According to the NMSS official, the council did not place people in the area as it is not suitable for building. "Most of the people now residing in Waterfront are victims of evictions from nearby smallholdings," he said.

Anna Mogoasi, a Waterfront resident since December 1997, says: "I was evicted from a farm in Honeydew because the farmers wanted us to pay rent and I could not afford it." She lives in her small shack with her baby, her husband, her younger brother, and a brother-in-law, who comes and goes.

Diepsloot, says the NMSS official, was intended to serve only as a reception area for people moved from Alex until suitable land was identified by the council. However, a shortage of land in the Northern Metropolitan area has resulted in a delay in moving the community to a more appropriate site.

Chapter 4

Race, Place, and Environmental Rights

*A Radical Critique of
Environmental Justice Discourse*

Greg Ruiters

oncerns about environmental justice, unlike those about political justice, raise a set of problems that go to the heart of inequality in spatial form and social processes. Political justice is often reduced to an aspatial, abstract judicial equality before the law. Environmental justice, on the other hand, invites a focus on the seemingly intractable material aspects of inequality.

But despite the inherently material nature of struggles for environmental justice, the bulk of this discourse has receded into a defensive mode that relies too heavily on juridical definitions of justice and fails to pay adequate attention to the spatial and production sides of environmental inequalities. The emphasis (wrongly) falls on the distribution of environmental hazards; the struggle for improved regulations; stricter enforcement; and better access to information about industries, their products, and workplace conditions. A deeper approach to environmental justice, however, requires a focus on the *production* and *prevention* of injustices.

In pre-democratic South Africa, the concept of justice was expansive. But since the negotiated political settlement in 1994, which largely preserved apartheid private property relations, this concept has gradually been reined in. A changed political opportunity structure—the Reconstruction and Development Programme, a democratic polity, and government-civil society partnerships have straitjacketed what was gloriously referred to as "the struggle" into juridical and corporate channels. The new "weapons" are, more often than not, the laws, the Bill of Rights, and the new Constitution, which provide only limited socioeconomic and environmental rights. Although the consultative government ethos provides opportunities for environmental groups to speak out and participate in policy formulation, it equally allows for moderation of demands and for cooption. Equity, rights, and partnerships between civil society and the state are key terms of the new policy style. By the mid-1990s nongovernmental organizations (NGOs) still had supportive relationships with mass organizations (unions, civics, youth, and women), but by the late 1990s, NGOs were increasingly marketing themselves as highly paid consultancies. At the same time, smaller and perhaps more critical NGOs have closed down. Ideals of deep changes in property and social relations developed in the African National Congress's (ANC) Freedom Charter and Congress of South African Trade Unions' (Cosatu) Workers' Charter are receding.

Having accepted the discipline of capital and the market, the ruling ANC has abandoned state-led development. The shift in South Africa has been towards a far more limited vision where capitalist styled "stakeholders," market efficiency, and institutions have gained hegemony. Social policy debate has moved to the right as market environmentalism has gained ground. The prevailing market environmental discourse stresses cost recovery and the conservation of scarce natural resources through commodification. All this has been grafted onto nation building and visions of an environmental movement that could unite South Africa, taking it beyond racial, political, and class divisions. Thus, a conflicting intellectual, legal, and policy context exists for understanding the place of environmental justice in South Africa.

In light of the above, this chapter's primary aim is to look into the rigor of the environmental justice discourse in a post-apartheid South Africa. Specifically, it examines competing ideas of environmental racism, concepts of rights and equity, and struggles over space and place, using the experience of the United States as a reference point. The chapter concludes with some ideas for a more materially grounded, "transitional" approach to environmental justice.

Environmental Racism

The notion of "environmental racism" has emerged from the 1960s American civil rights movement, black churches, and grassroots activists who share the perception that racism in social policy, housing, and urban environmental management is still widespread. Race is seen as the overwhelming factor in environmental injustice in the United States (Bullard 1993; Bryant and Mohai 1992). For example, Robert Bullard (1993, 7), a leading American environmental justice scholar, rails against "environmental apartheid" in the United States that "continues to cluster people of color in urban ghettoes, barrios and rural poverty pockets." According to Bullard, race is *the* determining factor in the siting of noxious industries and waste in the country. He has shown empirically that color rather than class explains the decision making of government and private industry alike. Given a choice between a poor white community and a poor black (or Hispanic) community for a place to locate a toxic disposal site, it is more likely to fall on the poor black community. Lead poisoning, for example, affects 68 percent of African-American children but only 38 percent of white children in families earning under $6,000 per annum (Bullard 1993, 21).

Not surprisingly, then, the United States environmental anti-racism movement uses terms such as "people of color being poisoned by white industries," "toxic colonialism," and the like. In the USA, "Communities of color across the land are questioning why their communities are used as receptacles for hazardous waste and polluting industries. . . . [They] feel they have the same right to clean air, water and an unpolluted land base as more affluent suburbanites have" (Bryant and Mohai 1992, 6–7).

The anti-racism movement in the United States also contests the "whiteness" of the mainstream environmental movement. In 1984, only four of the two hundred environmental NGO professionals in Washington, D.C., were black (Bullard 1994, 96). Although the situation has improved somewhat, environmental groups in the United States remain largely white, and rather than integrating into these mainstream bodies black environmentalists have chosen (or been forced) to create their own environmental associations addressing their own environmental concerns. As Dorceta Taylor (1993, 41) points out, "In these newer groups, minorities and the poor can associate with others like themselves—instead of joining a group where they would be with only a few or no other minority persons."

The parallels with South Africa are, of course, strong. The effects of apartheid on the material living conditions of black South Africans have been well documented, and black South Africans, both rural and urban, have been forced into overcrowded Bantustans and group areas with poor infrastructure and have borne the brunt of environmental hazards in the country (Durning 1990; Cock and Koch 1991; Ramphele and McDowell 1991; Hallowes 1993; IDRC 1995). The segregation of people based on the color of their skin was accompanied by an equally racialized distribution of waste sites, sewerage treatment plants, and dirty industries—all of which was enforced by a strong police state and racist ideology.

These spatial legacies persist today, with the overwhelming majority of environmentally hazardous industries and waste sites still located near, or within, black communities. White communities, meanwhile, were generally located in the most environmentally desirable rural and urban locations, and remain relatively free from the undesirable effects of industry and waste. Although this kind of overt environmental racism is no longer tolerated under the new South African Constitution, anecdotal evidence suggests that it still pervades environmental decision making at the local government level (McDonald 1997).

With the unbanning of anti-apartheid political parties in the early 1990s, the American language of environmental justice and environmental racism quickly took hold among environmental justice groups. In the highly politicized context of South Africa there was a mushrooming of new environmental groups and a new set of environmental debates. But as Farieda Khan points out in chapter 1 of this volume, the environmental movement in South Africa remains dominated by mainstream environmental groups that in turn remain largely white and middle-class in their composition and outlook. Many of these "old order" environmental organizations have taken on environmental justice issues as part of their organizational platforms and discourse, but their membership and primary activities belie their stated concerns. The major difference in South Africa, as Khan points out, is that black environmental groups have not been as successful as their American counterparts in establishing effective and well-resourced environmental justice organizations. Most of the "township-based" environmental groups are small, underfunded, and poorly organized, and there is no single organization that can claim to be nationally representative of black environmentalists.

This focus on environmental racism is important for at least three reasons. First, it challenges the claim that green politics transcends race and ideology in South Africa. Not only do the majority of black people face a very different set of environmental injustices on a regular basis from those faced by whites, they also face a very different struggle in trying to combat them. On a more positive note, it can also be argued that a focus on race is itself a form of resistance, and one that is deeply felt. As Michael Dorsey (1998, 505) argues in the American context, activism around environmental racism has proved that (a) blacks are interested in environmental issues, and (b) black environmental groups have organizational skills and a capacity to mobilize that sets them apart from white environmental groups. Environmental anti-racism has the potential to help people reject the "facts" of their oppressive everyday lives and emphasizes the self-confidence and dignity that can be gained from organizing against environmental and self degradation.

But there are also some problems with the racial-equity focus in environmental justice discourse as it has developed in the United States. The first problem is defining racism. Is it a discrete, empirical event involving overt acts? This narrow definition ignores the fact that racism takes covert multiple forms, from financial red-lining, to police bigotry, to all sorts of symbolic violences (e.g., advertising) and attacks on the dignity of people (Young 1990). Can racism and its effects be isolated so that we may catch it in the act? Is there a single form of racism? A quantitative analysis of racism provides a very partial lens.

A second reason why it is important to dissect the focus on environmental racism is that the race-equity focus tends to narrow the scope of environmental justice to equal treatment: "siting toxic waste and incinerators rather than broader social justice questions, workers rights, coalition building, eliminating risks and community participation" (Gottlieb and Fisher 1996, 193–201). While demands for an end to racial disparities in the siting of landfill are important, moving waste around is no solution either. For in the end it will land on the doorstep of the weakest community (even on another continent). The environmental racism movement has a predilection for putting distributive justice above the issue of why environmental "bads" are produced in the first place.

Thirdly, a "shallow" racial approach that "emphasizes only racism and race . . . and a homogenous community not fractured by class" means "we ultimately fetishize skin color . . . instead of developing a broader and deeper understanding of how inequality is produced" (Pulido 1996, 155). Pulido (1996, 151) sees the race discourse as "a *political* choice in which class inequalities and political weakness are rarely if ever discussed." She argues that a statistical approach derives from legal and courtroom requirements and policy debates, but that the environmental justice movement needs a wider lens on racism: a lens that allows for movement building. One does not want to reject the insights of environmental racism entirely, she argues, only its narrow empirical methodology.

Environmental Rights

We now consider legalistic notions of environmental justice. As with environmental racism, the notion of environmental rights emerged from the civil rights movement in the United States where they have become institutionalized as "Title Six Rights" by the Environmental Protection Agency.[1] In South Africa, the role of environmental rights has grown in large part because of the new Constitution and the changed political structure. The National Environmental Management Act (107 of 1998) promises that "adverse environmental impacts shall not be distributed in such a manner as to unfairly discriminate against any persons, particularly vulnerable and disadvantaged persons." The Act also seeks to empower citizens by allowing for private prosecutions as well as protection from liability for court costs if the action is in the public interest. The Human Rights Commission also has an environmental rights component, although few cases seem to have been channeled there thus far.

These new options for environmental litigation have opened opportunities for pursuing environmental justice. Indeed, in the American context, Bullard (1993, 204) sees the equitable enforcement of law and legal principals as the indispensable requirement and, "where applicable laws already exist, the environmental justice framework demands that they are enforced in a non-discriminatory fashion." To arrive at an environmentally just society Bullard suggests protection should be a right not a privilege and that both intended and unintended consequences of policies and practices need to be addressed.

But there are problems with this legalistic focus. First, and most obvious, are the high costs of litigation and the expertise required to engage effectively in the legal system. Few communities in South Africa have the resources and technical know-how to prove their cases of environmental injustice or to demonstrate that a specific polluting source is to blame (White 1991, 254). And, communities often have to endure hazardous conditions until after successful litigation, which may take years. More fundamental is the argument that the pursuit of justice through litigation and more effective regulation does not address the problem of class injustices; that it in fact entrenches private property rights. As Michael Ryan (1989, 150) notes, rights theory is paradoxical: "It provides instruments of (collective) struggle such as the right to unionize, actions against corporations for negligent harm, assertions of the right for equal treatment and so on . . . [but] there is no right to establish a socialist society because the doctrine of rights is welded to claims of property ownership." The courts' first principle is the sanctity of contracts and private property, not the wider social interest.

Robert Lake (1996) challenges the environmental equity position "both for its naïve faith in procedural justice in social conflict settings and in the inability of distributional notions of fairness to problematize the structural and institutional sources of injustice." Mackinnon (as cited in Schneider 1991, 319) takes the argument one step further by arguing that rights discourse has the potential to "keep people passive and dependent on the state, because it is the state which grants them their rights." Individuals are only allowed to "exercise their rights to the degree that the state permits. Legal strategies tend to weaken the power of the popular movement by allowing the state to define the movement's goals." Rights discourse may therefore be as paralyzing as it is enabling. It may mobilize, but also immobilize; it delimits the range of programmatic options, thereby narrowing outcomes.

This is not to deny the value of legalistic routes to addressing environmental injustices. Not to use interdicts and the law courts in South

Africa would be foolish. But legalistic justice can easily become too defensive, oriented solely to the issue of equal protection under the law. It also eviscerates the anger and force of moral arguments for justice and arrives after the damage has been done.

To move beyond the chimera of legalistic forms of distributional equity requires a critical exploration of the foundations of social power. In contemporary society the rules are framed by fair commodity exchange, private ownership, and "uncoerced" contracts. With the decline of feudal relationships and the rise of bourgeois society, humans became "legal bearers of rights" as opposed to bearers of customary privileges. The result of this efflorescence of rights is that the workers' dependence on capital does not appear to be a coercive relationship but rather to be a voluntary one, a "freedom." Freedom of movement and the right to choose a place of residence are hallowed liberal principles as long as the means of production and reproduction are monopolized by a single class. A worker who works in a South African mine has done so "freely," even if he or she is likely to die in the mine or emerge from it without his or her limbs. Would fair monetary compensation be sufficient to constitute justice? Many environmental justice movements would say yes.

Bourgeois rights pose issues of equality in abstract terms, and the rule of law is seen as neutral. However, capitalist relations presuppose a prior process of "forced and complete separation of workers and the ownership of the conditions for the realization of their labor. . . . Capital not only maintains this separation, but reproduces it on a constantly extending scale" (Marx 1977, 873–74). The moment of compulsion and force is a historical precondition and is active in the discipline over the workers inside the factory, ensuring control over minutes and seconds. It is precisely these relations of class domination that the legal form tries to spirit away. Marx shows "free workers" as bonded in the double sense that they are forced to sell their labor power and at the same time forcibly separated from the means of production. The same liberal illusion afflicts notions of environmental justice through the "even handed" application of the law.

Marx also highlights the inequality in the doctrine of equal rights: "One worker is married, another is not; one has more children than another. Thus, given an equal amount of work done, one will in fact receive more than another." Hence he observes, "to avoid defects, rights would have to be unequal rather than equal" (Marx in Fisk 1993, 31). Applied to environmental questions this would not mean equal exposure but *better* relative conditions for vulnerable and historically "disadvantaged" groups. As Chris Arthur (1978, 25) argues, "The demand for equality, or for equity in economic and legal arrangements, does not grasp the qualitative break with previous forms. Equality is the highest concept of bourgeois politics. It is not accidental that Marx never issued any programmatic declaration for it."

The problem with bourgeois theories of justice, as Iris Young (1990) points out, is that they seek to detemporalize—that is, they present themselves as fixed and unchanging standards. This, she contends, is "too abstract to be useful in evaluating actual institutions and practices." Thus, "everyday discourse about justice certainly makes claims, [but] these are not theorems to be demonstrated in a self-enclosed system. They are instead, claims upon some people by others" (Young 1990, 4–5).

Space, Place, and the Construction of Environmental Injustices

We now turn our attention to the questions of space and place. If it is the case that capitalist dynamism and competition produce injustices in new forms all the time, how do we understand the spatial dimensions to these injustices and what does the environmental justice literature have to say about it? It is important to stress that questions such as "who gets what" need to be underlined by time and space considerations such as when and where goods and services are received.

Capital relocations offer a classic case of market injustices. Capital, if it can, will move to places of lower intensities of class conflict and to less organized communities, setting in motion permanent instability and uncertainty. This "continuous restructuring of spatial configurations is a normal feature of capitalist competition that has become more pronounced under globalization. The results are all kinds of spatio-social differentiation—deindustrialization, suburbanization, ghetto formation, gentrification; in short, a pluralization of injustices" (Harvey 1982, 426). This instability undermines the institutional bases for long-term agreements that may have promoted stability, a sense of place, trust, equity, and justice. The paradox here is that as soon as justice has been won in some place, capital threatens to relocate.

Capital mobility accelerates creative destruction and changes the relative strengths of classes and the ability of workers to limit capital's mobile powers. Corporate job blackmail, municipal boosterism, and corporate welfare entail justice for shareholders and little justice for the communities whose livelihoods are under threat (Korten 1995; Hirst and Thompson 1996). Concessions won by legal means are eviscerated in space and time, since capital changes the scale of contestation or recoups losses in other ways (e.g., passing on costs of devaluation to consumers). This is not to say that capital always wins but that it tends under normal conditions to have superior command over space. Environmental and justice arguments must therefore confront the spatial power of capital.

From a materialist standpoint, territorial considerations attach to justice questions in specific ways. As Litfin (1994, 36) notes, "Environmental problems inject temporal and spatial understandings into the policy process . . . tendencies that are amplified as the problems take on intergenerational and planetary proportions." Injustice is as much national and local as it is international. But the tendency to see it only in the local, national, or group-specific terrain is very widespread. As a result, justice becomes wrapped in territorial colors and coalitions:

> The capacity of most social movements to command place better than space puts a strong emphasis upon the potential connection between place and social identity. The consequent dilemmas of socialist or working class movements in the face of universalizing capitalism are shared by other oppositional groups—racial minorities, colonized peoples, women, etc.—who are relatively empowered to organize in place, but disempowered when it comes to organizing across space. In clinging to place bound identity, such oppositional movements become a part of the very fragmentation which a mobile capitalism and flexible accumulation can feed upon. . . . Place bound organizations may be excellent bases for political action but they cannot bear the burden of radical historical change alone. (Harvey 1996, 302–3)

Harvey (1996, 303) sees "the general struggle against capitalism as always being made up of particular struggles against specific kinds of socio-ecological projects." Here a universal is not understood as the summation of particularities, but as dialectical, in that the universal and particular define each other. If justice cannot be adjudicated only at the local, or at a north or south or particularistic level, then new global coalitions and political formations are needed.

Given the volatility of capitalism, injustice is thus not a thing or a steady state, or merely about implementing national laws and constitutions. Rights embedded in the law and in a specific place (as in national welfare rights) are severely limited by capital's superior command of space—as opposed to labor's relative immobility and the severely limited spatial options of the poor. Hence space, place, and environmental justice are tightly interwoven. The poor are trapped by space and their predicament is reinforced by symbolic cultural labels suggesting pollution, dirt, and waste.

Equal protection cannot overcome this entrapment while abstract universals such as "our common future" appeal to a false impartiality. Equal protection, the liberal justice project, is doomed as a systematic approach. If social conflict drives justice, as this chapter argues, it also has the normative implication that membership of one's class or group needs to be valorized in an environmental perspective that establishes a new basis for universal values. It is thus quite conceivable that a variety of criss-crossing identities come into play in mobilizing against the many faces of injustice.

A Transitional View of Justice

The challenges posed in the previous section suggest the need for a threefold view of environmental justice transitions: time, identity, and scale. First, environmental justice should not be minima that rulers are willing to concede, nor be confined to positive law. Rather, demands must be transitional, capable of being both defensive and of being extended and redefined over time. Second, the demands of environmental justice must be able to increase the self-confidence and the collective power of the disempowered so that "people can learn to map their own environments from their own experiences" (Gottlieb 1993, 305–6) and discover new forms of self-awareness. Justice is a process—a complex product of existing local knowledge, identity, the balance of class and collective forces, experience, and the definition of future goals. And finally, as part of a counter-hegemonic struggle, justice means the creation of new institutions to mediate particular claims. A wider scale often reveals much about the roots of injustices: the more organized people are over a wider range (local, regional, international) the more expansive their demands for justice become. The boundaries of community and solidarity and the conception of needs and rights need to be seen as provisional and in transition. Group self-definitions, boundaries, and interests may change from initial formative demands and contexts.

In struggles for justice, particular individual identities are not "frozen patches." Temporary and open to reconstruction, these changeable identities are crucial in moving towards social transformation driven from below. An example may help here. Viewed from the standpoint of building towards a classless society working-class identity is temporary but it is an identity akin to a social prison. The working class, according to Marxist classics, has to abolish this identity. Yet the paradox of its struggle is that it has to constitute itself as a class along the way to its self-liquidation. A dynamic view of self-identity posits the latter as interwoven and produced by multiple interactions with the world. A related concept whereby "blackness" constructs "whiteness" as opposed to essentialist views of identities as frozen "things" allows for a pursuit of a class politics that can protect rather than suppress gender and race interests. Harvey (1998, 64) notes that "A politics that tackles underlying conditions that give rise to social injustice looks rather different from one that tries to give full play to identities once they have arisen. The loss of identity on 'solving' the problem shows that the mere pursuit of identity politics cannot be an end itself."

It is crucial in the pursuit of justice to make room for diverse and culturally sensitive notions of it. Justice is not confined to a minimalist or basic needs approach based on some *a priori* calculations about feasibility in the context of "limited resources." It is as much a struggle *for* as *over* justice. Universality or solidarity is viable only as a three-dimensional concept: "It must have its social material roots in the past, maintain itself in the present and branch out with enduring ramifications towards the future" (Meszaros 1989, 348). According to socialist modernizers like Meszaros (1989, 464),

"We cannot give up the search for global solutions to our global problems," otherwise "we withdraw into the little world of local skirmishes."

By way of conclusion I will note two points. First, justice and solidarity need to be synthesized if blind communitarianism with all its essentializing notions of identity and exclusions is to be avoided. Yet we cannot leap outside the imperatives of particularities. Militant particularism is still a vital force with which to challenge injustices and may be even more powerful if allied to wider struggles. If these dilemmas show anything, it is that environment and social justice are inseparable, that justice requires a global approach, proactive on all scales and infused with an understanding of how environmental problems are produced, rather than merely with their distribution.

Second, "realism" and "practicality" are insufficient criteria for an environmental justice movement. Justice is not simply "whatever capital is able and willing to concede from its fluctuating margins of profitability" (Meszaros 1995, 205). Positive law is a crucial stepping-stone towards more active citizenship and greater equality, but a radical justice discourse challenges in a way that goes beyond pragmatic, assimilative politics. Watering down justice to "basic" needs, while a major preoccupation of "experts," lowers the morale of the masses and meshes well with "Third World" standards for justice. Justice has to be viewed not as an end state, or as a thing or quantity, or as a set of rights, but as a process. From this standpoint, counter-hegemonic struggles for justice are also about the construction of different universals and values.

Note

1. More than sixty countries have included environmental rights in their constitutions, as does the International Covenant on Economic, Social and Cultural Rights (Sachs 1995, 46–47).

References

Arthur, C. 1978. "Introduction." In E. Pashukanis. *Law and Marxism*. London: Ink-links.

Bryant, B., and P. Mohai. 1992. *Race and the Incidence of Environmental Hazards.* Boulder, Colo.: Westview Press.

Bullard, R. 1993. *Voices from the Grassroots.* Boston: South End Press.

———. 1994. *Unequal Protection.* San Francisco: Sierra Club Books.

Cock, J., and E. Koch. 1991. *Going Green: People Politics and Environment in South Africa.* Cape Town: Oxford University Press.

Dorsey, M. 1998. "Race, Poverty and Environment." *Legal Studies Forum* 22 (1, 2 and 3).

Durning, A. 1991. *Apartheid's Environmental Toll.* Worldwatch Paper, 95. Washington, D.C.: Worldwatch Institute.

Fisk, M., ed. 1993. *Justice.* Atlantic Highlands, N.J.: Humanities Press.

Gottlieb, R. 1993. *Forcing the Spring.* Washington, D.C.: Island Press.

Gottlieb, R., and A. Fisher. 1996. "Feeding the Face: Environmental Justice and Community Food Security." *Antipode* 28 (2): 193–203.

Hallowes, D., ed. 1993. *Hidden Faces. Environment, Development, Justice: South Africa and the Global Context.* Pietermaritzburg: Earthlife Africa.

Harvey, D. 1982. *The Limits to Capital.* Oxford: Basil Blackwell.

———. 1996. *The Justice Nature and the Geography of Difference.* Oxford: Basil Blackwell.

———. 1998. Marxism, Metaphors and Ecological Politics. *Monthly Review,* April.

Hirst, P., and G. Thompson. 1996. *Gobalization in Question.* Cambridge: Polity Press.

IDRC (International Development Research Centre). 1995. *Building a New South Africa: Environment, Reconstruction and Development.* Ottawa: International Development Research Centre.

Korten, D. 1995. *When Corporations Rule the World.* West Hartford, Conn.: Kumarian Press.

Lake, R. 1996. "Volunteers, Nimbys and Environmental Justice: Dilemmas of Democratic Practice." *Antipode* 28 (2).

Litfin, K. 1994. *Ozone Discourses: Science and Politics in Global Environmental Cooperation.* New York: Columbia University Press.

McDonald, D. 1997. "Neither From Above Nor From Below: Municipal Bureaucrats and Environmental Policy in Cape Town, South Africa." *Canadian Journal of African Studies* 31 (2).

Marx, K. 1977. *Capital Volume One.* New York: Vintage Books.

Meszaros, I. 1989. *The Power of Ideology.* London: Harvester Wheatshelf.

———. 1995. *Beyond Capital.* New York: Monthly Review Press.

Pulido, L. 1996. "A Critical Review of the Methodology of Environmental Racism Research." *Antipode* 28 (2).

Ramphele, M., and C. McDowell, eds. 1991. *Restoring the Land: Environment and Change in Post-apartheid South Africa.* London: The Panos Institute.

Ryan, M. 1989. *Politics and Culture: Working Hypotheses for a Post-revolutionary Society.* Baltimore, Md.: Johns Hopkins University Press.

Sachs, A. 1995. *Eco-justice: Linking Human Rights and the Environment.* Washington, D.C.: Worldwatch Institute.

Schneider, E. 1991. "The Dialectic of Rights and Politics: Perspectives from the Women's Movement." In K. Bartlett and R. Kennedy. *Feminist Legal Theory.* Boulder, Colo.: Westview Press.

Taylor, D. 1993. "Environmentalism and the Politics of Inclusion." In R. D. Bullard, ed. *Confronting Environmental Racism: Voices from the Grassroots.* Boston: South End Press.

White, J. 1991. "The Teeth Need Sharpening: Law and Environmental Protection." In J. Cock and E. Koch, eds. *Going Green: People, Politics and the Environment in South Africa.* Cape Town: Oxford University Press.

Young, I. 1990. *Justice and the Politics of Difference.* Princeton: Princeton University Press.

Where Basic Services Are Only a Pipe Dream

Mpume Nyandu

> *There are no nearby toilets, we have to walk a distance to the other side to ask if the owners of the toilets can let us use their toilets. Sometimes people lock their toilets.*
> —Zamithemba Mxhashimba, Site B, Khayelitsha

> *If one house burns, nearby houses also burn, especially when it's windy.*
> —Mr William Bothman, Philippi

> *There are no crèches and pre-schools, and we need real houses so that we can be free from living in leaking and burning shacks.*
> —Nosisi Gladile, Langa, Zone 25

South Africa has many informal settlements. Khayelitsha, Philippi, and Langa in Cape Town are just three examples of settlements with growing populations and very few or no basic services like housing, water, sanitation, electricity, refuse collection, and proper roads. The list is endless. "One has to walk about ten minutes before one finds a toilet. At night it's not easy and not safe to walk that far, so one often looks for a corner nearby where one can relieve oneself," says Ndyebo Sibutha (25), who came originally from Queenstown in the Eastern Cape and has lived in Khayelitsha for close to two years.

Khayelitsha is one of the largest townships in the Western Cape Province and it is situated twenty kilometers to the east of Cape Town. According to information from the Khayelitsha Education Resource and Information Centre (KERIC), the township covers an area of more than thirty-five square kilometers and is built exclusively on sand dunes. Because no significant statistics have been compiled to date, population estimates vary from 500,000 to more than a million. Unemployment, according to KERIC, is in the range of 65 percent.

In 1995, KERIC submitted a project proposal to the Reconstruction and Development Programme office that included a general clean up campaign, the creation of a park, and the construction of an environmental center. But the restructuring of the municipalities at the time hindered progress on this project because consideration was being given to incorporating Khayelitsha into the Tygerberg substructure.

"On hot days we cannot sit outside because there are flies all over the place coming from the dump behind our shack. During rainy seasons the dump has a very bad smell. The big problem is that children play in this rubbish dump and they then develop sores and diseases like tuberculosis," complains Nosipho November (18), who's been in Khayelitsha for just over a year. She came from a rural area in the Transkei to babysit a two-year-old child whose mother is a sleep-in domestic worker in Cape Town. She adds: "We have water and toilet problems. We have to walk far to get to the nearest tap." According to Ndyebo Sibutha, when it rains the shacks leak. "Sometimes it's because the corrugated iron used is too old. This means that one has to move furniture around, often changing the bed position in the middle of the night, and placing containers where the water comes in."

These problems are not unique to Khayelitsha residents. William Bothman (55), who has lived in Philippi for ten years, lives on the edge of a stagnant pond. He says: "When it rains the pond fills up with water. The water doesn't come only to my house, everyone else in the area struggles in water. Sometimes the council comes and takes people to Gugulethu hostels for about two months while waiting for the water to soak down." When it comes to clean drinking water there is only one tap servicing Philippi residents. The tap was installed about six years ago. According to William Bothman's wife, Noli Jastile (41), before the tap arrived "people used to open up the storm water drain next to the road for water to drink. We did not mind that the water was dirty, we just removed the [visible] dirt and drank the water."

Another problem common to all three areas is fires. Because the houses are so closely packed, if one house burns the neighboring houses catch fire, leaving huge numbers of people homeless. When it is windy, hundreds of houses can burn in one night. The source of fire is said to be candles or paraffin lamps commonly used because there is often no electricity in these areas. "Can you see," says William Bothman, pointing at his house, "I put the fence around my house very far because I don't want other people next to me. If my house burns, my place must burn alone, you see!"

Because of the high unemployment rate, people scavenge in the waste dump for food, and for scrap to sell. In Philippi, trucks from supermarkets illegally dump rotten fruit, vegetables, and other expired foodstuffs. Trucks from building companies and scrap yards dump rubble and scrap. As soon as the trucks approach, people from Philippi flock in great numbers towards the dump. In Noli Jastile's words: "We earn our living through the waste products. We clean old bricks and sell them to get food. We wait for the Seven-Eleven supermarket trucks where we try and get some potatoes to eat so that we go to bed with something in our tummies. I am not saying these vegetables from the dump site aren't poisonous but what do you do when you are hungry and there's a bag of potatoes in front of you?"

With solid waste identified as a key problem in the Western Cape informal settlements, some community based organizations (CBOs) and NGOs involved in environmental work have tried to educate people about waste management. In Langa an NGO called TSOGA (meaning "wake up" in Sotho) has been working closely with Zone 25 on a waste management program which started in mid-1997 and seems to have worked well, according to the residents who are involved in the program. Nosisi Gladile (27), one of the women in the Waste Management Group, says: "We started by collecting waste, and we visited recycling centers. Our area is now much better than it used to be, it's not the same anymore." Zone 25 residents and the TSOGA team hope that this waste management project will have a ripple effect on other sections of Langa. Langa Zone 25 was initially a hostel area built for black men working in the surrounding industrial areas of Cape Town. But since early 1994 there has been a significant influx of people from all over the country. Today Langa has a population of close to 100,000 and covers hundreds of hectares.

Despite the problems, the Langa Zone 25 Waste Management Group is quite positive about the future of waste management, realizing that part of the solution lies with people doing things for themselves. They are also conscious that, in light of the larger problems they face (among them leaking and fire prone shacks), this is only a fraction of the solution. Nosipho November of

Khayelitsha feels that if the problems of the township cannot be solved, the government should move residents to another area with better living conditions.

In Philippi, the area committee is involved in a process of trying to get government to buy them the land they are currently occupying. They hope that once the land is legally theirs the council will take them seriously and start providing them with basic services. Toilets and waste management are major priorities. In the words of one of the residents: "We have churches here, people are praying, but I don't think they get answers from God. Not in a place like this. God wants a clean place."

Chapter 5

From Colonial to Community-Based Conservation

Environmental Justice and the Transformation of National Parks (1994–1998)

Jacklyn Cock and David Fig

nvironmental racism took many extreme forms in apartheid South Africa. This chapter will focus on one dimension of it: the separation of black South Africans from their rights in national parks. This abrogation of rights involved the expulsion of black South Africans from lands later used to create national parks. It further saw their exclusion from physical access to and managerial control of national parks.

Since the 1994 democratic elections in which the government led by the African National Congress (ANC) came to power, considerable efforts have been made to redress these injustices. These initiatives, although incomplete, are part of the transformation process within the national parks system and broader society.

The History of National Parks in South Africa

In 1994 the post-apartheid government inherited seventeen national parks, the flagship of which is the second oldest national park in the world, the Kruger National Park (KNP). Established more than a century ago, in 1898, the KNP now covers nearly two million hectares and is unrivaled in the diversity of its life forms, with 147 species of mammals and 507 species of birds. The other national parks in South Africa are smaller, but constitute part of an attempt to develop the conservation of a representative sample of each of South Africa's diverse ecological systems.

These protected areas reflect the relations of power and privilege that have shaped South African society. Under apartheid the majority of South Africans were subjected to a double exclusion from the national parks: black South Africans were denied access as visitors and were excluded from power, authority, and influence in decision making and policy formulation within the national parks.

From 1926 these parks were administered by the National Parks Board, the name confusingly used both for the governing body of non-executive board members (technically the Board of Curators) and for the organization as a whole. In 1996, the National Parks Board was renamed South African National Parks (SANP), after a public competition was held to find a new name.

Before 1994 board members were exclusively appointed from the ranks of white males who were generally closely aligned with Afrikaner nationalism. Specifically, board members developed "close bonds with the Nationalist government after 1948 (when the latter came to power)" (Carruthers 1995, 81). These bonds were cemented with the inclusion on the board of the centrally appointed provincial administrators. The organization as a whole was therefore white-controlled and largely reflected the culture and practice of apartheid. For example, until the 1980s, black visitors to the Kruger National Park were only allowed accommodation at Balule, a tented camp, established in 1932 with very rudimentary facilities. Access for black visitors was also restricted by economic factors such as entry fees and the need for motorized transport, both difficult conditions given the levels of deprivation and impoverishment imposed on black people by apartheid.

Furthermore, under apartheid the Kruger National Park was used for a variety of military purposes including the training of South African Defence Force soldiers, the covert supply of material to Renamo in Mozambique, and even the launch of a chemical weapons attack on Frelimo troops in 1992 (Cock 1993).

The parks were surrounded by overcrowded and degraded rural areas. Overall, they reflected the worst aspects of "colonial" conservation. For example, there was a total neglect of the archaeological record that shows that some of the parks—particularly Kruger—were the sites of settled African mining and trading communities for hundreds of years. The prevalent colonial philosophy of exclusion and domination of indigenous peoples involved forced removals at gunpoint.

The only Africans allowed to remain in Kruger were low-paid laborers (Carruthers 1995), reflecting the culture of the white administration with its racist employment and housing practices. In terms of jobs in the Kruger National Park, preference was given to laborers from Mozambique rather than to South Africans, on the grounds that the Mozambicans were prepared to work for extremely low wages. Within the organization there was no overt acknowledgment that it was the labor of the thousands of black workers that made the national parks possible. It was seldom recognized that the ranging, tracking, and other skills provided by black workers made a "scientific" contribution to conservation, whereas whites with these skills were often regarded as doing so, and given promotions accordingly.

The organization was dominated by conservationists exclusively concerned with preserving biodiversity while neglecting human needs and social issues. The notion of pristine wilderness and human exclusion, as exemplified by colonial attitudes, was sectional, and exacerbated national divisions along racial lines.

Rather than being a means of nation building, the parks worked against national unity to reflect and maintain the privileges of the white minority. Clearly, after 1994, this had to change.

The Rationale for Change

In October 1995 a new Board of Curators was appointed. Nine members were chosen by a subcommittee of the national cabinet through a process of public nomination, while a further nine were nominated by provincial premiers. The new board is more representative than its predecessors in racial terms. It is also marked by diversity of party political allegiance, and includes some members from the apartheid era. This diversity reflects the fact that the post-apartheid Government of National Unity was a coalition between the ANC and the former ruling party. Thus, while it is debatable to what extent all members share the same vision of the transformation of South African society, they do generally share a commitment to a fresh, transparent, and participatory policy framework.

The new board's transformation statement reads as follows:

> South African National Parks is striving to transfer power and control of resources from the minority that had been appointed and privileged by an undemocratic system, to the majority that participates in the new democratic process. It is also directing the benefits of its activities to providing for all South Africans, rather than the more wealthy and privileged sections of society.

This new policy signaled a dramatic shift in the dominant notions of conservation.

While the statement is strongly aspirational, it must be remembered that the transition to democracy in South Africa was not the result of a "miracle" or of the seizure of power, but of a negotiated settlement that involved many explicit and implicit compromises that left key elements of apartheid privilege and power intact. For example, until 1996, the cabinet minister responsible for national parks hailed from the former ruling National Party. Similarly, all the bureaucrats in central government responsible for biodiversity protection were members of the old guard, with transformation occurring only from 1998 onwards. Within the SANP, key officials, whether in the parks or in head office, were from the former white-ruled establishment, and continued to reflect similar values after democratization. In the national negotiations that established a democratic order, a "sunset clause" was approved that guaranteed old-order civil servants their jobs; however, the SANP made provision for the early retirement of some officials at the age of fifty-five to allow space for the racial diversification of management.

Linking Conservation to Social Justice

The SANP is informed by a new conception of conservation that is radically different from that generated during the country's colonial and apartheid past. This new vision centers on the inclusion rather than the exclusion of people and on linking conservation to human needs. "Until very recently the dominant understanding of environmental issues in South Africa was an authoritarian conservation perspective" (Cock 1991, 1).

This perspective is not unique to South Africa. Taylor has noted that environmental organizations throughout the world focus on survival issues "as they pertain to endangered species, national parks, preserves, and threatened landscapes. These survival debates are not linked to rural and urban poverty and quality of life issues" (cited in Harvey 1996, 386). This narrow preservationist notion of conservation was established throughout Africa by colonial authorities and, it has been argued, is exemplified in the notion of national parks (Adams and McShane 1996). Throughout Africa the establishment of national parks and conservation areas involved the removal, social dislocation, and exclusion of indigenous communities. As Carruthers (1995, 101) writes: "In the African version of wildlife conservation history, the experience has been that game reserves are white inventions which elevate wildlife above humanity and which have served as instruments of dispossession and subjugation."

The SANP is now committed to promoting a different concept of conservation, one linked to issues of development and human needs. It is a concept that implies a harmonious relationship between people and parks and builds on traditional conceptions of wilderness and wildlife in African indigenous cultures. The key to the new concept of conservation is that it attempts to link the protection of biodiversity to human benefits ranging from employment of local people to their access to the sustainable utilization of resources within the parks. The shift could be described as the move away from a colonially inspired model of conservation focused on preservation to a more indigenously conceived model.

The most significant aspects of this process of change relate to six spheres in which transformation has been attempted. These spheres are summarized below.

Land Restitution

One of the key issues of environmental justice that the new board has attempted to address is that of land restitution. Land restitution is also an aspect of reinstating an indigenous concept of conservation. While only

4 percent of South Africa's land area is devoted to protected areas, this must be understood in the context of the land shortage created by the Land Acts of 1913 and 1936 which restricted African land ownership to only 13 percent of the country. This is one of the most unjust legacies of colonialism and apartheid. Africans, who make up 70 percent of the population, were confined to eroded, overcrowded reserves. Although the laws have been repealed, white South Africans continue to control more than 80 percent of the country's total agricultural land. Since 1994, the post-apartheid government has embarked on a multifaceted program that aims to correct this injustice (Letsoalo 1987; Ramphele and McDowell 1991, 27ff.; Marcus, Eales, and Wildschut 1996).

The pattern of dispossession of rural people as a consequence of the creation of national parks and game reserves is not unique to South Africa; it can be seen in many countries in both the North and the South. In the 1850s, for example, U.S. troops flushed the final Ahwahneechee Indians out of the Yosemite Valley (Rothenberg 1995). The difference lies in the scale on which this dispossession has occurred. For example, the first warden of Kruger National Park, Colonel James Stephenson-Hamilton, earned the nickname Skukuza (which derives from XiTsonga to mean "he who sweeps away") for the way he forced the indigenous inhabitants out of the park from 1902. The outcome is that for many black South Africans dispossesion is the other side of the conservation coin.

Social justice in a democratic South Africa demands that the land claims of dispossessed local communities should be addressed, a factor recognized by the inclusion in the Constitution of provisions for land restitution and related legislation. Legally recognized land claims have the potential to unravel conservation efforts and dismantle many protected areas in the name of social justice. With this in mind the new Board took the initiative of establishing a Land Claims Committee and set out in a policy document its commitment to settling claims by negotiation, mindful of the need to balance social justice and its mandate to conserve biodiversity (South African National Parks 1998a). The Land Claims Committee has access to parks officials, the relevant land claims commissioners, government departments, advocacy groups, and affected communities and their legal representatives.

Claims are submitted to one of the five regional Land Claims Commissioners who are charged with researching the claims and attempting to resolve them in collaboration with the landowners and the claimants. In the case of state-owned land, a number of government departments may be involved, including Public Works, Land Affairs, Minerals and Energy (should prospecting or mineral rights be a factor), Defence, and Environmental Affairs (the host department of the SANP). Should the state acknowledge the legality of the claim, settlement can be negotiated between it and the claimant community. Any agreement must be endorsed by the Land Claims Court, which would also adjudicate in cases where no agreement has been reached.

Complex negotiations have resulted in at least two communities regaining their land while at the same time proclaiming their intention to retain existing land use. The first example of the resolution of a land claim in national parks was that of the Makuleke community, forcefully removed in 1969 from its traditional land between the Limpopo and Levhubu rivers in the Pafuri area. This was a particularly horrific removal which involved three thousand people being forced at gunpoint to burn their own homes. Their land was subsequently incorporated as the northernmost part of the Kruger National Park.

This area of the park has long been the site of contestation. After the removals, the National Parks Board secretary warned: "I foresee in this gain of today, if we acquire the Pafuri, the future germ of destruction of the whole park" (Carruthers 1995, 98).

The Makuleke community demanded that their rights to the Pafuri area be reinstated. After tough negotiations, agreement was reached returning to them full ownership of and title to their former land, amounting to 25,000 hectares. In turn the Makuleke people have guaranteed that they will use the land in a way that is compatible with conservation. The agreement makes it clear that in future no mining, farming, or permanent settlement will take place without the permission of the SANP. The conservation status of the land is therefore protected. This is in recognition both of its unique ecological features, its great scenic beauty, and the fact that its tourism and conservation potential are seen to outweigh any potential income from agriculture or cattle keeping.

A "contract park" will be established for a period of fifty years and will be managed by a Joint Management Body on which the SANP will be represented. This model follows an earlier example of a contract with the communities in the Richtersveld National Park in the Northern Cape, who in 1991 successfully prevented the SANP from imposing more authoritarian arrangements. In order to manage its interests in relation to the park, the Makuleke community has formed a Community Property Association and it aims to establish low-impact tourist lodges. The SANP remains responsible for conservation activities, while the community will be responsible for all tourism activities in its portion of the park. Capacity building and employment creation programs, supported by development aid from foreign donor organizations, aim to ensure that the community can, in time, also take responsibility for the conservation management of the land. The agreement also provides that some 5,000 hectares outside of the Kruger National Park will also be included within the contractual area in the community park. In essence, therefore, the size of the Kruger National Park has been expanded as a result of this settlement.

The agreement has been described as "a unique attempt to harmonize the protection of biological diversity with the interests of rural people" (Koch 1998, 71). The agreement has important implications for the mobilization of indigenous culture in support of conservation. One of the values of the ceremony marking the agreement in May 1998 was the reassertion of the sense of identity of the Makuleke which is closely linked to the land and fauna of the Pafuri triangle. This link was expressed in the form of a play performed at the signing ceremony by members of the community. Since the ceremony the agreement has been endorsed by the Land Claims Court and proclaimed by Parliament in early 1999.

A second land claims agreement was reached on Human Rights Day, 21 March 1999. This involved communities in the southern Kalahari. The gKhomani San form part of the indigenous hunter-gatherer peoples of Southern Africa, of whom approximately five hundred individuals survive. The San were acknowledged to have residential status within the Kalahari Gemsbok National Park when it was first proclaimed in 1931. The park manager was regarded as their legal guardian. Nevertheless, from 1937 there were efforts to expel them from the park. Under apartheid the San were reproclaimed "coloured" and were removed from the park in the mid-1970s. Having lost their access to the land, many became farm workers in the adjacent Mier community (a "coloured" reserve), whilst others were scattered in various parts of the subcontinent. In the intervening years they became impoverished and lost their language and culture. Anthropologists declared the N/u language extinct more than thirty years ago. During the course of the claim, sociolinguists were able to trace an old woman, Elsie Vaalbooi, whom they thought was the last speaker of the N/u language. In 1997, another ten speakers of the language and a dialect variety, !Kabee, were rediscovered (Crawhall 1999, 63).

The land restitution process has been extremely important for the gKhomani San, linking all the components of their diaspora and giving them a sense of common identity for the first time in many decades. The signing ceremony had an extra significance: it brought the entire community, including the last eleven speakers of the N/u language, together. This event has had major implications for the restoration of gKhomani culture, reinstatement of authentic place names, and the consolidation of the community's history and identity.

The deal with the gKhomani also includes the Mier farming community, who live on the southern fringe of the park, and who also lost land to it. South African National Parks have agreed to relinquish control over an area of 55,000 hectares. This area will be divided equally between the Mier and the San, who will gain title, but have agreed not to alter the land use of the area. There is a strong possibility that the Mier community will provide additional land for the new contract park; thus there will be a net gain in the amount of land in the southern Kalahari devoted to conservation. For residential purposes, the Department of Land Affairs will purchase some Mier-owned farms to the south of the park for the San, and compensate the Mier by providing 30,000 hectares of substitute land to add to the Mier commonage. Many of the details of the contract park have still to be finalized, but it is envisaged that the San will regain cultural and commercial rights—including the operation of certain ecotourism activities—in the park as a whole.

The Kalahari Gemsbok National Park also lies across the border from Botswana's Gemsbok National Park. Binational negotiations have produced a common management plan, and the fences between the parks will come down to create the first transfrontier park in Southern Africa. The new management plan has not yet factored in the future role of the gKhomani San. Given that the Botswana government has been involved in forced removals of the San from its Central Kalahari Game Reserve, and continues to disrespect San traditions, the settlement on the South African side could provide something of a positive role model for Botswana's future dealings with the San minority.

Petrus Vaalbooi, who chairs the Southern Kalahari San Association, responded to the agreement with the comment: "I feel very positive now. A year ago I wouldn't have said this. But from the words I hear now, I believe we have nearly crossed the bridge. I don't believe that land will solve the problems of the San, but at least we have a future and a life. We will be the owners of our own land" (Anon 1999, 16).

The historic Makuleke and gKhomani/Mier agreements were reached because the communities were willing to participate in ecotourism and conservation. This may not always be the case with land claims. At Riemvasmaak in the Northern Cape, the community appears divided about whether to enter into an agreement to use part of its land, Melkbosrand, as a contract national park. This land is currently within the Augrabies Falls National Park, but a community majority may effect its deproclamation.

The agreements that have been reached require SANP to pay more attention to the joint management of protected areas, and to provide more resources to ensure effective empowerment of partner communities.

Change from Within: Eliminating Racism and Sexism

Environmental justice also involves significant internal changes in South African National Parks. Specifically it means ensuring that all levels of the internal organization of the body reflect the demographic structure of South African society. In the past, black men and women occupied the manual and a few semi-skilled positions in the organization but were largely absent from scientific and managerial positions. Within the past five years, the human resources and affirmative action policy of the SANP has attempted to redress this problem. In line with national employment policies, targets have been set for the employment of black people, women, and the disabled across all employment categories.

The new board has taken steps to appoint black leadership to the executive directorate of the SANP in the form of a chief executive and three other directors, two of whom are women. The first black director of the flagship Kruger National Park is among the new appointees. Black people now account for 50 percent of the directorate.

Despite the institution of an affirmative action policy in 1996, this situation has not yet been replicated throughout the organization where, as is evident from Table 1, the upper employment categories are still dominated by whites. Conversely, unskilled and semi-skilled workers are over-whelmingly African and coloured. Women are severely underrepresented in the upper categories, as are Asians in all categories. Changing these dynamics is a significant challenge.

Table 1: Employment Profile of South African National Parks, January 1999 (Numbers of Employees)

Occupational Level	Male				Female				Total
	African	Asian	Coloured	White	African	Asian	Coloured	White	
Management	30	1	9	165	11	1	5	9	231
Skilled	66	3	24	148	15	2	7	96	360
Semi-skilled	716	2	220	9	92	2	73	100	1,214
Unskilled	1,489	0	82	3	756	1	97	4	2,432
Total	2,301	6	335	325	874	6	182	208	4,237

Source: South African National Parks 1999b

In January 1995 the board appointed a Transformation Task Team to set up transformation committees in every part of the organization. These committees monitor the application of non-racist and non-sexist policies at local level. Staff have been introduced to the transformation process through participatory, sensitizing, and value-sharing workshops through which racist and sexist incidents have been drawn to the attention of management, part of whose job description requires the absolute elimination of such incidents within the SANP. The organization's housing, schooling, employment, and promotion policies were formerly racially based, and the transformation structures have assisted the organization to make substantial progress in overcoming its discriminatory legacy.

Increasing Community Involvement

> The future of conservation lies in getting the cooperation,
> understanding and participation of the local people.
> (Adams and McShane 1996, 139)

Traditionally, the logic of conservation in South Africa's national parks saw surrounding communities as inimical to biodiversity conservation. Neighbors were regarded as potential poachers and competitors for land and water, and their poverty was seen as an embarrassment to tourism. Park officials saw their relationship with neighbors as being predominantly one of policing and maintaining fences between them. There was no notion of SANP having any social responsibility toward neighboring communities. Taking a narrow view of the National Parks Act, officials saw their responsibilities as limited only to one side of the fence. "Why should we privilege the neighbors, when our mandate should be one of serving the entire nation?" was another typical refrain.

Neighboring communities, on the other hand, saw the SANP as usurpers of land, wildlife, and medicinal resources. Some communities resented the parks for fencing access to water in times of drought when their livestock came under risk. The perennial problem of rogue animals escaping from parks and destroying crops or farm animals was constantly reiterated. Legally, escaped animals were not the responsibility of the SANP but of the provincial conservation authorities, who were often not easily accessible. Instead of assuming this responsibility, SANP allowed relations to deteriorate and resentments to fester.

Under pressure from NGOs such as the Group for Environmental Monitoring, whose "People and Parks" program had raised community awareness and challenged the conservation agencies to make better arrangements with neighbors, the SANP began in the mid-1990s to establish a series of community forums linking communities along the borders of the Kruger National Park. However, very few resources were allocated to the successful functioning of these liaison bodies.

Nevertheless, the former SANP Chief Executive, Dr G. A. Robinson, had become sensitized to community issues, especially after taking a personal interest in the establishment of the first community-owned contract park, the Richtersveld National Park, in 1991. Robinson saw the need to systematize community relations, and appointed a general manager for what was called "social ecology."[1] Thus began the first systematic attempt to restore relations with the parks' rural neighbors.

The new board placed great emphasis on the organization's need to commit itself to an active strategy of interaction with neighboring communities, and to stimulating community-based development through conservation and tourism. It has promoted a new conservation ethic that demands new practices. In recognition of this, the Social Ecology Unit of SANP was in 1997 promoted to the status of a full directorate of the organization and is charged with implementing such practices.

The practices include the formalization of interactions between national parks and neighboring communities through structures such as the Richtersveld Management Plan Committee and the five community forums adjacent to the Kruger National Park. These forums incorporate as many role players as possible, including tribal authorities, youth leaders, educationalists, other conservation bodies, village development committees, NGOs, and government departments. They deal with issues such as water problems, problems of marauding livestock, employment, and other economic opportunities. In all, ten national parks now have community forums operating in adjacent communities, while others such as the West Coast National Park and the Tsitsikamma National Park have social ecologists who are involved in local community affairs.

Community forums are not the only mechanism for participation in park policy formulation. The SANP's commitment to a participatory and transparent policy process has resulted in extensive consultations with various stakeholders on issues such as elephant, water, and fire management in the Kruger. In the board's formulation of the organization's land claims policy there was extensive consultation with interested and affected parties. This commitment to broad participation involves recognition that "environmental management is no longer seen to be the exclusive provenance of governments or the nation state" (Harvey 1996, 379).

The new approach has also put in place public consultation with the relevant stakeholders in the creation of new national parks, such as at Agulhas and the Namaqualand Coast. The consultations have smoothed the way for public acceptance and a sense of public ownership of new conservation endeavors, in contrast with the former exclusive and exclusionary approach.

Improving Accessibility

The Directorate of Social Ecology is also committed to providing human benefits by making the parks more accessible to the majority of South Africans. This involves improving visitor services and changing the culture of places such as the Kruger National Park. In the past Kruger was operated as a highly subsidized tourist playground for whites in general and Afrikaans-speaking civil servants in particular. The management culture was authoritarian. Kruger, the size of Wales or Connecticut, was seen as the fiefdom of a hardy and dedicated group of conservationists. With democratization, this culture of exclusivism needs to be supplanted.

It will take a considerable time to change the demographics of park visitors. Although just under 820,000 tourists visited Kruger during 1997, the vast majority were white South Africans or foreign tourists. No racialized statistics are kept by National Parks on its visitor profile and until that happens, redress and replanning will be difficult.

The commitment to changing the social composition of visitors is a shared theme in contemporary South Africa and the United States. According to one source: "Young, white, above all, healthy, if not wealthy, middle-class families overwhelmingly dominate the camping sites and visitor centers" of American parks (Rothenberg 1995, 37). In both the United States and South Africa these visitors experience highly managed, sanitized experiences of wilderness (Rothenberg 1995, 171). This is especially true of the Kruger National Park where visitors are confined to cars, public roads, and their camps after sunset. Wilderness trails were introduced very recently and operate on a very limited basis. However, these are being extended, and urban black youth are being given new opportunities to enjoy wilderness experiences through the Imbewu Project, which organizes youth walking trails in the parks.

This outdoor education is linked to the SANP's growing emphasis on environmental education in general among black schoolchildren. The focus of the environmental educational efforts of the Directorate of Social Ecology is on local schools and youth clubs. A total of fifty-one schools was visited during 1997 and a series of workshops was held. In September 1998, a very successful Youth Summit was held in Mopane camp in the Kruger National Park. For most of the two hundred young African participants, this was their first experience of wildlife outside a zoo. The youth formulated a Charter which was sent to President Mandela and which reflected a holistic understanding of the environment. In addition to committing themselves to "protecting resources" and to "fight against air, water and soil pollution," the Charter included items such as a commitment to "recognise the value of elders as a rich resource of indigenous knowledge and oral history which needs to be researched and recorded," the "conservation of cultural sites," and "respect for different cultures and cultural objects."

The SANP has committed itself to improving the lives of the majority of South Africans, not only through provision of environmental education, recreational opportunities, and wilderness experiences, but also through the provision of economic opportunities to the communities bordering the parks.

Tourism and Income Generation

The provision of goods and services in the national parks was traditionally tendered out mainly to larger urban-based and white-owned corporations. One of the key strategic areas for transformation accepted by the board in January 1997 is ensuring that such economic opportunities and contracts are open to black entrepreneurs, manufacturers, consultants, and suppliers of goods and services. In particular, the tendering arrangements have been altered to ensure that small and medium-sized enterprises can participate. This is of particular importance to entrepreneurs in communities adjacent to the parks.

In addition there are a number of projects under way which have created partnerships aimed at the economic empowerment of neighboring communities. These include facilitating the establishment of ecotourism ventures, developing markets for the sale of local crafts in the national parks' shops, the training of tour guides to transport local people into parks, the organization of local producers to supply fresh produce to the parks, the creation of cultural groups to perform traditional dances for tourists, facilitating the sustainable use of renewable resources such as wood and grass, and setting up nurseries to ensure that traditional healers are availed of supplies of herbal medicines.

One example of such a project is the provision of a sales outlet for woodcarvers at Numbi Gate (one of the entrances to the Kruger National Park), which has meant substantial increases in revenue. In the past the artists were not allowed into the park and had to rely on passing vehicles for an occasional sale. The Skukuza Alliance Arts and Craft Project has created a craft center for them and this in itself has increased sales from R2,000 to R40,000 per month, with membership increasing from sixty-nine to four hundred artists by June 1998. Another project was initiated with a group of twenty women in the Lubambiswano forum area adjacent to the Kruger Park. It aims to establish gardens to raise produce to be marketed in the park's shops and restaurants. While the income generated by these initiatives is comparatively low, it can sometimes mean physical survival in the extremely impoverished communities that surround the park.

The SANP has traditionally received a significant subsidy, about R59 million per year, from the state. Given the fiscally conservative economic policy of the state, the contribution to biodiversity conservation is unlikely to increase. The SANP will probably experience increasing cuts in its annual subsidy, despite the fact that South Africa's national parks are a key drawing card for tourism and foreign exchange. The organization has recognized that it will be expected to pay an increasingly larger share of its way. At present, only three national parks—Kruger, Tsitiskamma, and Cape Peninsula—make a profit. However, profit accounts for only 10 percent of the parks' operating income (South African National Parks 1999a). The state subsidy is thus vital to the organization. Yet although the subsidy may seem large "from the point of view of financial self-sufficiency there are few if any national parks systems in the world that rely so little on state support as the SANP" (Msimang 1998, 4).

To overcome this economic situation the board has taken three steps:

- Instituted organizational restructuring requiring each park to operate as a business unit, with decentralized decision making informed by a three-year Business Plan.
- Created and filled a new post of Director of Commercial Development and Tourism.
- Accepted the principle of outsourcing, commercialization, concessioning, and partnering of non-core functions.

The general opinion emerging from a series of workshops held between March and June 1998 to discuss outsourcing was that the core business of the SANP includes the formulation and implementation of policy, nature conservation, access to the parks, and interpretative services. Tourism infrastructure and other services were viewed as ancillary provided they do not negatively affect the core business, although there is some debate about who should operate trails and night drives. Non-core functions were seen as services such as laundries, hut cleaning, security services at the entrance gates and shops, and road maintenance. Initial experiments are taking place with outsourcing the SANP magazine, a shop, some film rights in Kruger, and some accommodation in the West Coast National Park.

While certain services may be outsourced, there is no question of privatization or the alienation of state assets. Yet outsourcing is going to require careful conditions to be put in place for the SANP to continue to regulate and monitor service delivery, especially to guarantee management in line with ecological principles. Ideally, outsourcing should be linked to black empowerment and transfer benefits to adjacent communities. This will require attention to capacity building in these communities to enable them to provide the necessary skills or resources.

Achieving a balance between commercial and conservation interests will present a significant challenge. Any concessioning needs to be scrupulously sensitive to the natural and built environments. Many South Africans are anxious to avoid the U.S. experience where intrusive commercialism has threatened the survival of the parks. In the United States, concessioning had its origins in the placating of the wealthy: "Allowing hotels and other visitor services was a way of bringing politically powerful people into conservation" (Interview, Kendall Thompson, U.S. National Parks Service, Yosemite National Park, 4 August 1998). By contrast, concessioning or outsourcing in South Africa has as one of its goals political and economic redress: the empowerment of burgeoning business interests in the black community formerly disadvantaged by apartheid. Outsourcing relieves the state of some of its obligation to support the sustainable use and conservation of biological diversity. It also creates a situation in which conservation and tourism services become market-driven. The existing SANP infrastructure is not well geared to becoming a regulator of private enterprise activities within its jurisdiction. Outsourcing is therefore fraught with these and a number of other potential problems.

The Development of Cultural Resources and Heritage Management

There is a new commitment within the SANP to developing cultural resources and historical sites within the parks. This is part of the emergence of a new understanding of heritage conservation, which links both cultural and natural heritage. The SANP has begun to realize this commitment by investing in historical, anthropological, and archaeological research. This has involved partnerships between parks-based social ecologists and leading academics and practitioners. Results of the research are shared with visitors through site museums, displays, publications, and educational and interpretive programs. Social ecologists in the national parks have received heritage management training, and, in August 1998, the Directorate of Social Ecology held an important international symposium entitled "Voices, Values and Identities" aimed at integrating cultural heritage into the management of national parks (Dladla 1999, i).

Newly excavated archaeological sites have been opened to visitors. The best example of one of these is the Thulamela site in the north of the Kruger, which provides evidence of a royal village, gold mining, and trading in the area dating back to 1460. Further south, the Masorini site is a reconstruction of a baPhalaborwa hill village displaying centuries-old iron smelting, grain storage, and hut-building activities. Still to be opened is the Mapungubwe site in the Limpopo National Park, which abuts Botswana and Zimbabwe. Excavations here in the 1930s revealed, among other things, a carved golden rhinoceros, now housed in the University of Pretoria.

The SANP's cultural heritage program could contribute towards nation building and the creation of a common society in South Africa based on cultural sensitivity and awareness. This would involve reversing the ethnic particularism and notions of conservationism enshrined under apartheid. The significance of national parks is not limited simply to their capacity to preserve biodiversity and promote ecotourism. In both the USA and South Africa they have promoted nationalist ideologies. In the USA the establishment of national parks has been described as an "attempt to forge a national identity out of national grandeur" (Beinart and Coates 1995, 75). According to another source, "the disappearance of European wilderness provided the young American nation with a new identity. Struggling with a cultural inferiority complex vis-à-vis Europe, the United States found a sense of self in celebrating its still pristine, 'virginal' wilderness areas. Wild landscapes took the place of the missing national and cultural history" (Rothenberg 1995, 119).

In South Africa, conservation was linked to a less inclusive national project: the notion of conservation was used to mobilize an exclusive Afrikaner nationalism to which a mythologized figure of Paul Kruger, after whom the Kruger Park is named, was central. It was only under extreme pressure from his supporters that Kruger finally proclaimed the Sabie Game Reserve in 1898 (Carruthers 1995). The "Kruger-wildlife-conservation myth" is particularly ironic in view of the fact that Kruger has been described as an "old man who never in his life thought of wild animals except as biltong [beef jerky]" (cited in Carruthers 1995, 61).

In the celebrations of the park's centenary, the SANP commissioned a video which has been extensively promoted, despite the misgivings of the board. The video celebrates the Kruger myth, and treats the park as if it is a pristine natural environment, shorn of any history of human habitation. "The video also manages to ignore virtually every significant piece of research on the history and human geographies of the Kruger National Park written in the last 20 years" (Bunn and Auslander 1999, 32). Clearly the values embodied in developing the new respect for cultural heritage are not shared across the institution, and will need to be inscribed much more deeply in the consciousness of all parks officials.

The Challenges Ahead

In sum, transformation to achieve environmental justice in South Africa's national parks involves the following goals:

- the ending of all forms of racial and gender discrimination;
- the development of human resources across all employment categories;
- the elimination of all discriminatory and exploitative labor practices;
- the formulation and implementation of new policy on partnerships and co-management arrangements with previously dispossessed communities resulting from the settlement of their land claims;
- the extension of environmental education to the society as a whole;
- the promotion of a new holistic understanding which links the conservation of both natural and cultural resources to development;
- the improvement of relations with, and the provision of material benefits to, neighboring communities;
- the recognition of the need to change the corporate culture of the

parks so as to make jobs, contracts, and visitor services more accessible to the majority of South Africans;

■ the generation of income and provision of more cost-efficient
services to visitors.

While the Transformation Task Team has been monitoring and
evaluating the transformation process within the SANP, it is clear that
there is a long way to go before fundamental transformation as opposed
to shallow restructuring is achieved. Leadership of this process must take
place at the highest level, so that the values of the new organizational
culture can be infused throughout the institution.

The SANP has not realized the full potential of partnerships with
communities. Much hope was expressed that the organization would
cut its teeth in terms of establishing a success story in joint management
of the Richtersveld National Park, where the Nama landowners con-
tracted their land into the park in 1991 after extensive negotiations. Yet
the joint management arrangements were never perfected in the Richtersveld, a community of six thousand people, and anticipated benefits
have flowed inadequately. This bodes ill for other contract parks, especially those resulting from successful land claims, where the SANP needs
to establish its good faith and friendship towards formerly dispossessed
communities. The Makuleke agreement was only reached after two years
of negotiations, and the Makuleke people expect benefits from ecotourism that have yet to materialize. A similar dynamic exists in the Southern Kalahari and may have an impact on other contract parks around
the country.

Community co-management of contract parks is a relatively recent
and untested mechanism for biodiversity protection. Power relations will
have to be monitored to ensure that the SANP, endowed with more technical resources and capacity, does not overwhelmingly dominate the
partnership. It will be crucial for the SANP to anticipate the need to make
such partnerships function well, and to take the necessary steps, including significant investment in appropriate human resources, to ensure that
this occurs. Failure will result in disempowered neighbors and disillu-
sioned social ecology professionals. It will reconfirm the suspicions of the
more traditional conservationists who, skeptically, see partnerships as
problematic and as examples of temporarily fashionable special pleading.

The difficulties of co-management are compounded by the fact that they have seldom succeeded elsewhere. For example, in Australia, the Anangu Aboriginal co-management of the Uluru-Kata Tjuta National Park (formally Ayers Rock and the Olga mountain range), which had a five-year start on the Richtersveld, is not yet an equitable arrangement. While the Anangu hold title to the land, the park has been leased back to the Director of the Australian National Parks and Wildlife Service (Cronin 1998, 248–49). A similar arrangement exists in the Kakadu National Park, another World Heritage Site in the Northern Territory of Australia (Cronin 1998, 272–73). Parks officials still dominate the co-management process, and on important issues such as land use Aboriginal people feel disempowered and do not have much of an authoritative voice. Weaver (1991, 314) found that in practice joint management systems in Kakadu did not exist.

Joint management structures have been established in two parks in northern Canada to provide aboriginal people with significant involvement in their operations, but on the basis of no "tested and true formula" (East 1991, 345). More recently, aboriginal peoples have invested efforts in claiming exclusive title to conservation areas and more often are seeking to set up their own management systems (Morrison 1997, 282–83).

Writing in the early 1990s, West and Brechin (1991, 396) concluded from a survey of the field that "true joint management involving true sharing of decision power on central issues of vital concern to resident peoples is thus an unfulfilled agenda with which the conservation community will need to come to grips."

Since the challenge to create viable, mutually beneficial co-management arrangements is not being met effectively in a number of countries, the urgency for SANP to become an important path breaker in this territory is further underlined. Its striving to be a world-class conservation agency will be significantly undermined if it passes up opportunities to make a cutting-edge contribution to the successful implementation of co-management arrangements with communities which own conservation land.

The difficulties of meeting this challenge can be attributed to problems of a lack of institutional capacity, political will, resources, and community cohesion. At times, the SANP has seriously marginalized the social ecologists, undermining their credibility and their ability to affect complex situations.

There are also deep-seated tensions at many levels within the organization. Sexist and racist practices still need to be challenged, community benefits are meager, community participation is shallow, and there is a history of strained relationships between the board and the directorate in regard to the boundaries between operational and policy issues. A number of actors, both within and outside the body, regard the changes since 1994 as reflecting a shallow restructuring rather than a fundamental transformation.

The transformation of the South African National Parks from an institution of colonial to community-based conservation is part of the wider project of transforming South Africa into a just, democratic, and non-racial society. However, in several respects, transformation has been supplanted by a restructuring which reflects the incorporation of the liberation movement into institutions serving elite interests.

The key objective of the liberation movement was the seizure of state power through popular armed struggle; the dominant discourse was of a revolutionary rupture, ungovernability, and a people's war. However, "instead of seizing power, the democratic movement negotiated its partial transfer. Instead of taking over and transforming the state, the movement found itself assimilated into it" (Marais 1998, 12). In this regard the SANP reflects some of the hallmarks of the South African transition to democracy: negotiation, appeasement, inclusion, and reconciliation. The SANP is a microcosm of how, in the words of Pallo Jordan, former Minister of Environmental Affairs and Tourism, "the [anti-apartheid] struggle has resulted in an unfinished revolution" *(The Star,* 3 September 1997).

The South African National Parks is at a crossroads. Ahead lies a choice between two visions: one that sees it as important to complete the transformation; and another which rests on alliances with remnants of the old order to block more thorough-going change. The new executive leadership charged with the day-to-day management of the organization may find itself caught between the two. Since late 1999, the Directorate of Social Ecology has been downgraded to a subdivision of the conservation directorate.

More recently, the organization has accepted, with World Bank and Cabinet support, a proposal to "commercialize" some parts of the Kruger and other national parks. In the name of private-public partnerships (which exclude local community interests), some areas of the Kruger will be set aside for the development of private lodges through commercial tenders and exclusive traversing rights over a substantial surrounding area for the companies operating these lodges. Leaving aside the dubious commercial logic of this proposal, it is extremely unclear how it might provide any community benefits. On the contrary, the realization of such a scheme may defeat any attempts by, for example, the Makuleke community to embark on successful community ecotourism ventures.

As a model, community-based conservation is once again under threat. Without an inclusive vision for nature conservation, its survival will depend on the whims of a few decision makers rather than on a large constituency whose interests might be served by such activities. The challenge in South Africa will be how to further a transformative vision for its national parks that builds on the basis of environmental justice.

Note

1. No relationship to the work of Murray Bookchin, who writes about ecological libertarianism under the label of "social ecology."

References

Adams, J. S., and T. McShane. 1996. *The Myth of Wild Africa: Conservation without Illusion.* Berkeley: University of California Press.

Anon. 1999. "San Celebration." *Timbila: Rhythms of the Earth* 1 (2): 16–17.

Beinart, W., and P. Coates. 1995. *Environment and History: The Taming of Nature in the USA and South Africa.* London: Routledge.

Bunn, D., and M. Auslander. 1999. "From Crook's Corner to Thulamela." In Y. Dladla, ed. *Voices, Values and Identities Symposium.* Pretoria: South African National Parks.

Carruthers, J. 1995. *The Kruger National Park: A Social and Political History.* Pietermaritzburg: University of Natal Press.

Cock, J. 1991. "Going Green at the Grassroots: The Environment as a Political

Issue." In J. Cock and E. Koch, eds. 1991. *Going Green: People, Politics and the Environment in South Africa.* Cape Town: Oxford University Press.

———. 1993. "The Impact of Militarisation on the Ecology of Southern Africa." Unpublished paper. Johannesburg: Group for Environmental Monitoring.

Crawhall, N. 1999. "Reclaiming Rights, Resources and Identity: The Power of an Ancient San Language." In Y. Dladla, ed. *Voices, Values and Identities Symposium.* Pretoria: South African National Parks.

Cronin, L. 1998. *Key Guide to Australia's National Parks.* Sydney: Reed New Holland.

Dladla, Y., ed. 1999. *Voices, Values and Identities Symposium: Record of the Proceedings, 25–27 August 1998.* Pretoria: South African National Parks.

East, K. M. 1991. "Joint Management of Canada's Northern National Parks." In P. C. West and S. R. Brechin, eds. *Resident Peoples and National Parks: Social Dilemmas and Strategies in International Conservation.* Tucson: University of Arizona Press.

Harvey, D. 1996. *Justice, Nature and the Geography of Difference.* Oxford: Blackwell.

Koch, E. 1998. "Ecofile." *Out There* (March).

Letsoalo, E. 1987. *Land Reform in South Africa: A Black Perspective.* Johannesburg: Skotaville.

Marais, H. 1998. *South Africa: Limits to Change: The Political Economy of Transformation.* London and Cape Town: Zed and University of Cape Town Press.

Marcus, T., K. Eales, and A. Wildschut. 1996. *Down to Earth: Land Demand in the New South Africa.* Johannesburg: Land and Agriculture Policy Centre.

Morrison, J. 1997. "Protected Areas, Conservationists, and Aboriginal Interests in Canada." In K. Ghimire and M.P. Pimbert, eds. *Social Change and Conservation: Environmental Politics and Impacts of National Parks and Protected Areas.* London: Earthscan.

Msimang, M. 1998. "Submission to the Kumleben Commission on Institutional Arrangements for Nature Conservation in South Africa." Pretoria: South African National Parks.

Ramphele, M., and C. McDowell, eds. 1991. *Restoring the Land: Environment and Change in Post-Apartheid South Africa.* London: The Panos Institute.

Rothenberg, D., ed. 1995. *Wild Ideas.* Minneapolis: University of Minnesota Press.

South African National Parks. 1998a. *Land Claims Policy.* Pretoria: South African National Parks.

———. 1998b. *Progress Report, Directorate of Commercial Development and Tourism 19 June.* Pretoria: South African National Parks

———. 1999a. *Financial Statements for the Year to Date, January 1999.* Pretoria: South African National Parks.

————. 1999b. *Report: Directorate of Human Resources January 1998–January 1999*. Pretoria: South African National Parks.

Weaver, S. M. 1991. "The Role of Aboriginals in the Management of Australia's Cobourg (Gurig) and Kakadu National Parks." In P. C. West and S. R. Brechin, eds. *Resident Peoples and National Parks: Social Dilemmas and Strategies in International Conservation*. Tucson: University of Arizona Press.

West, P. C., and S. R. Brechin. 1991. "National Parks, Protected Areas, and Resident Peoples: A Comparative Assessment and Integration." In P. C. West and S. R. Brechin, eds. *Resident Peoples and National Parks: Social Dilemmas and Strategies in International Conservation*. Tucson: University of Arizona Press.

Chapter 6

The Fox in the Henhouse

The Environmental Impact of Mining on Communities in South Africa

Thabo Madihlaba

Since the discovery of diamonds and gold in the late 1800s, mining has been one of the defining features of South African society. From the use of migrant labour to Cold War politics over rare minerals like platinum, the mining industry has played a central role in the political, social, and economic fabric of the country.

The mining industry has also had an enormous environmental impact on South Africa. Not only is the industry the largest single producer of solid waste, accounting for almost two-thirds of the total waste stream, it has had an indirect impact on a wide range of land, air, and water resources. It has also had far-reaching implications for environmental justice in South Africa, impacting as it does on worker and community health and safety, particularly in poor communities adjacent to mining activities.

The purpose of this chapter is to explore the relationship between the mining industry and environmental justice in post-apartheid South Africa and to determine what gains (if any) have been made over the last decade by those most directly affected by the environmental impacts of mining. The chapter begins with a brief overview of the mining industry and its environmental record and then discusses the development of policy to address these environmental concerns and the role of civil society in pushing for environmental reform. A case study of the community of Clewer, near the mining town of Witbank, illustrates the kinds of environmental justice struggles that poor communities continue to face and the enormous gap between policy rhetoric and environmental practice. The power of the mining industry to call the shots when it comes to environmental assessment and monitoring is an issue that needs to be addressed by both government and civil society and the Clewer case is but the tip of the iceberg of civil society's ongoing struggle for effective and just environmental participation.

Overview of the Mining Industry in South Africa

Although it has declined in importance to the overall South African economy, the mining industry continues to be one of the economic mainstays of the country. Gold is by far the most significant contributor to the mineral economy (accounting for as much as 65 percent of the value of mineral exports and R18.8 billion in sales in 1990) and South Africa is the largest gold producer in the world. The importance of gold to the economy is bound to weaken with its recent fall from grace among central banks around the world as a store of wealth, but gold is not the only important mining activity in South Africa. Coal, the dominant source of fuel, ran a close second to gold in total sales in 1990 (R7.7 billion, of which 45 percent came from exports), and created 90,000 jobs. South Africa is also the largest producer in the world of vanadium, chrome ore, ferrochromium, aluminoscilate, and manganese (IDRC 1995, 107–8). South Africa is the only country other than Russia where platinum is mined. Not surprisingly, the mining industry has always been, and remains, dominated by large private, white-owned corporations. Fully 90 percent of all mines are held privately, the majority of this ownership controlled by six major mining corporations. In fact, "no other country in the world, except for the United States , has given so many mineral rights to the private sector" (IDRC 1995, 110). Black empowerment consortiums have begun to make inroads into the mining sector, as they have in virtually all sectors of the South African economy, and small-scale, independent mining operations do exist, but the general composition of the mining sector has changed little since the days of apartheid. Plans made during the anti-apartheid struggle to nationalize the mining industry were quickly shelved once post-apartheid negotiations began, and the sanctity of private mine ownership appears well protected for the foreseeable future.

One aspect of the mining industry that has changed, however, is the forced removal of black South Africans from their ancestral lands to make way for mining operations. One example of this policy was the removal, on 31 August 1963, of the Baphalane people from Schilpadnest—land which they had been occupying and to which they had had the title deeds since the early 1700s. Backed by armed police, bulldozers destroyed houses, crops, and community buildings. Approximately eight hundred people were loaded onto trucks and dumped in an unserviced area called Varkvlei (Mantsere) in what was later to become part of the "independent" homeland of Bophutatswana. They were not compensated for their land and were given very little compensation for their destroyed homes. The land was leased to Gencor, a large mining interest, to mine platinum and chrome. The Baphalane people are still living in shacks and substandard houses. The land to which they were removed is barren and overcrowded, and water is scarce. Some of the older members of the community never recovered from the removal and were said to have died of broken hearts.

The Environmental Impact of Mining

Much has been written about the general environmental impact of mining in South Africa (Durning 1990; Felix 1991; Crompton and Erwin 1991; Gandar 1991; Fig 1991; Coetzee and Cooper 1991; Flynn 1992; IDRC 1995) and there is no need to go into detail here. It is, however, worth summarizing this impact to underscore the effects of the industry on land, water, and air resources.

As noted above, mining is the largest producer of solid waste in the country. For every ton of metal that leaves the mills, 100 tons of waste is created (Durning 1990, 15). This waste is generally deposited onto enormous mine tailing dumps, many of which are located in close proximity to poor black communities. The mine dumps create hazards for residents—

particularly for children—and leave a legacy of unsightly mountains of industrial waste. The mountains of gold mine trailings that blot the landscape of Johannesburg are perhaps the most infamous examples.

More important than aesthetics, however, is the fact that mine trailing heaps leach contaminants into scarce ground and surface water supplies (a situation aggravated by the fact that most mining in South Africa occurs in the upper reaches of major water catchments) and contributes to localized air pollution. Mining processes have also contributed to water contamination, salination, and siltation. It has been estimated, for example, that 60 percent of the salt load entering the Vaal Barrage is caused by the effluence from four mines (Coetzee and Cooper 1991, 133) and South African newspapers regularly report stories of wetlands contaminated with radioactive mine materials, arsenic from gold mines found in drinking water, and slimes dams containing high concentrations of cyanide bursting their banks. Meanwhile, the decommissioning of slimes dams adds to air pollution with toxic particulates contributing to a wide range of respiratory, eye, and ear infections. Air pollution also results from the thermal processes used by some mines which yield enormous amounts of smoke as well as the spontaneous combustion of stock piles of low-grade coal. There are even some abandoned coal mines in the Witbank area of Mpumulanga where underground burning continues almost a half century after the mines were closed.

It is the environmental impact of the mining industry on workers and adjacent communities that are the most immediate and most pressing, however. The tens of thousands of deaths that have occurred among mine workers as a direct result of accidents over the last century have been coupled with an untold number of deaths and debilitating diseases from work-related illnesses like asbestosis. The dust and noise of open pit and underground mines, added to exposure to toxic chemicals used in the mining process, places mine workers on the very front line of environmental injustices, and miners arguably bear the most direct and serious environmental impacts from mining.

It is not much better for those who live next to a mine. Noise, dust, and dangerous equipment and vehicles are constant threats to psychological and physiological health and safety, and the quality of air and water is invariably poor. These adjacent communities are generally poor and black and have had little, if any, choice about the location of a mine near their homes. Often it is the miners themselves and their families who live in these affected communities. At one school in Soweto, located next to a disused slimes dam, the students have had to contend with radioactive gases and constant dust. The situation became so bad that the front door to the school had to be boarded up and newspapers stuffed into open crevices in an (unsuccessful) attempt to keep the dust out (*Mail & Guardian*, 19 September 1997).

Progress in the 1990s?

With the unbanning of anti-apartheid parties in 1990 and the start of negotiations for a new political dispensation in South Africa soon thereafter, the mining industry and the South African government began to look at the need for reforms. The National Party introduced a new Minerals Act (50 of 1991) that began to address environmental considerations by recognizing the health and safety concerns of workers and the need for land rehabilitation after and during mining operations. In 1993 the Act was amended to require each new mine to have an Environmental Management Program Report (EMPR) prepared before it broke ground. These EMPRs were intended to force mining companies to outline all the possible environmental impacts of the particular mining operation, from start to finish, and to make provision for environmental management (financial and otherwise). The reports were then to be approved by all relevant government departments (e.g., Water Affairs and Forestry, and Agriculture).

These legislative changes represent an important step forward, but critics have pointed to several major flaws. First, the mining companies are allowed to "draw up their own EMPRs and prescribe their own solutions for management of adverse environmental impacts. They also determine the level of finance to be set aside for rehabilitation and closure [of a mine] . . . and the company can identify some of this material as confidential so that the public cannot scrutinize it" (IDRC 1995, 111). Second, the regional director of the Department of Minerals and Energy (DME) can, at his or her discretion, simply exempt an applicant from EMPRs altogether. Third, it has been argued that EMPRs are not as rigorous as the more established national and international criteria for environmental impact assessments (EIAs) and "do not question whether the decision to mine is an appropriate environmental choice" (IDRC 1995, 111). But even if the EMPR is consid-

ered a sound strategy on paper, the lack of resources to monitor its implementation means that very little enforcement (let alone litigation) actually
takes place. This lack of enforcement is further complicated by the fact that
the policy standards of the different ministries with which the mining
company must comply vary and there is no clear hierarchy of which standards should prevail. Finally, public consultation is not required for the
mining EMPRs, making a mockery of participatory governance.

In October 1998 the Department of Minerals and Energy released a
White Paper entitled "A Minerals and Mining Policy for South Africa"
(RSA 1998) which included a section on "Environmental Management."
At the most general level, the White Paper makes it clear that environmental management must be taken seriously: "Government, in recognition of the responsibility of the State as custodian of the nation's natural
resources, will ensure that the essential development of the country's
mineral resources will take place within a framework of sustainable development and in accordance with national environmental policy, norms
and standards" (Section 4.2). But the paper also adds that any environmental policy must ensure "a cost-effective and competitive mining industry" (Section 4.1.iii) and makes it very clear that the Department still
supports EMPRs (Section 4.1.vi).

Though these concessions to the mining industry raise doubts
about how serious the government is about change, the White Paper
does emphasize the need for more rigorous environmental reporting
and appears committed to applying the more stringent environmental
standards of Integrated Environmental Management (IEM) (Section 4.2):

> The principles of Integrated Environmental Management
> (IEM) will be applied to environmental management in the
> mining industry. These must be amplified to include cradle-
> to-grave management of environmental impacts in all phases
> of a mine's life, effective monitoring and auditing procedures,
> financial guarantees for total environmental rehabilitation
> responsibilities, controlled decommissioning and closure pro-
> cedures, procedures for the determination of possible latent
> environmental risks after mine closure and the retention of
> responsibility by a mine until an exonerating certificate is
> granted.

The White Paper also supports the inclusion of a "no go" option whereby a decision could be made to refuse a mining permit altogether on environmental grounds, and argues that the "polluter pays" principle should apply: "The mining entrepreneur will be responsible for all costs pertaining to the impact of the operation on the environment" (Section 4.2).

On the issue of the differences in environmental standards set by different government departments, the White Paper says that mining companies will have to comply with "a single national environmental policy and governance within a framework of co-operative governance." It is not entirely clear where this single framework will originate, however: "While Government has appointed the national Department of Environmental Affairs and Tourism [DEAT] as its lead agent for this role, the DME will, in support of the lead agent and in accordance with national principles, norms and standards, develop and apply the necessary policies and measures to ensure the mining industry's compliance with the national policy on environmental management and other relevant policies such as the national water policy. Similarly, due recognition will be given to the Department of Water Affairs and Forestry as lead agent for the national water resource" (Section 4.2). But the wording here is vague, and there are apparently already considerable inter-departmental tensions between DEAT and the DME. Managing this cooperative form of environmental governance will no doubt prove difficult, and will probably necessitate much clearer guidelines of responsibility.

The element most relevant to this discussion is the call in the White Paper for more public participation in the environmental decision-making process (Section 4.2): "Equitable and effective consultation with interested and affected parties will be undertaken pro-actively to ensure public participation in the decision-making process and the *audi alteram partem* [hear the other side] rule shall apply to all decision-making. The decision-making process shall provide for the right to appeal. Access to information shall be in accordance with the requirements of the Constitution." Furthermore, "Mining companies will be required to comply with the local Development Objectives, spatial development framework and Integrated Development Planning of the municipalities within which they operate and will be encouraged to promote social participation by conducting their operations in such a manner that the needs of local communities are taken into consideration."

Promises do not always translate easily to reality, though, and concerns have been raised about the development of a tripartite statutory board on which labor, government, and industry make all the major decisions, while marginalizing input from "other interested parties" (i.e., community organizations and NGOs). Furthermore, given the limited capacity of many community organizations and NGOs to gather the information and technical insights necessary to challenge effectively large multinational corporations like Anglo American, it is questionable how much of an impact civil society would have on mining decisions, even if it were given reasonable access to decision makers.

In December 2000 the Department released a Mineral Development Draft Bill. The same tensions outlined above persist, however. And although the Draft Bill (Section 38.2.f and g) proposes that an applicant for a mining right must provide "a social plan containing details of the socioeconomic impact of the proposed mining project, as well as the measures to remedy any negative socioeconomic impacts during the life of the mine and after closure; [and] a scoping report reflecting the expected environmental impacts," much of the responsibility for monitoring and evaluating these socioeconomic and environmental impacts rests with the mining firms themselves. As we shall see in the case study below (as well as in the narratives included in this volume about the impact of mining on workers and communities), there are problems with placing faith in the mining sector's ability to conduct adequate social and environmental impact evaluations.

Nonetheless, the growing activism on the part of civil society about issues of environmental justice and mining in South Africa means that it will play an increasingly important role in these debates whether industry and the state like it or not. Many environmental NGOs—the Environmental Justice Networking Forum (EJNF), Environmental Monitoring Group (EMG), and Earthlife Africa for instance—now have staff and/or programs dealing specifically with mining issues, and several community-based organizations like Mafefe Environmental Committee, Tikologo Development Organization, and SA Green Revolutionary Council are also involved in the debates. The EJNF has been particularly active in this area.

Clewer—The Machines Next Door

Clewer is a small community near the town of Witbank in the province
of Mpumalanga. The community began to experience serious mining-
related problems in 1994 when a coal mine was opened less than thirty
meters from the nearest home. The community was not consulted when
the mining license was issued to the company, and heavy mine machinery and trucks began moving in without any warning. Only after residents inquired about the deafening noises from the blasting were they
told that it was an open cast mining operation.

Besides the noise from the blasting and the heavy trucks rattling
through the streets twenty-four hours a day, there was constant dust. As
conditions worsened, the community organized themselves into a group
called Clewer Concerned Residents in order to bring their concerns to the
attention of the mine owners and government authorities. After several
unsuccessful attempts to get mine management to listen to them, the residents sought legal representation. A meeting was arranged between mine
managers and the community representatives and their lawyer, but no
concrete plans were made to change the operation of the mine. Interestingly, the local newspaper refused to publish the community's side of the
story "because they are fighting a very big company."

The situation reached the point where the blasting was causing the
walls of houses to crack and roofs to collapse, the underground water was
depleted and contaminated, and tarred streets turned into dusty gravel
roads. To make matters worse, the community was deeply indebted to the
lawyer assisting them and could no longer afford the legal fees.

After struggling for two and a half years the community turned to
the Environmental Justice Networking Forum for help, and this author
became directly involved in its campaign for environmental justice. It
emerged that at some stage the mine had hired someone they claimed
was a geo-hydrologist to test the groundwater that the community
claimed was polluted. Based on the results of the tests the mine maintained that the water was clean and good for human consumption. Only
later was it discovered that the *expert* was not a geo-hydrologist, and the
water was in fact contaminated, an example of the deceitful manner in
which mine management was dealing with the community.

EJNF wrote an urgent letter to the Department of Environmental

Affairs in the province asking it to intervene. The Department responded quickly by sending environmental officers to investigate and initiated a series of multi-stakeholder meetings which included representatives from the Departments of Water Affairs and Forestry, and Minerals and Energy, the residents of Clewer, and the mine management.

EJNF also worked with the community to organize media coverage, and the story was covered on national television and in the mainstream press. This media coverage put considerable pressure on the mine and the government to speed up the discussions and to address the problems the community was facing. To give further impetus to the discussions, the residents organized a protest march against the mine. EJNF arranged for placards and persuaded four other organizations to pledge solidarity with the Clewer community by joining the march. The protest action succeeded because it seriously affected mining activities, with residents blocking the routes to and from the mine from as early as two in the morning. As a result, mine operations came to a standstill for eight hours on the day of the protest.

Mine personnel attempted to create friction between the community and the mine workers by claiming to the trade union that the residents had intimidated the miners, preventing them from going to work. The tactic ultimately backfired because many of the workers belong to the community, share its concerns, and even took part in the march.

Immediately after the march the mine filed a lawsuit against the community (specifically identifying individual leaders) for losses incurred. During the same period the community alleges that pamphlets were distributed (in the name of EJNF) calling for the closure of the mine. This appears to have been an attempt by mine officials to sow discord between the community and the mine workers who would lose their jobs should the mine be closed. The ploy failed because the National Union of Mineworkers (NUM) is a member of EJNF and the misunderstanding was cleared up.

The community then asked EJNF for legal help and, after the Legal Resources Centre was brought in, the mining company temporarily suspended legal action. After months of negotiations and endless meetings, the company finally agreed to take responsibility for (most) of the damage that had been caused. Together with the community, the mine would appoint an independent assessor to evaluate the damage and pay for repairs. Mine officials also agreed to drop their charges against the community and to settle its debt with the first lawyer it had briefed. To date the mine has repaired the streets, reimbursed residents whose water pumps had burnt out because of groundwater depletion, and compensated some of the residents for their damaged houses. The groundwater problem has yet to be solved, however, and in some cases residents have not yet been compensated for their damaged houses because the mine does not accept responsibility for all the damage. Nevertheless, the community has seen some progress—progress that would have been unthinkable ten years before.

Conclusion

Change is coming to the mining industry in South Africa, but it is happening slowly and communities, NGOs, and unions will have to be vigilant every step of the way to ensure that mine owners adhere to the more rigid environmental (and participatory) standards laid out in new policy documents. Of greatest concern is the fact that the Department of Minerals and Energy seems determined to allow the mining industry considerable latitude when it comes to monitoring its own environmental impact. Environmental Management Program Reports and Environmental Impact Assessments are an important step forward but they leave much of the decision-making power in the hands of corporations—a situation akin to leaving the fox in charge of the henhouse.

Clewer illustrates the enormous obstacles facing civil society in this regard, but it also represents the enormous potential for change in the post-apartheid era. Whether more communities in South Africa will have the political acumen and the necessary allies and resources to do what the people of Clewer have done remains to be seen.

References

Coetzee, H., and D. Cooper. 1991. "Wasting Water." In J. Cock and E. Koch, eds. *Going Green: People, Politics and the Environment in South Africa.* Cape Town: Oxford University Press.

Crompton, R., and A. Erwin. 1991. "Reds and Greens." In J. Cock and E. Koch, eds. *Going Green: People, Politics and the Environment in South Africa.* Cape Town: Oxford University Press.

Durning, A. 1991. *Apartheid's Environmental Toll.* Worldwatch Paper, 95. Washington, D.C.: Worldwatch Institute.

Felix, M. 1991. "Risking Their Lives in Ignorance." In J. Cock and E. Koch, eds. *Going Green: People, Politics and the Environment in South Africa.* Cape Town: Oxford University Press.

Fig, D. 1991. "Flowers in the Desert." In J. Cock and E. Koch, eds. *Going Green: People, Politics and the Environment in South Africa.* Cape Town: Oxford University Press.

Flynn, L. 1992. *Studded with Diamonds and Paved with Gold: Miners, Mining Companies and Human Rights in Southern Africa.* London: Bloomsbury Publishing Ltd.

Gandar, M. 1991. "The Imbalance of Power." In J. Cock and E. Koch, eds. *Going Green: People, Politics and the Environment in South Africa.* Cape Town: Oxford University Press.

IDRC. 1995. *Building a New South Africa: Environment, Reconstruction, and Development.* Ottawa: International Development Research Centre.

RSA (Republic of South Africa). 1998. White Paper: "A Minerals and Mining Policy for South Africa." Pretoria: Government Printers.

When Gold Becomes a Nuisance

Dudley Moloi

After three decades of suffering from the environmental fallout of a 240-hectare slimes dump perched on the edge of their community, residents of Kagiso township, southwest of Johannesburg, finally decided to take the owner of the land, the mining company that produced the slimes dam material, and the Minister of Mineral and Energy Affairs to court on the grounds that all three had failed to adhere to, or enforce, laws regulating the closure of mining operations. Two Kagiso residents, Terrence Motsumi Mokhene and Irene Anna Mogotsi, initiated the court order and cited the nuisance factor of slimes dump dust, as well as its health and environmental effects on the community.

Two of the most affected Kagiso areas, the Father Martin section and Extension 8, were built right beside the dump site between 1984 and 1986 at a time when gold was being actively mined north of the township. When the gold was extracted from ore, the waste product (or tailing) in the form of sludge was pumped into a slimes dam located some distance from the residential areas. However, the dam was eventually expanded to the extent that it now lies less than thirty meters from some houses. The mining operation closed in 1991, but the dried sludge continues to be a problem in the form of dust.

A study conducted by the National Council for Occupational Health concluded that the dust particles in the area contained alpha quartz, which causes silicosis. South African National Civic Organization (SANCO) publicity secretary for Kagiso, Uruhu Moiloa, said that "preliminary research on the dust particles indicated a 45 percent existence of alpha quartz. . . . We are informed that, by any standard, this is an unacceptably high level. Silicosis dries lungs up and turns them into stone."

But Kagiso residents, whose anecdotal testimony of the effects of the dump site dates back as far as 1972, believe it does not take scientific experience to confirm that the dust fallout is higher than the tolerable level. In a sworn affidavit, Mokhene said: "The dust affects my health and my well-being. Especially during the months when the dust levels are high, I cough and suffer from an irritated throat. . . . The dust causes my eyes to itch, burn, and water. When I experience these symptoms, my eyes are red. Many residents complain of the same problem."

Besides the health impact of the dust fallout, Mokhene and other Kagiso residents say the dust is a nuisance and makes their lives uncomfortable. People living particularly close to the slimes dump even have to seal their houses with cotton wool to minimize the dust that accumulates on everything in the house. The residents add that their properties have been devalued as no potential buyer would want to live in these conditions.

According to SANCO's Moiloa, discussions on the problems associated with the Kagiso slimes dump began as far back as 1989 but have been hampered by constant changes in mine ownership. After one mining house, *Luipaards Vlei Gold Estate,* had been pinned down and had agreed to rehabilitate the dump, the company closed mining operations and residents had to go after the owners of the dump.

Out of frustration, said Moiloa, the community sought the assistance of an environmental NGO, the Group for Environmental Monitoring (GEM), and the Legal Resources Centre to "exploit the possibility of resorting to existing environmental laws." The basis of the court case is therefore intended to test an individual's constitutional right, among other things, to a "healthy and clean environment." By including the Minister of Minerals and Energy as a respondent, the claimants hope to force the department to ensure that the appropriate laws are implemented.

Moiloa believes that the Kagiso residents' challenge to the mining industry to clean up the mess left by its mining operations is in the interest of all South Africans. He adds that government organizations such as the National Council of Occupational Health must disclose information revealing "the extent to which mine owners have been irresponsible and abused the environment."

Moiloa also quotes the late Harry Oppenheimer, former Chair of Anglo American: "There's no doubt that we have indeed left deep and dangerous holes underneath the soils of South Africa. . . . There's also no doubt that when we leave this part of the earth, we'll have left a great civilization." Far from a "great civilization," what Kagiso residents see when they look outside their homes is a nuisance left behind by a mining company.

Chapter 7

The Rule of Law

*Opportunities for Environmental Justice
in the New Democratic Legal Order*

Jan Glazewski

he legal system has played a controversial and even contradictory role in the history of South Africa. Under apartheid, the judiciary upheld racist and exclusionary legislation—some of which contributed directly to environmental injustices—but it was also a vehicle for resistance and liberal reforms (see for example Abel 1995). With the end of formal apartheid the legal system has been dramatically revamped and South Africa now has one of the most progressive constitutions in the world including a Bill of Rights (chapter 2 of the Constitution of the Republic of South Africa 108 of 1996) with its section (s24) on environmental rights.

The inclusion of an environmental right, and other rights with a distinct socioeconomic flavor implying a positive duty on the state, raises tremendous challenges in the context of South Africa's developing country status. It was pointed out in *Soobramoney v Minister of Health, KwaZulu-Natal* (1997 (12) BCLR 1696 (CC), para. 8), a case concerning the right of access to health care services (s27(1) of the Constitution) that: "We live in a society in which there are great disparities in wealth. Millions of people are living in deplorable conditions and in great poverty. There is a high level of unemployment, inadequate social security, and many do not have access to clean water or to health services." The constitutional directive for the delivery of a healthy environment must accordingly be seen in this context. In the same vein, the constitutional right to "sufficient food and water" (s27(1)(b) of the Constitution) imposes potentially onerous obligations on the state.

So what do all these constitutional changes mean for environmental justice in South Africa? Can the new legal system be expected to bring about meaningful change? More specifically, to what extent can the Bill of Rights and new environmental legislation be translated into concrete reality for the millions of South Africans who were denied environmental justice under the apartheid regime?

This chapter attempts to answer these questions by examining the Bill of Rights and newly enacted legislation in detail to see what legal gains (if any) have already been made, and the potential of the legal system to address environmental justice in the future. The chapter examines the environmental, property, administrative justice, access to information, enforcement of rights, right to equality, and the right to dignity clauses of the Bill of Rights to see if they have any bearing on formalizing the otherwise abstract notion of environmental justice. It then looks at the National Environmental Management Act, the National Water Act, and the Marine Living Resources Act, all of which have been enacted since the transition to democracy in South Africa, as well as developments in the reform of other areas of environmental law, particularly those concerning pollution control and waste management.

It is argued that legislative reforms have come a long way in giving precise legal definition to the notion of environmental justice and concrete parameters for judicial actions but there is still a long way to go before the legal system can play a more effective role in the resolution of environmental justice issues, particularly insofar as they entail the delivery of socioeconomic goods. It is argued further that there is more evidence of legislative reform in the area of resource management (land, water, forestry) than there has been in pollution control and waste management, the impact of which are often borne by poorer communities.

The Bill of Rights

The Bill of Rights includes not only an environmental clause but a number of other clauses which have made, or have the potential to make, a significant contribution toward environmental justice in the country. The all-pervasive effects of these clauses on the law is illustrated in *The Director: Mineral Development Gauteng Region and Sasol Mining (Pty) Ltd v Save the Vaal Environment and others* (1999 (2) SA 709 SCA) concerning the application of the *audi alterem partem* (let the other side be heard) rule in the granting of a mining license. In upholding the right of an environmental NGO to have the environmental effects of mining considered prior to the granting of a mining authorization, Judge Olivier, delivering the judgment of the Supreme Court of Appeal, stated that: "Our Constitution, by including environmental rights as fundamental justiciable human rights, by necessary implication requires that environmental considerations be accorded appropriate recognition and respect in the administrative process in our country" (at page 719).

Environmental Clause

The environmental clause is made up of two components. The first of these, subsection 24(a), provides that "everyone has the right . . . to an environment that is not harmful to their health or well-being." This subsection has at least the flavor of a *fundamental right*. Subsection 24(b), on the other hand, is framed more in the nature of a principle of state policy. It has the character of a *socioeconomic right* rather than a fundamental right, as it imposes a constitutional imperative on the state to secure the right of individuals to "reasonable legislative and other measures that":

  i. prevent pollution and ecological degradation;
  ii. promote conservation; and
  iii. secure ecologically sustainable development and use of natural resources while promoting justifiable economic and social development.

In this regard the environmental clause mirrors the pattern of the Bill of Rights as a whole, including both traditional fundamental rights, for example the right to dignity and equality, as well as socioeconomic rights such as the right to housing, health care, food, water, and social security. Many countries, India and Namibia for example, have put fundamental rights and socioeconomic rights in separate chapters of their constitutions implying that they are to be accorded different treatment. But South Africa has included both in one chapter, implying that they are equally justiciable. As observed by the Constitutional Court in *Government of the Republic of South Africa and Others v Grootboom and Others* (2000 (11) BCLR 1169 (CC), 1183D), a case concerning the application of the right of access to adequate housing (s26 of the Constitution): "Socio-economic rights are expressly included in the Bill of Rights; they cannot be said to exist on paper only. . . . The question is therefore not whether socio-economic rights are justiciable under our Constitution, but how to enforce them in a given case."

The question of implementing socioeconomic rights in the environmental context, more specifically the right to a basic water supply enshrined in s27 of the Bill of Rights, was considered in *Thulisile Manqele v Durban Transitional Metropolitan Council* (unreported, case No.2036/2000 dated 7 Feb 2001, Durban and Coast Local Division). The applicant, an unemployed thirty-five-year-old woman who resides in a Durban Metropolitan council flat with four of her own children and three other children, had her water supply disconnected by the council as she had not paid her water account. The applicant sought an order invalidating the discontinuation of her water supply on the grounds that (a) the relevant provisions in the Water Services Act (108 of 1997) had not been complied with, and (b) that in any event she had a right of access to a basic amount of water both under this Act and under s27(1)(b) of the Constitution.

The court dismissed both these arguments, the first, on the rather spurious ground that the Water Services Act provides for the passing of regulations to stipulate how much water constitutes a "basic water supply" and that such a determination had not been made under the Act. The court considered this a policy question in which it should not get involved. This despite the fact that the council had adopted a policy of providing the first six kiloliters free of charge for non-defaulters. The second ground, the constitutional argument, was also dismissed because the papers before the court had not adequately laid the grounds for it. It appears, however, that constitutional challenge remains an avenue to pursue in the future.

As will be shown in the next section, apart from socioeconomic considerations, environmental justice may be secured by means of several of the other clauses in the Bill of Rights. Examples are the right to administrative justice, the right to access to information, and the right to dignity. This raises the question: What contribution does the environmental clause make to the cause of environmental justice? To put it another way: Given the environmental protection afforded by other clauses in the Bill of Rights, do we really need the environmental clause? How does s24 take the environmental justice cause further?

Subsection 24(a) of the environmental clause creates a right with two aspects. Firstly, it commences by stating that everyone has a right to an environment "that is not harmful to their health." Clearly, this goes beyond the right to health care established by s27 of the Bill of Rights concerning the provision of health care services. A particular environment may be damaging to people's health, yet not fall foul of s27 as it does not infringe a person's right to health care services. Given the serious health consequences of air and water pollution, the siting of waste disposal sites, and so on, health is unarguably a component of environmental justice and within the ambit of s24. This means that, if air pollution or the placement of disposal sites is to be subjected to constitutional challenge on the grounds that people's health is being damaged, the challenge will have to be brought in terms of the environmental clause not s27. However, the environmental clause must encompass more than health, otherwise we would be simply referring to environmental health, a function of the National Department of Health, leaving no obvious role for the Department of Environmental Affairs and Tourism.

In this regard we must examine a second aspect of the right created by subsection 24 (a) that is perhaps even more significant. The clause goes on to provide for a right to an environment that is not harmful to one's "well-being." A person's well-being is harmed if his or her interests are harmed. Many of our interests are protected by other clauses in the Bill of Rights, but some are not. If one's environment harms one of these interests—an interest important to one's well-being and yet not protected elsewhere in the Bill of Rights—one will have to turn to the environmental clause for relief.

The aspect of subsection 24(a) concerning well-being provides environmentalists with a potentially powerful weapon. People do not only have an indirect interest in their environment, they also have a direct one. A clean and undisturbed environment does not only have instrumental value because it secures other things of value such as good health or tourist related income, it also has an inherent and intrinsic value. In this respect, the environment can be likened to many cultural objects: a Pierneef painting; a Herbert Baker building; San rock art. These objects certainly have instrumental value insofar as they generate tourism, but they also have intrinsic value. Thus, we have a direct interest in their preservation.

In the environmental context, the possibilities suggested by a right to well-being are exciting, but potentially limitless. The words nevertheless encompass the essence of environmental concern, namely a sense of environmental integrity; a sense that we ought to utilize the environment in a morally responsible and ethical manner. If we abuse the environment we feel a sense of revulsion akin to that felt when a beautiful and unique landscape is destroyed, or a wild animal is cruelly treated.

The right to an environment conducive to well-being also embraces a sense of stewardship; people are the custodians of the environment for future generations which are specifically referred to in subsection 24(b). The latter notion was to some extent captured in MacDonald's statement in *King v Dykes* (1971 (3) SA 540 (RA), 545) in which he said:

> The idea which prevailed in the past that ownership of land conferred the right on the owner to use his land as he pleases is rapidly giving way in the modern world to the more responsible conception that an owner must not use his land in a way which may prejudice his neighbors or the community in which he lives, and that he holds the land in trust for future generations.

Apart from the "Save the Vaal Environment" case referred to above, the only other reported case which has referred to the environmental right, albeit under the Interim Constitution of 1993, is *Minster of Health and Welfare v Woodcarb (Pty) Ltd and Another* (1996 (3) SA 155). The Minister of Health and Welfare brought an application for an interdict under the Atmospheric Pollution Prevention Act (45 of 1965) to stop the respondent from operating a scheduled incineration process at his sawmilling plant. It was alleged that the respondent was doing so without the registration certificate required under the Act. In addition the Minister had received a series of complaints from occupants of neighboring properties concerning the emission of smoke from the respondent's plant. In addition to finding that the respondent had been operating the burning process without the necessary certificate, the court found that "the generation of smoke in these circumstances, in the teeth of the law as it were, is an infringement of the rights of the respondent's neighbours to 'an environment which is not detrimental to their health or well-being' enshrined in the Interim Constitution." In doing so, the presiding judge nudged the traditionally private law maxim *sic utere tuo ut alienum non laedas* (use your property in a way which does not harm another) into the public law realm. This dictum therefore lays the groundwork for further application of the environmental clause to promote environmental justice, particularly where communities are suffering the ill-effects of industrial pollution in their neighborhoods.

This case illustrates the fundamental question of whether the environmental right has only "vertical" application or whether it has also "horizontal" application. In other words, is the environmental clause only enforceable against organs of state or can it also be invoked in disputes between private parties? On this point, Alfred Cockrell (1997, 1–17) makes an important distinction between "direct" and "indirect" horizontality. By direct horizontality he means that a right in the Bill of Rights could be used to ground a substantive right held by one private person against another private person; by indirect he means that the right may only influence a court's interpretation and development of an existing common law principle. He points out that while the final Constitution allows for greater scope for the horizontal application of the Bill of Rights, it in no way allows for "full-scale" direct horizontality. A twofold enquiry is necessary under the Constitution. Cockrell argues that the first enquiry is whether the right binds a private agency. In this enquiry, regard must be had to the nature of the right and the nature of any correlative duty. If it does so apply, the second stage of the enquiry entails the court developing the common law.

It is suggested that the nature of subsection 24(a) of the environmental clause is such that it is undeniably applicable to private persons because of its close resemblance to the common law principle of neighbor law based on the Roman Law *sic utere tuo* principle referred to above. Neighbor law essentially governs private law relationships, and s24(a) appears to extend this principle into the public law realm, as illustrated in the *Woodcarb* case.

By including an environmental right the constitution makers have put environmental justice issues squarely into the realm of government responsibility. The clause entails formidable challenges both to the judiciary, which will have to put some flesh onto the notion of well-being, among other matters, and to the legislature which, given the "injustice of our past" referred to in the Preamble to the Constitution, and apartheid's environmental legacy, is obliged to put in place a comprehensive body of environmental law. As outlined below, a good start has been made with other clauses of the Bill of Rights.

The Property Clause, Land Reform, and Protected Areas

From a historical perspective environmental issues and land dispossession in South Africa are closely linked, as the establishment of many of South Africa's protected areas fell under the broader land dispossession policy of previous governments. The property clause (s25) prevents the arbitrary deprivation of property and provides for compensation where property is expropriated for a public purpose or in the public interest. Furthermore, it specifically provides that property is not limited to land, and that for the purposes of the section "the public interest includes the nation's commitment to land reform, and to reforms to bring about equitable access to all South Africa's natural resources" (s25(4)).

Property rights can be asserted to resist legitimate land-related aspirations. In *Diepsloot Landowners and Residents' Association v Administrator, Transvaal* (1993 (1) SA 577 (T)) the Applicant, the landowners association, challenged the Administrator's decision to settle the "Zevenfontein" squatters near a residential area. Among the arguments used in the then Transvaal Provincial Division was that the Administrator's decision, made under authority of the Informal Townships Establishment Act, would interfere with the Applicant's private rights. These included the fact that the settlement would allegedly create a nuisance and would amount to an unwarranted interference with private property rights. The landowners alleged that their property rights included an environmental component and that the settlement would affect the environment by creating dust and smoke and polluting the underground water. The application was granted on other grounds but was dismissed later by the Appellate Division (1994 (3) SA 336 (A)).

The claims and aspirations of people who were dispossessed of their land under the apartheid regime are acknowledged in a specific sub-clause of the property clause, which provides as follows: "A person or community dispossessed of property after 19 June 1913 as a result of past racially discriminatory laws or practices is entitled to the extent provided by an Act of Parliament either to restitution of that property or to equitable redress" (s25(7)). In consequence, the Restitution of Land Rights Act (22 of 1994) provides for the restitution of such rights and establishes a Commission on Restitution of Land Rights, regional land claims commissioners, and a Land Claims Court.

A number of specific claims for restitution of land rights in protected areas under the Restitution Act have been considered in the recent past. These include: claims for the restitution of land rights in a portion of the Kruger National Park by the Makuleke Tribe; a submission by the Mbila Land Committee in relation to the Sodwana State Forest in the district of Ubombo in KwaZulu-Natal; the restitution of land rights in the northern portion of the Cape Vidal State Forest and for a portion of the Cape Vidal State Forest and Eastern Shores State Forest, both in the magisterial district of Hlabisa, also in KwaZulu-Natal.

The general approach to resolving these claims is to negotiate a mutually amicable agreement whereby both community and environmental interests can be accommodated, while taking into account the specific needs and circumstance of each individual case. While some of the above-mentioned claims have not yet been resolved, the first, that of the Makuleke people who once occupied about 20,000 hectares in what is now the Pafuri region of the Kruger National Park, as well as in the Madimbo corridor in the Northern Province, was successful (see chaps. 1 and 5 in this volume). A similar negotiation process is currently underway regarding certain claims in the Dwesa and Nkambathi areas on the Wild Coast in the former homeland of Transkei.

The Administrative Justice Clause

Administrative law is central to the judicial pursuit of environmental justice, as conflicts over natural resource exploitation and development invariably entail the exercise of administrative decision-making powers. Some hypothetical examples of such decision making would include a local and provincial authority approving a controversial industrial development in the vicinity of an established community; authorization being granted by national or provincial government to commence a pollution-generating activity which poses a threat to groundwater quality; the Minister of Environment Affairs and Tourism granting a fisheries quota which has not taken account of the needs of previously disadvantaged communities as is required in terms of the objectives of the recently enacted fisheries legislation described below.

The inclusion of a Just Administrative Action clause (s33) in the final Constitution not only codifies the existing common law but also provides authority to extend the standard of review. The courts have traditionally been constrained from entering into the merits of administrative decisions and have confined their observations to fairly narrow grounds such as the decision maker failing to apply his or her mind to the matter. One of the leading cases illustrating this approach was *Union Government (Minister of Mines and Industry) v Union Steel Corporation (South Africa) Ltd* (1928 AD 220). Over time the courts developed the "symptomatic unreasonableness" test that entitled them to question the decision only when it was grossly unreasonable.

The administrative justice clause of the Bill of Rights changes the picture. It provides that:

1. Everyone has the right to administrative action that is lawful, reasonable and procedurally fair;
2. Everyone whose rights have been adversely affected by administrative action has the right to be given written reasons;
3. National legislation must be enacted to give effect to these rights and must—
   a. provide for the review of administrative action by a court or, where appropriate, an independent and impartial tribunal;
   b. impose a duty on the state to give effect to the rights in subsections (1) and (2); and
   c. promote an efficient administration.

According to the Transitional Arrangements set out in the Constitution, this Just Administrative Action clause must be given effect to by specific legislation and Parliament has duly enacted the Promotion of Administrative Justice Act, the impact of which remains to be seen.

The equivalent provision in the Interim Constitution was worded differently and provides a significant opportunity for the courts to depart from the traditional approach described above. Subsections (c) and (d) are of particular relevance to the standard of judicial review providing as they do that:

Every person has the right to:

(c) be furnished with reasons in writing for administrative action which affects any of their rights or interests unless the reasons for that action have been made public; and

(d) administrative action which is justifiable in relation to the reasons given for it where any of their rights is affected or threatened.

Etienne Mureinik (1994, 40) expressed the view that this sub-clause deals a mortal blow to the doctrine of unreasonableness and gives the courts an opportunity to develop a theory of what is justifiable. Jaques De Ville (1994, 360) cogently argued that the subsection opens the door for the continental doctrine of proportionality to be accepted into our law. This doctrine states that the action taken must be reasonable in relation to its consequences. According to De Ville, the new standard of judicial review requires administrative action that is "suitable and necessary to attain the statutory prescribed purpose and which does not result in harm to individual(s) which is out of proportion to the gains to community."

De Ville's arguments were specifically endorsed by the Cape High Court in *Roman v Williams* (1998 (1) SA 270 (C), 281 E–F) where a decision of the Commissioner of Correctional Services to re-imprison a probationer under the Correctional Services Act (8 of 1959) was subjected to review proceedings. The judge decided that the common law review grounds were no longer relevant and that they had been overtaken by the constitutional test of legality. He stated that, "administrative action, in order to prove justifiable in relation to the decisions given for it, must be objectively tested against the three requirements of suitability, necessity and proportionality which requirements involve a test of reasonableness. Gross unreasonableness is no longer a requirement for review."

It is suggested that this more rational approach will have profound implications for administrative decision making generally and the promotion of environmental justice specifically. In the environmental justice context this has been illustrated by cases such as *Corium (Pty) Ltd v Myburgh Park Langebaan (Pty) (Ltd)* (1995 (3) SA 51 (C)) and *Van Huysteen v Minister of Environment Affairs and Tourism* (1995 (9) BCLR 1191 (C)) both of which concerned controversial development proposals in the vicinity of the ecologically sensitive Langebaan lagoon in the Western Cape. Finally, it is suggested that the inclusion of the right to environmental health and well-being in the Constitution as well as the advent of a comprehensive set of statutory environmental management principles in the National Environmental Management Act of 1998 will provide further impetus for the inclusion of considerations of fairness and equity in administrative decision making concerning the environment.

The Access to Information Clause

In the context of South Africa's transition to democracy, more specifically as regards the information clause in the Interim Constitution, it has been said that "access to information is . . . a necessary adjunct to an open democratic society committed to the principles of openness and accountability" (*Quzeleni v Minister of Law and Order* 1994 (3) SA, 625 E).

The Access to Information clause of the final Constitution provides:

(1) everyone with the right to access to
    (a) any information held by the state; and
    (b) any information that is held by another person and that is required for the exercise or protection of any rights.

(2) National legislation must be enacted to give effect to this right, and may provide for reasonable measures to alleviate the administrative and financial burden on the state.

But as in the case of the Just Administrative Action clause discussed above, national legislation must be enacted within three years of the Constitution taking effect to give effect to the obligation referred to in subsection 2. Parliament has accordingly enacted the Promotion of Access to Information Act, a potentially invaluable tool in the hands of NGOs concerned with promoting environmental justice. It provides for detailed rules and procedures for access to information from both public and private bodies. Although certain circumstances warrant exemption from the provision of the Act, these are significantly trumped by "an imminent and serious public safety or environmental risk" (ss36(1)(a) and 70(1)(a)). It again remains to be seen how effective this Act will be in practice.

The constitutional Access to Information clause has been subject to judicial scrutiny in a number of cases including some related specifically to the environment. The relief sought by the applicants in *Van Huyssteen NO and Others v Minister of Environmental Affairs and Tourism and Others* ((1995) (9) *BCLR* 1191 (C)) concerning a controversial proposal to construct a steel mill at Saldanha Bay, included an application for an order compelling the Respondent Minister to furnish all available documentation concerning the project. The judge acknowledged that the right of access to information is not absolute and unqualified, but held that in the present case there was no question of a possible limitation under the limitation clause of the Interim Constitution. The Applicants were accordingly entitled to the documentation they sought.

This line contrasts with that adopted in *Goodman Bros (Pty) Ltd v Transnet Ltd* (1998 (8) *BCLR* 1024 (W)) where the Applicant unsuccessfully tendered to supply goods to the Respondent. He applied for a similar order under the access to information clause, compelling the release of documents concerning the evaluation of the tender, as well as for an order under the Administrative Justice clause described above, compelling reasons to be furnished. The Applicant was successful in relation to the request for reasons but not in relation to the documentation under the information clause. The judge quoted with approval an unreported judgment dated 22 March 1998 (*SA Metal Machinery Co Ltd v Transnet Ltd*) where it was held that an unrestricted right of access to documents in possession of a public body can easily lead to abuse, but acknowledged that some protection had to be afforded against the oppressive consequences of state secrecy which previously existed. In *SA Metal Machinery* it had been held that there had to be a reasonable basis for believing that the disclosure of documents in the possession of the state would assist in the protection of a person's rights. The judge furthermore emphasized that the section did not entitle the Applicant to information to determine whether a right was threatened or infringed. More than simply an unsubstantiated apprehension of harm would be needed to invoke the section. The application was accordingly dismissed.

A further general but pertinent question that has been considered by the courts specifically in the context of s23 is whether the reference to rights in the section includes rights other than those contained in the Bill of Rights. In *Directory Advertising Cost Cutters v the Minister for Posts Telecommunications and Broadcasting and Others* (1996 (3) SA 800), the judge expressed the view that the term "rights" as used in the Bill of Rights referred to the fundamental rights in Chapter 3 (of the Interim Constitution), "nothing more, nothing less."

However, a different view was expressed by the presiding judge in *Van Niekerk v City Council of Pretoria* (1997 (1) All SA305T). The appellant sought an order under the Access to Information clause compelling the release of a report in the possession of the respondent concerning damage to his property. The judge, after giving examples of a number of rights which were not mentioned in the Bill of Rights, concluded that the approach taken in the Directory Advertising case was unwarrantably narrow and that "the limitation of 'rights' envisaged in s23 to the fundamental rights envisaged in chapter 3 is untenable."

The National Environmental Management Act, discussed below, has substantially elaborated on the right of access to information. The relevant provisions are specifically to apply until such time as the legislation envisaged in s32(2) of the final Constitution is passed, and must be seen against the backdrop of the important set of environmental management principles that constitute the foundation stones of the Act. The relevant principle (s2(3)(k)) provides that "Decisions must be taken in an open and transparent manner, and access to information must be provided for in accordance with the law."

This principle is developed in part 2 of chapter 7 of the Act entitled "Information, Enforcement and Compliance," which outlines two broad approaches regarding access to information. Firstly, it details the right of access to information both for the citizen and for the state. As regards the citizen, "every person is entitled to have access to information held by the State and organs of state which relates to the implementation of this Act and any other law affecting the environment, and to the state of the environment and actual and future threats to the environment, including any emissions to water, air or soil and the production, handling, transportation, treatment, storage and disposal of hazardous waste" (s31(1)(a)).

It provides that "organs of state are entitled to have access to information relating to the state of the environment and actual and future threats to the environment, including any emissions to water, air or soil and the production, handling, transportation, treatment, storage and disposal of hazardous waste held by any person where that information is necessary to enable such organ of state to carry out their duties in terms of the provisions of this Act or any other law concerned with the protection of the environment or the sustainable use of natural resources" (s31(1)(b)). The section goes on to detail circumstances in which such information can be refused.

Secondly, there is set of innovative provisions aimed at protecting "whistle-blowers" who disclose environmental information from both civil and criminal consequences. A person who discloses under the Access to Information clause evidence of environmental risk is protected from being dismissed, disciplined, prejudiced, or harassed because of having furnished such information. The section only applies in limited circumstances, namely if the information was disclosed to a committee of Parliament or a provincial legislature, an organ of state responsible for protecting the environment or emergency service, the Public Protector, the Human Rights Commission, or an attorney-general. It also applies if disclosure is necessary to avoid a serious and imminent threat to the environment and to ensure that such threat is properly and timeously investigated or to protect a person against serious or irreparable harm from reprisals (s31(5)).

The Enforcement of Rights Clauses and Legal Standing

The South African legal system, like many others, has traditionally required that in order to have standing to challenge administrative unlawfulness an individual must show that he or she has some degree of personal interest in the administrative action being challenged (Baxter 1989, 650). The *locus standi* rule, as this requirement is also known, has traditionally been a significant impediment to those wishing to litigate in environmental matters because it denies public-spirited litigation access to the court.

This has not always been the case. Roman law recognized the *actio populari*, or citizen's action, whereby any member of the public could bring an action in the public interest. Similarly legal standing was not a requirement in South African law in the nineteenth century, as is apparent in the case of *Dell v The Town Council of Cape Town* ((1879) 9 Buch 2), a case with distinctive environmental undertones, where the court found that the depositing of rubbish on Woodstock beach by the Council of Cape Town constituted a nuisance to the public at large, and granted a temporary interdict to Dell, the local railway traffic manager. The court had no difficulty in acknowledging *locus standi,* for an action brought in the public interest, holding that Dell "is entitled to make this application to restrain the nuisance in any public place in the town." In the context of the health component of the environmental clause in the Bill of Rights discussed above, it is interesting to note that the court also stated that although Dell did not specifically state that his health was likely to suffer, it was implicit that this would be the case as he worked in the vicinity of the rubbish.

However, in a triumvirate of cases decided at the turn of the century, *Patz v Green & Co* (1907 TS 427), *Bagnall and Colonial Government* (1907 24 SC 470), and *Dalrymple & Others v Colonial Treasurer* (1910 TS 372), the tide turned, and the general requirement that an individual required a special interest peculiar to himself before being given a hearing was imported into our law from the English law. This turnabout in the historical position severely curtailed the ability of both individuals and groups to litigate in the public interest and the ramifications were evident throughout the field of public interest law. In the environmental context, the strictures of the requirement were vividly illustrated, for example, in *Von Moltke v Costa Aerosa* (1975 (1) SA 255 (C)), where the Applicant, a nature lover and resident of Llandudno, a suburb on Cape Town's Atlantic seaboard, sought an interdict prohibiting a developer from starting building operations at Sandy Bay, a popular nudist beach a few kilometers from his residence. The operations were allegedly illegal because the requisite planning permission had not been obtained under the Townships Ordinance, the planning legislation applicable at the time. The court nevertheless refused to entertain the Applicant's case, holding that "the party seeking relief must show some injury, prejudice or damage or invasion of right peculiar to himself and over and above that sustained by the members of the public in general."

More recently, in *Minister of Health and Welfare v Woodcarb,* the air pollution case referred to above, the Respondent took the point that the Applicant lacked the necessary *locus standi* on the grounds, *inter alia,* that the Atmospheric Pollution Prevention Act (45 of 1965) provided for criminal sanctions and not for the civil remedies the court was asked to grant. This argument was rejected by the court, which held that the whole purpose of the legislation was to control the installation and use of scheduled processes and that the Applicant was implicitly entitled to bring this particular application. In so doing the court relied to some extent on the environmental clause in the Bill of Rights.

The Enforcement of Rights section (s38) of the Bill of Rights thus dramatically changes the position. It provides that anyone listed in the section may approach a competent court alleging that a right in the Bill of Rights has been infringed or threatened. The list of such persons includes "anyone acting as a member of, or in the interest of, a group or class of persons; anyone acting in the public interest; and an association acting in the interests of its members."

It should be noted that the section refers to a person who alleges that "a right in the Bill of Rights" has been infringed. Thus, although the judgments referred to above in the context of the Access to Information clause assert that "rights" are not limited to those contained in the Bill of Rights, it is clear that in the context of s38, the term "rights" is so limited. So, while an individual or an NGO may now approach a court in the general environmental cause, such a person or organization would still have to assert that a constitutional right, rather than a general common law right, has been infringed or threatened. The obvious right to assert in this context is the environmental clause. This raises the question discussed above of whether it has horizontal as well as vertical application.

The National Environmental Management Act of 1998 liberalizes the position even further. Part 2 of chapter 7 of the Act, titled "Information, enforcement and compliance," s32(1), firstly, extends the matters for which relief may be sought, to include "any breach or threatened breach of any provision of this Act, including a principle contained in chapter 1, or any other statutory provision concerned with the protection of the environment or the sustainable use of natural resources." It thus extends the constitutional clause which only grants *locus standi* in cases of threats to rights in the Bill of Rights.

Secondly, it comes to the aid of potential litigants by including innovative provisions regarding the award of costs. Costs are typically an inhibiting factor in bringing public interest actions, including those in the environmental interest. A novel provision, s32(2), specifically gives the courts the discretion not to award costs against a litigant "if the court is of the opinion that the person or group of persons acted reasonably out of concern for the public interest or the interest of the protection of the environment and that no other means had been reasonably available for obtaining the relief sought." This provision has the potential significantly to ameliorate the position of environmental applicants who might in the past have been reluctant to litigate because of the possibility that an unsuccessful outcome would be accompanied by an onerous costs award against them.

Conversely, under s32(3)(a), where such an applicant or plaintiff secures the relief sought, the court is granted discretion to "award costs on an appropriate scale to any person or persons entitled to practice as an attorney or advocate in the Republic who provided free legal assistance or representation to such person or group in the preparation for or conduct of the proceedings." Finally, the court is also granted the discretion to rule that the party against whom the relief is granted pay to the person or group concerned any reasonable costs incurred in preparing for the proceedings under s32(3)(b).

This liberalization by the Bill of Rights of the *locus standi* requirement, coupled with the extension of the circumstances in which one may litigate in the public environmental interest considerably enhances opportunities for public interest litigation in the environmental sphere. It should be noted that these provisions apply in respect of court proceedings only and not to other tribunals. The legislation is so new that its effect has not yet been tested.

The Right to Equality

It is not inconceivable that the Right to Equality (s9) could be invoked directly to promote environmental justice. Inequality may be alleged in the fact, for example, that garbage may be collected twice a week in a wealthy area but only once a week in a poorer township falling under the jurisdiction of the same local authority. The question arises whether the equality clause that provides that "everyone has the right to equal benefit of the law" and that includes the full and equal enjoyment of all rights and freedoms, as well as an affirmative action provision to advance equality, could be invoked in the environmental cause.

In the United States context, Robert Bullard (1997, 103) has observed that "The charge of environmental racism has heightened the debate surrounding social inequities that exist in the larger society. Environmental racism exacerbates existing social inequities." To illustrate this point he cites *Bean v Southwestern Waste* (482 F Supp 673 (SD Tex)) where evidence was provided linking municipal solid waste siting with the race of the surrounding residents.

The equality clause has been considered in a number of cases, including *Stadsraad van Pretoria v Walker* (1998 (3) *BCLR* 257 (CC)), concerning unequal rates and taxes in a particular residential area; *Prinsloo v Van der Linde* (1997 (6) *BCLR* 759 (CC)), concerning an action for fire damage under the Forest Act (122 of 1984); *President of the Republic of South Africa v Hugo* (1997 (6) *BCLR* 708 (CC)), concerning the State President's pardon of women prisoners who were mothers; *Harksen v Lane NO* (1998 (1) SA 300 (CC)), concerning differentiation under the Insolvency Act (24 of 1936); and others.

The equality clause comprises a number of components. One of these provides a right to equal protection and benefit of the law and is not elaborated on here. A second concerns the right not to be unfairly discriminated against, and the question arises in the environmental context whether the environmental racism scenarios described above could fall under this clause.

No environmental issue has yet been considered by the courts under the discrimination provision of the equality clause and one can only speculate as to how it will be applied. It is predicted, however, that sooner or later such a case will come before the courts. The general approach in equality cases thus far has been to enquire whether there has been differentiation and, if so, whether it is discriminatory. The object here is to establish whether the state has acted rationally. Where there has been discrimination, the second enquiry is whether it is unfair. Here the issue is whether the instrument in question entailed "treating persons differently in a way which impairs their fundamental dignity as human beings, who are inherently equal in dignity" (*Prinsloo* at para 31).

The Right to Dignity

In considering whether the discrimination is unfair, the courts have relied on the right to human dignity which is included in s10 of the Bill of

Rights. This section, which provides that "Everyone has inherent dignity and the right to have their dignity respected and protected," perhaps goes to the heart of environmental justice. However, this right has not been invoked directly by the courts but has instead, as seen above, been referred to in the equality cases to determine unfair discrimination.

Legislative Developments and Environmental Justice

The first five years of the new government's term of office saw a flurry of legislative activity, including the passage of laws with a direct bearing on environmental justice. These have all been preceded by intensive public consultation processes culminating in both Green and White Papers and in official Acts. Among them are the National Environmental Management Act, the National Water Act, the Marine Living Resources Act, and developments in the area of pollution and waste management. In each case, the relevance to environmental justice is discussed.

The National Environmental Management Act

The National Environmental Management Act (107 of 1998) was preceded by an extensive four-year nationwide consultative process known as CONNEPP (the Consultative National Environmental Policy Process) that commenced relatively soon after the new government came to power. It culminated in the White Paper on "Environmental Management Policy for South Africa" which specified amongst its objectives that new environmental legislation was necessary to give effect to the constitutional environmental clause. The White Paper includes environmental justice as one of the principles that is to underpin new environmental legislation. It states that to "comply with the requirements of environmental justice, government must integrate environmental considerations with social, political and economic justice and development in addressing the needs and rights of all communities, sectors and individuals." Moreover, policy, legal, and institutional frameworks must:

- redress past and present environmental injustice;
- take account of the need to protect and create employment;

- recognize that workers can refuse work that is harmful to human health or the environment;
- ensure that everyone is able to make known environmental or health hazards without fear of the consequences;
- ensure equitable representation and participation of all with particular concern for marginalized groups.

The White Paper was closely followed by the National Environmental Management Act, which is built on the concept of "sustainable development," as elaborated on in s2(4)(a) of the Act. The Act also sets out landmark national environmental management principles that provide the basis for environmental management throughout the country. Included in the set of principles are two that are directly relevant to environmental justice:

Environmental justice must be pursued so that adverse environmental impacts shall not be distributed in such a manner as to unfairly discriminate against any person, particularly vulnerable and disadvantaged persons (s2(3)(c)); and

Equitable access to environmental resources, benefits and services to meet basic human needs and ensure human well-being must be pursued and special measures may be taken to ensure access thereto by categories of persons disadvantaged by unfair discrimination (s2(3)(d)).

The Act envisages that these principles will be converted into concrete reality through environmental management and implementation plans which each organ of state will be required to prepare under chapter 3 of the Act, titled "Procedures for Co-operative Governance." It remains to be seen how these principles will be applied in practice.

The National Water Act

The passage of the National Water Act (36 of 1998) represents a dramatic departure from South African water policy of the past. South Africa's water law in the past three centuries was molded and shaped by the needs and aspirations of white settlers who trekked into the interior and,

in colonizing the land, fashioned laws that primarily served their domestic and agricultural needs (Rabie 1989).

It is generally acknowledged that the apartheid regime denied vast
sectors of the populace access to basic resources, including water. In the
White Paper on a National Water Policy for South Africa which preceded
the new law, it was pointed out that between twelve and fourteen million South Africans do not have access to safe water, and more than
twenty million are without adequate sanitation. The Department of
Water Affairs and Forestry has made significant strides in redressing this
state of affairs with its Work for Water and other programs. The primary
aim of the program is to eliminate alien vegetation and, in doing so, the
program has created much needed employment. Other spin-offs have
been the establishment of secondary industries and a poverty relief
fund. The new water law accordingly reflects a new democratic spirit by
giving effect to the constitutional right of access to water referred to in
s27 of the Constitution. It also prioritizes current environmental, economic, and other needs as well as shaping water law in the context of
the Southern African region.

An important innovation relevant to environmental justice is the
concept of a "reserve" provided for in chapter 3 of the Act, dedicated to
Protection of Water Resources. The "reserve" is defined as "that quantity
and quality of water required to (i) satisfy basic human needs for all
people who are, or who may be, supplied from the relevant water resource; and (ii) to protect aquatic ecosystems in order to secure ecologically sustainable development and use of the relevant water resource"
(s2(n)). It is evident that there are two distinct components of the reserve. The first is a basic needs component which embodies Principle 8
of the Fundamental Principles: "The water required to ensure that all
people have access to sufficient water shall be reserved." These are not
property rights but rights to claim delivery of water up to a defined
quantity. The second aspect is the ecological component embodied in
Principle 9 which states that the "quantity, quality and reliability of
water required to maintain the ecological functions on which humans
depend shall be reserved so that the human use of water does not indi-
vidually or cumulatively compromise the long term sustainability of
aquatic and associated ecosystems."

Basic needs and the ecological reserve accordingly enjoy priority over other claims to water. Moreover the use of water for all other purposes shall be subject to authorization under a uniform licensing system introduced under the Act. The question of what exactly constitute "basic needs" was addressed in the White Paper, which suggested a provisional quantity of 25 liters per person per day as a short-term target. It acknowledges that this is a relative concept that should increase as standards of living increase. It is anticipated that the courts will in due course hear cases regarding the application of a basic right.

The quantification of the environmental or ecological component is more problematic. How much water is necessary in a particular catchment area to protect aquatic ecosystems in order to secure ecologically sustainable development? The White Paper acknowledged that a methodology is needed and suggests a range of methods based on the introduction of a national resource protection classification system. However, many questions remain unanswered and there will in all probability be some head-scratching in this regard, particularly among the scientific water community, including freshwater biologists, who will be called upon in particular cases to assess the quantity of water constituting the reserve. In practice, the scientific community has already resorted to making a so-called rapid reserve assessment.

A number of other innovations in the National Water Act reflect a clear commitment to more equitable access to the nation's scarce water resources. These include the abolition of the system of riparian rights to water, a uniform system of licensing, and the placement of all water resources under the custody of the state.

The Marine Living Resources Act

The South African fishing industry provides substantial employment to people in the four coastal provinces and makes a significant contribution to the economy. An unabashed reason for replacing the previous Sea Fishery Act (12 of 1988) with the Marine Living Resources Act (18 of 1998) is to give concrete reality to the constitutional imperative to redress "the injustices of our past." To this end, the White Paper which preceded the Act, and whose drafting offered opportunities for intensive public consultation, devotes considerable effort to highlighting the need to address transformation and equitable access to the country's lucrative fisheries resources.

One section of the White Paper, entitled "Access and Access Rights" (part 4, para 4.3.17), deals with the percentage share of the Total Allowable Catch (TAC) held by the commercial fisheries sector, commenting that "the present concentration of access may be elaborated by introducing the aspect of colour or ethnic group associated with the respective quota holders. If so analyzed, the picture displays an overwhelming quota-holder dominance by the formerly advantaged sector of the population." A clear imperative of the White Paper is to redress these past imbalances and the Act reflects this in many of its provisions.

S2 of the Act sets out its "Principles and Objectives." Included in the list of general fisheries management principles are the need to achieve optimum utilization and ecologically sustainable development of marine living resources, the need to conserve marine living resources for both present and future generations, and the need to apply precautionary approaches in respect of the management and development of marine living resources. However, a uniquely South African principle is the specific objective "to restructure the fishing industry to address historical imbalances and to achieve equity within all branches of the fishing industry." A further principle emphasizes the need to utilize marine living resources to achieve economic growth, human resource development, capacity building within fisheries and mariculture branches, and employment creation.

Similarly, the institutions created under the Act, namely the Consultative Advisory Forum for Marine Living Resources (the CAF), and the Fisheries Transformation Council (s29) both embody the transformation philosophy and thus pursue the ideal of environmental justice in the sphere of access to natural resources. The specific object of the latter is "to facilitate the achievement of fair and equitable access" to fishing rights (s30). While this may be laudable, a curious omission and a departure from the past is the exclusion of any form of scientific evidence—a crucial component of fisheries management—from these bodies. The bodies are simply to be "broadly representative and multi-disciplinary." The Council's objective is to lease rights to and to assist in the development and capacity building of historically disadvantaged persons and small and medium-size enterprises.

The section providing for the granting of rights of access by the Minister to key sectors of the industry refers specifically to the objectives in s2 referred to above, and stipulates that the Minister must have particular re-

gard to "the need to permit new entrants, particularly those from historically disadvantaged sectors of society" (s18(5)). Such rights may be granted
for: commercial fishing; subsistence fishing; the conduct of mariculture;
and the operation of a fish processing establishment (s18(1)). A further
overtly social engineering provision provides that the Minister may allo-
cate rights to the Transformation Council (s31(1)). Interestingly, no mention is made of recreational rights, although "recreational fishing" is
defined in the definition section and referred to in other sections of the Act.

Pollution Control and Waste Management

As noted previously, a primary concern of the environmental justice
movement is the equitable and even distribution of air, land, and water
pollution burdens. The problem is particularly acute in South Africa as
past, racially based land-use planning, policies, and practices have exacerbated inequities so that waste sites, industrial plants, and so on are invariably located in close proximity to poorer sectors of South African society.

The link between poor air, poor health, and poverty is evident in
particular regions of South Africa and results from particular activities,
for example mining. Lack of access to electricity and the resultant use of
coal- and wood-burning appliances in many townships have exacerbated
the problem. The net result has been an increased incidence of respiratory diseases in certain areas. Scientific studies initiated by the Department of Minerals and Energy have shown, for example, that domestic
fuels, particularly coal, are a significant source of air pollution and have
adverse affects on children's health, particularly in the Vaal Triangle's
Sebokeng/Lekoa urban area (Terblanche, Nel and Opperman 1992). A
further study carried out in the Vaal Triangle shows that children living
in non-electrified homes run a 30 percent higher risk of developing respiratory illness than their counterparts living in electrified homes (Terblanche and Pols 1994).

One of the most vivid and tragic recent illustrations of an environmental justice issue is undoubtedly the Thor Chemicals saga (see chapter
1 and the narrative "Crippled for Life by Mercury Exposure" in this volume). A criminal charge was brought against the directors of Thor SA who
were found guilty of contravening the Occupational Health and Safety
Act but acquitted on a charge of culpable homicide. A Commission of

Inquiry headed by then Professor Dennis Davis (now a High Court judge) found that a range of national, provincial, and local authority departments were culpable. The Commission found that "the evidence reveals a pattern of government commission and omission which allowed the problem to develop. The acts of commission afforded Thor the authority to continue with the practices . . . while the omissions meant that Thor was never adequately held to account" (para 2.2.7.2). A second phase of the Commission of Inquiry dealing with the environmental aspects of the mercury waste is still pending.

Clearly much needs to be done with regard to the implementation and administration of pollution control legislation in South Africa. One approach would be to streamline and coordinate the various laws controlling pollution in the country through Integrated Pollution Control, a mechanism which has been adopted in the UK and in many European countries (Kidd 1995; Stein 1997). Progress has been slow in this regard. In 1991 the Council for Scientific and Industrial Research (CSIR), commissioned by the Department of Environment Affairs and Tourism, produced a baseline report "The Situation of Waste Management and Pollution Control in South Africa." The report noted that South Africa has no comprehensive all-embracing national statute dealing with waste, and found, amongst other matters, that there were thirty-seven national statutes, sixteen provincial ordinances, and numerous local authority by-laws relevant to land-based pollution. Today, with the advent of nine new provinces and a number of new laws on the statute book, the numbers have probably increased.

In 1992, the Department initiated a project to develop a National Holistic Policy for Integrated Pollution Control, and more recently (August 1998) a Draft White Paper on "Integrated Pollution and Waste Management for South Africa" was produced. The draft remains a draft. Despite the amount of effort and time that went into creating this document it is rather disappointingly general and lacks any rigorous analysis of the legal system regulating and administering pollution control. Among its proposals is yet another envisaged study intended to produce a National Waste Management Strategy. While these studies may generate voluminous reports often at donor expense, there is little evidence that there have been any changes to the status quo, particularly the conditions of the poorer communities that bear the brunt of pollution.

Conclusion

This chapter has attempted to show that while it is difficult to give a precise legal definition to the abstract notion of environmental justice, the inclusion of an environmental clause in the Bill of Rights has added considerable momentum to its legal development. In South Africa this has been done both judicially and legislatively by the new government's clear commitment to give effect to the imperative of the environmental clauses to enact legislative and other measures for environmental protection. However, there has been more evidence of legislative reform in the domain of resources rather than in pollution control. Thus, while we have seen new legislative developments in the areas of land, water, and forestry, we have yet to see significant developments in pollution control and waste management. These areas are being considered in the context of the Environmental Law Reform Programme currently being undertaken by the Department of Environmental Affairs and Tourism, and its outcome is eagerly awaited.

References

Abel, R. 1995. *Politics By Other Means: Law in the Struggle Against Apartheid, 1980–1994.* New York and London: Routledge.

Baxter, L. 1989. *Administrative Law.* Cape Town: Juta and Co.

Bullard, R. D. 1997. "The Threat of Environmental Racism." In R. V. Percival and D. C. Alevizatos, eds. *Law and the Environment.* Philadelphia: Temple University Press.

Cockrell, A. 1997. "Private Law and the Bill of Rights: A Threshold Issue of 'Horizontality.'" In *Bill of Rights Compendiun.* Durban: Butterworths.

De Ville, J. 1994. "Proportionality as a Requirement of the Legality in Administrative Law in Terms of the New Constitution." *SA Public Law* 360.

Kidd, M. 1995. "Integrated Pollution Control in South Africa: How Easy a Task?" *South African Journal of Environmental Law and Policy* 37.

Mureinik, E. 1994. "A Bridge to Where?: Introducing the Interim Bill of Rights." *South African Journal on Human Rights* 40.

Rabie, A. 1989. "The Conservation of Rivers in South African Law." *SA Public Law* 1 and 204.

Stein, R. 1997. "Regulation of Waste Management in South Africa: A Case for Integration." *South African Journal of Environmental Law and Policy* 253.

Terblanche, A. P. S., and A. Pols. 1994. *Characterisation of Risk Factors Associated with Household Fuel Usage in South Africa*. Department of Minerals and Energy Report No. EO 9303. Pretoria: Department of Minerals and Energy.

Terblanche P., C. M. Nel, and L. Opperman. 1992. *Health and Safety Aspects of Domestic Fuels*. Pretoria: Energy Branch, Department of Minerals and Energy.

Fearing Asbestosis

Mpume Nyandu

Dorcas Matemane of Mafefe, a small village situated in a remote corner of the Northern Province, is the mother of eight children. Now in her early fifties, she was forced to go job hunting when she was only ten years old. It seems the only job available at the time was at an asbestos mine in Mafefe. So, at the tender age of ten, totally uninformed about the dangers of asbestos, she became a worker, grinding asbestos. She worked at the mine until she was in her late teens when she stopped because she was soon to marry a man from Tzaneen, away from Mafefe. Years later her husband died and her brothers brought her back to Mafefe with her children.

Many years after leaving the mine she started experiencing chest pains and exhaustion. She went to see a doctor about her problem and was told that her chest problems were related to her history of exposure to asbestos. She says: "I am now weak and experiencing chest pains and I can hardly climb a small hill because I have short breath."

Dorcas would like to continue working to get her children through school, but cannot do so because of her health problems. "Because I cannot work now I am just waiting and hoping to get a pension from the government so that I can take care of my children," she laments. The Mafefe Asbestos Committee helped Dorcas claim compensation from the Commission on Occupational Diseases in 1997. With the R30,000 she received, she bought "three beds, cups and plates, wardrobes, two uniforms for two of my children at school, cement, sand, door frames, and windows to build a house because I never had all these things before," she says. Although the money will not reverse her health problems, it has certainly brought a few positive changes in her life. She's been able to acquire a house and her very first bed, things she thought she would never own.

When the Mafefe Asbestos Committee was formed in 1988 it focused on asbestos issues and on helping people with the compensation process, but now it does much more.

Illnesses such as those arising from asbestos exposure, mesothelioma and asbestosis, for example, not only ruin people's health but also bring other problems. William Nakaphala, for instance, was diagnosed with asbestosis in 1958, a few years after he stopped working at an asbestos mine. His wife left him when she realized he was ill and could not find another job. He has been living on a disability grant ever since.

In Mafefe, it is not only the former workers on the mine who live in fear of being diagnosed with asbestos-related illnesses; the whole village is concerned. Between 1991 and 1995, 581 of the 18,000 villagers were diagnosed as suffering from asbestosis and pneumocolosis. Fifteen people died of mesothelioma.

Asbestos pollution pervades Mafefe. The busiest road in the village is literally covered and leveled with a layer of asbestos fiber. As William puts it, "Asbestos has been spread all over the place, especially here at the bus stop. People stand here and inhale it from the dust caused by cars and buses." The wind is not the only agent for spreading asbestos pollution. During rainy seasons soil contaminated with asbestos fibers is often washed into the nearby rivers where people and animals drink.

The only primary school in Mafefe was built with asbestos bricks, which were originally plastered with cement, and painted. In most parts of the school the paint is peeling and the cement is falling off the walls, revealing the bricks and exposing the pupils to asbestos fibers on a daily basis. The asbestos exposure does not end in the classrooms and in the school grounds where there are patches of asbestos fibers. Most of the children come from homes built of asbestos bricks. As a result, many of them are likely to be diagnosed with asbestosis and mesothelioma at some point in their lives.

The nearest town to Mafefe is Pietersburg, about three hours away by car. People travel long distances to find jobs. So when asbestos mining started in the area it was seen by many of the villagers as a great opportunity for employment.

Although mining no longer takes place, the residents of Mafefe are still feeling the effects. The biggest sources of pollution are the dumps that are situated all over the village. On the beautiful green mountains surrounding the area one can still see scars and patches left behind by asbestos dumping. Some of the scars are currently being rehabilitated through tree planting, but this is only a small part of the solution to the asbestos problem that prevails in the area. What will happen to the school? What about the road that's covered in asbestos?

No one knows how long it is will take to deal with problems faced by the Mafefe community. William Nakaphala feels that part of the solution is to understand the extent of the damage. This should be done, he believes, by screening every member of the village and giving medical assistance to those diagnosed with asbestos-related illnesses. Continuous pressure on the government to play an active role in assisting the Mafefe community is seen as another part of the solution.

Chapter 8
Doublespeak in Durban

Mondi, Waste Management, and the
Struggles of the South Durban Community
Environmental Alliance

S. (Bobby) Peek

> *Pollution often seems to occur where black people live. This*
> *is the rubbish of history which we have to deal with today.*
> —Kader Asmal, former Minister of Water Affairs and
> Forestry, *The Mercury*, 3 November 1998

T here are various interpretations of environmental justice. In the context of a democratic South Africa, it is about the challenges facing poor and vulnerable people in developing their capacity to translate their hard-won democracy into reality and interpreting and putting into practice the environmental policy gains of the new democracy.[1]

This chapter will examine how local communities in South Durban are attempting to give teeth to democratic rights by undertaking environmental justice action to improve their neighborhoods, physically and socially. Specifically, this case study follows the struggles of the South Durban Community Environmental Alliance (SDCEA), a multi-ethnic and multi-racial alliance of ten community based organizations (CBOs) and two NGOs in South Durban, against Mondi Paper (Pty) Ltd, which operates a paper mill in the area.

The history of this struggle will be documented to highlight the practical implementation of environmental justice action and to draw lessons for environmental movements in other parts of the country. A brief overview of South African civil society's engagement with government and industry against waste sites will form the departure point, after which a history of environmental justice campaigning in South Durban, and the Mondi struggle in particular, will be provided.

The South African Waste Site Struggle

A cursory glance at the history of waste management practices in South Africa reveals an abysmal record of ineptitude, poor monitoring, and environmental injustice. In a report commissioned by the apartheid-era Department of Environmental Affairs and Tourism (DEAT 1992, 3), it was found that "conditions that could lead to contamination exist at more that half the landfill sites [in the country] on which information was collected." In 1996, the submission by Earthlife Africa (ELA) Pietermaritzburg to the Thor Chemicals Commission of Enquiry stated that only 20 percent of the landfill sites in South Africa could be considered safe. Particularly damning was the admission by Dave Baldwin, Technical Director of Waste-tech, the largest private waste management company in South Africa, that "none of the Waste-tech landfill sites are without problems, which includes inter alia, problems associated with leaching/leaking into the ground water" (Earthlife Africa 1996, 26).

Between 1994 and 1996 most of the toxic waste sites in South Africa were brought to the public's attention because civil society campaigned and highlighted poor management practices or the inappropriate location of these sites. Visserhoek, in the Western Cape; Margolis, Chloorkop, and Holfontein in Gauteng; Aloes in Port Elizabeth in the Eastern Cape; and Umlazi in South Durban all received media attention because of public protests and legal battles, as did the Thor Chemicals Commission of Enquiry, in which Earthlife Africa and the Environmental Justice Networking Forum (EJNF) played an important role. The new government's

Minister of Water Affairs and Forestry, Kader Asmal, whose ministry was responsible for landfill sites, also paid attention to community concerns.

On 22 July 1995, the EJNF held its first national meeting to plan a joint strategy at a national level in the campaign against the landfill sites. EJNF called on Asmal to "develop more effective means of enforcing existing laws," and requested that steps be taken to ensure that the Department of Water Affairs and Forestry's (DWAF) past record in failing to prosecute repeat offenders did not continue.[2] Minister Asmal welcomed these interventions and subsequently took a decision that monitoring committees should watch over the operations of landfill sites and inform the DWAF about problems.

Although this move was welcomed, communities demanded more from the monitoring committees than mere monitoring. Because of the impact of landfill sites on residential areas, communities wanted a direct say in the management of these sites.

This demand was well articulated in South Durban in relation to the Umlazi IV hazardous landfill site negotiations. It was agreed that the Umlazi Closure and Rehabilitation Monitoring Committee (UCRMC), which included community members, CBOs, NGOs, government, and Wastetech, would "jointly decide, negotiate, monitor and evaluate matters relating to pre- and post-closure, including the management of the landfill site" (Singh 1996, 5). This was the first time in the history of engagement between waste site contractors, government, and communities that communities had input over the management processes at a landfill site and could determine its closure and/or re-opening.

All the above-mentioned stakeholders were involved in the development of the Umlazi landfill site permit, as required in terms of section 20 of the Environment Conservation Act. It was agreed that the site's closure date should only be extended "after consensus had been reached with the [Umlazi Closure and Rehabilitation] Monitoring Committee, Provincial and Local Government."

EJNF continued to campaign about waste sites, and in 1998 held a second national strategic planning meeting which was attended by CBOs and NGOs from around South Africa who were active in waste management issues. Thirty-six organizations participated in this two-day meeting. The workshop galvanized opposition to poor waste management practices, with organizations resolving to engage not only with the DWAF and the Department of Environmental Affairs and Tourism at a national level, but also with various environmental and health departments in the provinces.[3]

The successful closure of the Umlazi and Margolis landfill sites, and the improved management at the Vissershoek and Holfontein sites, were offset by a series of setbacks in the waste management struggle. One of these was the case of the Aloes community in early 1995. In this case, DWAF, although aware of the environmental problems posed by the site, unilaterally renewed the permit to allow dumping there. This was done despite the fact that Minister Asmal had written to his Director-General on 8 May 1995, stating that "there is a serious dispute between Waste-tech and the communities" and therefore, "for the moment we should not renew that company's permit until we have found amicable solutions jointly with Waste-tech and the communities concerned."[4] Asmal's urgent request came six days too late, however, for the permit had already been issued. But continued protest by community members resulted in a promise by the Port Elizabeth mayor a year later that the permit for the Aloes Landfill site would not be extended (Earthlife Africa Pietermaritzburg 1996, 26).

These battles over the siting and management of waste in South Africa have helped to heighten the profile of environmental justice struggles and to move environmental debates in the country in general away from the physical, technocratic, and conservation-oriented focus of the past to a more human rights centered approach. This shift was reinforced in May 1998 when EJNF hosted the "Speak Out on Poverty Campaign" at Aloes. A total of twenty-nine people representing urban and rural CBOs and NGOs from various parts of the country gave presentations during the three-day hearing, which was chaired by Archbishop Njongonkulu Ndungane. In all, 109 written submissions were made.[5] During these hearings, environmental issues were interpreted broadly: poor provision of services; land degradation in rural areas; the harmful effects of acute exposure to poisonous chemicals and/or pollutants from dirty industries and mining operations; exposure to hazardous waste sites, incinerators, and informal dumping sites; and poor forestry practices (EJNF 1998). This process provided civil society with an opportunity to portray the environment in a new light.

Also in May 1998, the South African Human Rights Commission

(SAHRC)[6] announced that it would investigate alleged human rights abuses by EnviroServ, South Africa's largest hazardous waste disposal company, against the Aloes community. EnviroServ had been granted permission by government to operate one of the two most hazardous commercial landfill sites in the country. Until September 1998 EnviroServ had also operated a medical waste incinerator adjacent to the Aloes community. The investigation, the first into alleged environmental human rights abuse, is still to be completed.

Within this new spirit of environmental democracy, all stakeholders (government, industry, labor, CBOs, and NGOs), under the guidance of DEAT, worked toward a National Waste Management Strategy (NWMS) that was finalized in the latter part of 1998 and welcomed by civil society. The NWMS addresses issues of waste management at an institutional and practical level. These issues include the registration of and issuing of permits for all waste facilities, including coal waste, by December 2004 (NWMS, Version D, 15 October 1999). However, while this positive strategy was being developed, the South African government chose to import hazardous waste from Australia (groundWork 2000), demonstrating the need for continued vigilance on the part of civil society.

Environmental activity in South Durban must be viewed in this broader context, where communities and organized movements have been provided with more space to challenge the environmental abuses of the past, but where the legacies of environmental racism and industrial indifference still persist.

South Durban—An Unfortunate History

South Durban was, until the 1940s, a thriving market gardening area. However, in 1938 the Durban City Council resolved that the district would be developed into an industrial estate with black residential areas providing a workforce (Scott 1994). This resolution was further stimulated by the introduction by the National Party Government of the Group Areas Act of 1950 and the land expropriation legislation enacted in June 1958.

These laws resulted in the South Durban communities being removed from land that was then rezoned for industrial purposes and led to industrial development adjacent to residential areas. As a result, South Durban is home to two petrochemical refineries (owned by Shell, BP, Petronas, and Engen), and seven recorded hazardous waste dumps (including a chrome dump) within, or adjacent to, black residential areas. The area is also home to various fiber plants, a paper mill, hazardous chemical storage facilities, an airport, and more than 150 smokestack industries which are largely dependent on crude oil imported via an offshore buoy through South Durban.

The resultant sulfur dioxide (SO_2) pollution has placed Durban in the dubious position of having one of the highest concentrations of ambient SO_2 pollution in the country (Wiley 1996, 6). In addition to suffering from the poor environmental practices in South Durban, the majority of the population also live in areas of urban decay caused by the housing policies of the apartheid regime.

With the end of formal apartheid and the election of the African National Congress (ANC) in 1994 some important steps have been taken toward resolving these inequities. In 1995, the environmental justice struggle received a particularly important boost when then President Nelson Mandela, during a visit on 25 March to the Engen oil refinery, was met at the gates by demonstrating community members calling for a reduction in the pollution produced by Engen. President Mandela granted the community an audience and called an inter-stakeholder meeting which included Engen, the various organizations representing communities living adjacent to the refinery, and various cabinet ministers including the Minister and Deputy Minister of Environmental Affairs and Tourism, the Minister of Health, and the Minister of Minerals and Energy (Wiley 1996, 11).

The meeting served to highlight the pollution debate as a holistic environmental and socioeconomic problem in South Durban, rather than an isolated industrial problem. This process also led to the first South Durban Multi-stakeholder Environmental Management meeting, which was chaired by the former Deputy Minister of the Environment, General Bantu Holomisa, on 4 May 1995 (Lombard and Associates 1995).

Soon after President Mandela's visit, local children, whose homes and playgrounds in South Durban bordered an industry called Chemico, owned by Engen, entered the unfenced and abandoned plant to play. They inadvertently consumed an unknown quantity of the organo phosphate *lindane* while playing with the substance found discarded at the plant. Two children were hospitalized as a result of this incident (*Daily News,* 7 April 1995). At the time, emergency services were unable to determine the cause of the children's vomiting and did not know how to treat them because the instructions on the storage containers for the chemical abandoned by the company were written in Chinese.

In a separate incident in June 1995, Minister Asmal, after public protest and lobbying by local South Durban community organizations, schools, and NGOs, visited the Umlazi IV hazardous landfill site owned by Waste-tech, which is now part of EnviroServ. Communities living across the road from the Umlazi site, and the school adjacent to the site, complained about the smell and the possible health effects. Community organizations vetoed the request by Waste-tech to extend the licence for the site for a further five years. Minister Asmal, like President Mandela, called for a multi-stakeholder approach to deal with the Umlazi hazardous landfill site problem.

All these campaigns have met with significant success, the most notable being the agreement by the Engen refinery in 1998 to reduce its sulfur dioxide pollution by 65 percent. The Waste-tech Umlazi hazardous site was closed on 28 February 1997; the children affected by the lindane were examined by an independent specialist approved of by the community; and Minister of Environmental Affairs and Tourism Mohammed Valli Moosa has resolved to develop an air quality environmental management plan for South Durban that will be replicated elsewhere in South Africa if it proves successful (Hallowes 2001).

These victories were attained through the united stance of a broad spectrum of communities, vigorous public campaigning, strong political lobbying, and assistance from NGOs such as the Legal Resources Centre, EJNF, and links to organizations abroad such as Communities for a Better Environment, the South African Exchange Program on Environmental Justice (SAEPEJ), and academic institutions based in the United States, such as Michigan State University.

In 1996, realizing that to succeed in the environmental justice struggles in their region, a strong unified community voice had to be developed, various local communities in South Durban established the South Durban Community Environmental Alliance in 1996. A vigilant, well-organized, and relatively well-resourced voice, the SDCEA plays an important role, not only because it represents people who are living amid "one of the largest concentrations of inherently dangerous petroleum and chemical industries . . . and hazardous waste" in South Africa (Wiley et al. 1996, 1), but also because of the industrial vision that the national government has for South Durban. South Africa's Trade and Industry Minister Alec Erwin's Strategic Development Initiative has earmarked South Durban as the biggest industrial center in the Southern Hemisphere, linking the production in the region with markets in South East Asia and the Pacific Rim.[7] In the long term this development may result in many more serious infringements of environmental justice in relation to established black neighborhoods in the area. A proposal in the recent Strategic Environmental Assessment (SEA) in South Durban undertaken by the Council for Scientific and Industrial Research (CSIR 1999) on behalf of the Durban Metropolitan authority suggests that there is even a possibility that residents will be relocated out of South Durban entirely.

Mondi Paper—The Struggle

Mondi Paper is a multinational corporation, with Anglo American (31.2 percent) and Anglo American Industrial Corporation (51.7 percent) its largest shareholders. Hazardous coal ash produced as waste by Mondi is dumped adjacent to the residential community in South Durban in a dump site for which they hold no permit,[8] and is the source of much of the tension between local residents and the company.

Conflict between Mondi and local communities dates back several decades, to 1968, when the company established its operations on what had been the community's recreational land. The apartheid Durban City Council sold the land to Mondi without any public consultation. The community then had to live with the dangers of heavy transport using the roads of residential areas. The death of a local resident in a collision with a Mondi truck in July 1989 (Weinberg 1991) led to a strong community campaign for safer traffic systems, and an alternate access route was built.

More recently, in 1997, Mondi attempted to expand the hazardous ash dump site in the direction of residential areas, despite the refusal by residents to endorse the expansion. It was this lack of consultation, and the subsequent space for opposition opened up by Mondi's official request to government for permission to expand the site, that galvanized community resistance and led to an intense campaign to stop the extension of the dump.

Most alarming of all to local residents was the absence of a permit to dump ash at the landfill site. The community was also frustrated by the delay of the local provincial office of DWAF in dealing with the dumping of the hazardous ash. As a result, the SDCEA decided to liaise directly with the Minister of DWAF. The Minister supported the community's concerns, questioning whether the provincial office "would have shown this high degree of tolerance if [the waste site] had been established in upper middle-class and white areas?"[9]

The obfuscatory manner in which the provincial DWAF office operated is summed up in their statement to Minister Asmal that the hazardous ash was historically not considered a waste requiring disposal, and was exempt from the permits required in terms of the Environment Conservation Act (73 of 1989).[10] However, in the scoping document produced by the consultants for Mondi in July 1997, it was stated that "the DWAF has implemented a programme to have all solid waste landfill sites permitted in terms of Section 20 of the Environmental Conservation Act. Mondi is thus required to apply for a permit to operate the ash waste site."[11] The lack of action by the DWAF meant that hazardous ash was being dumped in an area where it was not possible to prevent pollution from entering the broader environment and affecting the residents adjacent to the dump.

This irregular *modus operandi* frustrated the community, and it also played a part in Mondi's strategy for dealing with the community. Inviting them to negotiate about alternative ways of disposing of the hazardous ash, Mondi made it clear that it intended to continue dumping in the area. This infuriated residents, who felt that they had been deliberately misled into attending a meeting to find real alternatives to the dumping of ash.[12]

When Mondi's consultants began investigating the options in 1997, the community made it clear that it considered the ash to be hazardous to the environment and to residents' health. This concern was not mentioned in the Background Information Document. Concerned about this, the community began its own investigation via the Internet. This highlighted the fact that coal ash from boilers contains heavy metals, selenium, and arsenic. At a meeting between the Mondi consultant and the community on 6 August 1997, the community, which had secured free legal representation, disclosed the information it had gathered. The consultant admitted publicly for the first time that the Durban Metro Department of Health had expressed concerns about public health.

The community's contention that the ash was hazardous was confirmed when its own sampling revealed lead, chromium, cadmium, and arsenic.[13] Mondi had maintained in 1998 that studies had shown that the ash was not hazardous. Mondi's consultants undertook a new analysis of the waste and declared that it was, indeed, considered to be hazardous.[14] As a result, community members questioned the credibility of these "independent" consultants, who had been appointed by Mondi with no consultation with the community. In the Umlazi IV hazardous landfill site case, by contrast, the UCRMC had chosen a consultant in consultation with other stakeholders.

The debate about the consultants was taken one step further when the SDCEA formally addressed the Durban Metro Exco on 16 November 1998, requesting that the Council liaise directly with communities rather than communicate via consultants. The SDCEA believed that "the practice of using consultants to manage [the city's] responses to the challenges of new developments must cease."[15] Communities were concerned about the use by industry and government of consultants because they felt that their input was "watered down" by the time it reached government.

By August 1998, the SDCEA's frustration had grown to the extent that it resolved to make another direct appeal to Minister Asmal. In its submission, the SDCEA accused the provincial office of DWAF of creating barriers to their participation in the Mondi process. This accusation was made on the basis that the answers to questions put to the DWAF were "evasive and weak" and impeded the SDCEA's capacity to deal with destructive environmental injustices left over from the past.[16]

Minister Asmal's response was direct and apparently unambiguous. He immediately corresponded with the provincial DWAF office, questioning its condoning of the ash landfill site. He also agreed to visit the site and investigate the problem for himself. This was his third visit in four years to South Durban to deal with toxic waste sites.

The SDCEA took the opportunity to campaign in the area, alerting the community to the impending visit. For the first time in South Durban's environmental justice history, the local medical profession, the

Bayport Independent Practitioners' Association, supported the community in its campaign. In a letter to the SDCEA, the Association stated that "there is no doubt that environmental pollution has a large role to play in the causation and exacerbation of many common disease processes seen by us throughout the year." A local doctor, who was part of the SDCEA, went on record attesting to an increase in upper respiratory tract infections and dermatitis. It was also mentioned that cancer-related deaths were common in the community. In a significant assessment, a local doctor stated that chronic pollution had an effect on mental health.[17]

With support from the medical association, as well as the religious fraternity and local educators, the SDCEA was more confident in its approach. Minister Asmal was met by placard-bearing demonstrators in the rain outside Mondi on 2 November 1998. After discussions with the various stakeholders he stated that the site must be closed by 31 July 1999. However, DWAF was again equivocal in the manner in which it dealt with this issue. Instead of giving a firm message, Minister Asmal stated that "should Mondi be able to demonstrate and prove to the satisfaction of my Department that further on-site ash disposal can be undertaken without detrimental effects to the environment, including the human environment, and that there is full compliance with the minimum requirements and relevant legislation, then my Department will be prepared to reconsider the decision regarding closure and further ash disposal."[18]

Although the SDCEA accepted this intervention with some relief, members were cautious because Asmal's statement conflicted with the DWAF's Minimum Requirements: "Buffer zones are separations between the boundaries of registered landfill sites and residential developments. They may vary between 500 meters and 1000 meters in width, depending on the classification of the landfill. No residential development may take place within a proclaimed buffer zone. At the discretion of the local authority and the state departments, however, developments such as industrial development may be permitted" (DWAF 1998, G-1). In this case, houses were less than 500 meters from the landfill site to the north and west. Furthermore, the landfill site is closer than 3,000 meters to the Durban Airport runway in a southerly direction, within the one-in-fifty-year floodline, within close proximity to the Mlazi river, developed on a wetland, and upwind of the residential area. All these factors violate the present DWAF Minimum Requirements.[19]

Importantly, the SDCEA has also been vocal about ensuring that Mondi develops cleaner technology. Specifically, it has questioned why Mondi declined to change to a cleaner gas firing fuel that would not produce the kinds of hazardous ash that currently need to be landfilled, stating that economics should not be the only factor involved in the decisions about which fuels to use.[20] In response, Mondi cited financial concerns, maintaining that their responsibility extends not only to the surrounding community but also to their shareholders.[21]

The SCDEA has also insisted that Mondi does not simply relocate its hazardous ash waste site near another poor (and less politicized) neighborhood in an attempt to move the issue out of the spotlight. When Mondi attempted to do this, the SDCEA alerted the DWAF. It also queried "the use of ash in the police car pound at Isipingo."[22] The community has also raised concerns that Mondi might seek to dump the ash at the closed Umlazi IV landfill site.

These concerns and actions by SDCEA suggest that communities in South Durban have moved beyond the 'not in my back yard' (NIMBY) syndrome and are pressurizing Mondi to think more holistically about a solution to the hazardous ash waste problem. The human rights aspect of the environment has also been strongly invoked by the community in South Durban in their struggle against Mondi. This was evident in the petition signed by residents adjacent to Mondi before Minister Asmal's visit to the site on 2 November 1998. The petition called for the "community's civil and human rights to be redressed and for environmental injustices to be challenged through effective implementation of appropriate legislation." Responding to the fact that Mondi would be allowed to continue dumping ash until July 1999, a local community member stated that "socially, culturally, and philosophically, the placing of a dump site adjacent to any community is not an acceptable practice. This is also reflected in the new minimum requirements. . . . Agreeing on further dumping for nine months is a compromise enough from the people who have suffered for the last 30 years" (*Daily News,* 3 November 1998).

Lessons for Environmental Justice Struggles in South Africa

This is not the first time that environmental justice struggles in South Durban have been the subject of inquiry.[23] The lessons learned from the Mondi case will be viewed together with the lessons learned from the report of Wiley et al. (1996) in the hope that they will help other communities better to understand environmental justice struggles and assist them in the successful implementation of their own campaigns.

Consultation and Negotiation

- Outcomes of agreements and studies will be accepted only if all stakeholders agree to accept the consultants chosen to manage these processes. In the Umlazi and Bul-Bul[24] hazardous site processes, the monitoring committees accepted the work of the consultants because the consultants were acceptable to all the stakeholders.

- Investigations into developments that will impact on the environment should not only deal with quantitative assessments. Qualitative investigative research techniques should also be used, and authorities must deal directly with the affected community rather than through consultants.

- There must be no ambiguity in the objectives of the various stakeholders when entering into multi-stakeholder negotiations. Mondi invited the community to discuss alternatives to ash dumping in the area but it became apparent to the SDCEA that Mondi's concept of alternatives included continuing to dump. Wiley et al. (1996) mention that those who initiate consultation must state clearly the proposed terms of reference, including the topic and ground rules.

- Communities must improve their negotiating skills if they are to succeed in their environmental justice campaigns.

Technical, Scientific, and Legal Capacity

- Environmental justice campaigning will not succeed without the necessary technical, scientific, and legal assistance. As Eddie Koch (1991, 29–30) argued a decade ago, the need for "a skilled organisation that can consult community groups and offer skillfully re-searched advice . . . and which can provide accurate data to activist groups" is crucial. This is as true today as it was then. Furthermore, without the equivalent of a U.S.-style Environmental Protection Agency, and with the onus of environmental monitoring placed on civil society in South Africa, community access to credible scientific, technical, and legal services is all the more crucial.

Campaigning

- Campaigns must be multifaceted to be successful—the fact that the SDCEA was a broad coalition was critical to its achievements.

The Authorities and Legislation

- A community's capacity to deal with local environmental injustice is built on engaging the responsible authority and questioning the basis on which decisions have been made. The SDCEA accused the DWAF of inhibiting the development of its capacity by not answering satisfactorily the questions put to it.
- Decisions made by government officials must be clear and unambiguous; contradictions must be avoided.
- Permit processes and environmental impact assessments allow space for communities to engage with authorities in sustainable decision making.

Conclusion

South Africa's young democracy is faced with many challenges that have to be met by all stakeholders. The challenges are daunting, yet exciting. In attempting to reverse centuries of injustice, South Africa has a new Constitution, new legislation, and a new government. However, to nullify the environmental injustice still suffered by the poor and vulnerable, communities throughout the country need to question industrial and government practices. They must do so with the aim of supporting government's intentions to implement the Constitution and to pressurize industry to improve its practices. Communities must use the political space created within the new South Africa to translate their newfound democracy into reality.

More importantly, civil society, and in this context, the environmental justice sector, has to redefine and reshape the role it plays in a post-apartheid South Africa and move beyond protest politics against an illegitimate government. The government is now legitimate but many believe it has yet to deliver on all its promises. The dilemma facing civil society is whether to sit down at the negotiating table with government stakeholders as partners, or to play a watchdog role, or both.

Notes

1. The terms community and civil society are used throughout this case study. For purposes of clarity, "community" will refer specifically to residents living in the area affected by the hazardous ash landfill site. "Civil society" will be used to refer to community members working in conjunction with a broad range of nongovernmental organizations.

2. Letter dated 11 August 1995 written by EJNF to Minister Asmal raising the concerns of various community activists about hazardous waste sites in South Africa.

3. Minutes of the EJNF National Waste Workshop, Kempton Park, 11–12 September 1998.

4. Letter from Minister Kader Asmal to his Director-General, 8 May 1995.

5. Nine of these submissions constitute the short narratives interspersed between chapters in this book.

6. The South African Human Rights Commission is a statutory body (chap. 9, s181 of the Constitution of the Republic of South Africa) set up for the protection, development, attainment, monitoring of, and access to human rights in the country.

7. Minister Erwin's speech at a fund-raising dinner of the local chapter of the ANC, in Isipingo, South Durban, on 17 March 1999.

8. The Department of Water Affairs and Forestry (DWAF), through a permitting system for landfill sites, manages and enforces the necessary legal requirements on these sites. The Mondi landfill site could not be managed by DWAF for it had no permit. It could only be managed by the local Durban Metro authority for nuisance impact.

9. Letter from Minister of Water Affairs and Forestry Kader Asmal to the KwaZulu-Natal provincial office of the Department of Water Affairs and Forestry, 31 August 1998.

10. Letter from the Minister of the KwaZulu-Natal provincial office of the DWAF to Minister Asmal, 2 September 1998.

11. Background Information Document, Permit Application for Westlands Waste Site at Mondi Paper Merebank, July 1997.

12. Minutes of the first Working Group Meeting held at Mondi, 12 November 1997.

13. Report by the M L Sultan Technikon, Department of Chemistry, 24 November 1998.

14. Letter from the Department of Water Affairs and Forestry to Mr. R. Barton, General Manager of Mondi, 17 December 1998, in which the ash analysis undertaken by Mondi's consultants is categorized as hazardous.

15. The SDCEA was granted permission to make a presentation to Durban Metro Exco after the SDCEA had laid an objection with the Durban Mayor regarding the manner in which the Durban Metro Environmental Department was dealing with the sale of the land adjacent to Mondi, which would result in the plant encroaching onto the buffer strip between the community and Mondi, an industry regulated by the Hazardous Installations Regulations.

16. Letter from the SDCEA to the provincial office of the DWAF in KwaZulu-Natal, 27 August 1998, in response to the DWAF answers to questions raised by the SDCEA.

17. Letter from Dr. L. L. Naidoo to Minister Asmal, 1 November 1999, highlighting health problems in the South Durban Merebank residential area.

18. Statement by Minister Asmal at the ash disposal site, 2 November 1998.

19. This summation was contained in the background document prepared by the SDCEA for Minister Asmal titled *Landfill—Mondi Ash Site: A General Review with Questions and Answers*. The document was based on the DWAF minimum requirements and other legislative requirements. It was presented to Minister Asmal on the day he made his decision to close the Mondi Ash site.

20. Letter from the SDCEA to Mr. J. Barton, Managing Director of Mondi, 22 September 1998. The Environmental Justice Networking Forum KZN also supported this call for "cleaner and safe technology" (Letter from the EJNF to the Facilitator of the Mondi Ash Landfill Site Monitoring Committee, 26 January 1999).

21. Letter from Mondi to the facilitator of the Mondi Ash Landfill Monitoring Committee, 4 March 1999.

22. Monitoring committee for the Mondi Merebank Ash Landfill Site, Minutes of Meeting, 3 December 1998.

23. In 1995, the Durban City Council chose South Durban as one of three case studies focusing on the implementation of the principles of Local Agenda 21. Wiley et al. (1996) studied the various consultations, negotiations, and partnerships between the various levels of government, the South Durban community, and industry in South Durban, and drew lessons which facilitate understanding of the elements of successful consultation.

24. The Bul-Bul hazardous landfill site is on the border between Umlazi and the community of Chatsworth. This entire site slipped down the slope in September 1997.

References

CSIR (Council for Scientific and Industrial Research). 1999. *Draft Integrated Report: Strategic Environmental Assessment South Durban.* Durban: Council for Scientific and Industrial Research.

DEAT (Department of Environmental Affairs and Tourism). 1992. *Hazardous Waste in South Africa.* Pretoria: Department of Environmental Affairs and Tourism.

Department of Water Affairs and Forestry. 1998. *Minimum Requirements for Waste Disposal by Landfill, Second Edition.* Pretoria: Government Printer.

Earthlife Africa. 1996. "Submission to the Thor Chemicals Commission of Inquiry." Durban.

EJNF (Environmental Justice Networking Forum). 1998. *Environmental Justice Networker.*

groundWork. 2000. "Press release: SA Hosts International Basel Workshop While Deliberately Undermining Basel Decisions." Pietermaritzburg.

Hallowes, D. 2001. "Action Plan for South Durban Pollution." *groundWork Quarterly Newsletter* 3 (1).

Koch, E. 1991. "Rainbow Alliances: Community Struggles Around Ecological Problems." In J. Cock and E. Koch, eds. *Going Green: People, Politics and the Environment in South Africa.* Cape Town: Oxford University Press.

Lombard and Associates. 1995. "Group Reports and Proceedings." South Durban Multi-stakeholder Environmental Management Meeting, Durban City Jubilee Hall, 4 May.

Scott, D. 1994. *Communal Space Construction: The Rise and Fall of Clairwood and District.* Ph.D. thesis, University of Natal, Durban.

Singh, P. 1996. "Proceedings." Workshop to Discuss the Closure of the Umlazi IV Landfill Site, Durban.

Weinberg, P. 1991. Fighting the Factories. *New Ground* (Spring).

Wiley, D. 1996. "Environmentalism in the New South Africa: Conflict and Co-operation in Durban's Petrochemical Basin." Paper presented at the 1996 Annual Meeting of the African Studies Association, San Francisco.

Wiley, D., C. Root, S. Peek, and S. Ramurath. 1996. "Report on the State of the Environment and Development in the Durban Metropolitan Area, South Durban." Durban.

Where You Taste the Smell

Mpume Nyandu

About two kilometers from the Aloes Waste-tech dump site in Port Elizabeth in the Eastern Cape, one is greeted by plastic bags of various colors clinging to fences, littering and lining the road. But these are nothing compared to what welcomes you as you get closer to the site.

The air changes and suddenly you are confronted by an unbearable smell coming from waste sites where toxic waste products of all sorts are dumped. This is no ordinary bad smell. You don't only smell it, you taste it too. If you hang around the dump site area long enough, you are sure to get a headache and your tongue starts to taste and feel rubbery. This is no exaggeration. I experienced all of these sensations on a visit to the site that lasted less than two hours.

There is a landmark that you cannot help but notice at the dump site: the medical waste incinerator. Its chimney constantly puffs dark fumes in all directions, depending on the wind, affecting nearby communities. The three closest communities (within a few hundred meters) are the Corobrick, Vermaak, and Motherwell townships. The Vermaak community is the worst affected as it is trapped between the dump site and the incinerator. The incinerator chimney is at almost the same level as the houses in Vermaak, so when the wind blows their way the medical waste fumes go directly into people's homes.

The Vermaak community is an informal settlement on a hill in the area called Aloes. It is estimated that the first people to settle in the area arrived approximately seventy years ago. People in the community felt that, despite the problems of transport and unemployment they shared with many other black communities, they were leading a reasonably good life. The dump site and incinerator pollution have changed that. When the dump site was started (twenty years ago) and the incinerator was built (six years ago), none of the local communities was consulted.

Since then illnesses such as nasal and chest infections, particularly tuberculosis, have plagued the community. Daniel Pienaar, aged 74, one of the oldest surviving members, who arrived in the Aloes area in 1949, says: "We have been very unhappy and uncomfortable since Waste-tech came into this area. They started burning all sorts of things with very bad smells. As a result of this pollution a lot of people are now dead." Daniel says Waste-tech burns a variety of plastic containers and other waste from hospitals, including amputated body parts. He knows this because he once worked at the Waste-tech incinerator. As he puts it, "When I discovered that people's legs and arms also get burnt here, I decided to quit, I said I am not coming back, after working for only a day. I took my money and left."

As a result of the illnesses caused by pollution some people have lost jobs and others have been forced by ill health to stop work and apply for government grants. Jane Tanyongo, one of the oldest members of the Vermaak community, says: "My life changed completely after Waste-tech came with their incinerator and waste dump. I started having a sore neck and throat, then the nosebleeds followed, that is when I decided to go to the hospital. At the hospital they said I got this from the polluted area that I live in. I used to work in Sydenham as a domestic worker, I had to stop working because of ill-health. I now earn a government grant and I have to visit the doctor every month. I also have constant leg problems because my house is forever damp. The water causing the moisture comes from the toxic liquid waste ponds situated at the dump site."

Accompanied by a Waste-tech official who gave us a guided tour, we visited the infamous sites, informally named Aloes 1 and Aloes 2. Both sites are huge. Aloes 1, which is the old site, covers 8.6 hectares and the new site, Aloes 2, covers 6 hectares. The old site, which is being closed down, is a huge piece of filthy land, with holes in the ground filled with toxic and non-toxic materials, some exposed, some partially covered. Because the area is windy and dry contaminated dust from the site covers it. Aloes 2 is being built and is close to completion. Although it looks professional and expensive, it also contains the very smelly leachate pond, which at the time of the visit was full to the brim.

The official who accompanied us admitted the company was spending about R100,000 a month in an effort to contain the smell but to date had been unsuccessful. The pitch-black liquid cannot be disposed of elsewhere because it contains so much chloride. The Waste-tech official assured us that the dump would be removed in five years, but the community is not convinced.

In Jane Tanyongo's words, "Waste-tech is here to stay, they can't just spend so much money building more ponds only to pack up and go after five years."

In 1995, the Aloes Environmental Monitoring Committee was formed. It comprises members of the affected communities, Waste-tech, the municipality, and the Departments of Health and Water Affairs. "The committee was set up to monitor the health of the people," says Joan Couldridge, one of its members. "Instead it became a monitor of the management of the site. The people are still unhealthy, we want a proper medical examination for the people. So far we have been refused." Couldridge, together with the community, took up the fight against Waste-tech and the government to put a stop to the ongoing pollution in the Aloes area.

Their efforts are finally paying off. The Vermaak and Corobrick communities have been promised that they will receive title to land in Well's Estate, away from the dump site and about four kilometers from a formerly whites-only community (much to the displeasure of the latter).

However, it will take some time to restore the Vermaak community's faith in government. "As far as I can see, we will end up dying here because the government is not paying any attention to our problems," says Mr Pienaar. He adds, "We voted the government into power but we are not seeing anything happening."

Chapter 9

A Political Economy of Dam Building and Household Water Supply in Lesotho and South Africa

Patrick Bond

We in South Africa need the water from the Lesotho Highlands Water Project to meet the increase in our demand, and, in particular, to meet the needs of previously neglected communities.

—President Nelson Mandela in a 1995 letter to World Bank President James Wolfensohn (cited in Asmal 1996, 2)

We are changing the very flow of water to bring development to our people.

—Minister of Water Affairs and Forestry Kader Asmal. Opening of the Lesotho Highlands Water Project, 22 January 1998

The [Lesotho Highlands Water] Project provides an opportunity to advance the debate that not all big dams are necessarily bad.

—John Roome, World Bank LHWP Taskmanager Project Appraisal Document for $45 million LHWP loan (World Bank 1998, 18)

The recent military intervention by South Africa and Botswana in Lesotho had demonstrated the Southern African Development Community's commitment to creating a climate conducive to foreign investment, Deputy

*President Thabo Mbeki told a high-powered investment
conference in the city yesterday.*
—Cape Times, 2 December 1998

*The fundamental problem is that of unrelenting capital
accumulation and the extraordinary asymmetrics of money
and political power that are embedded in that process.
Alternative modes of production, consumption, distribution
as well as alternative modes of environmental
transformation have to be explored if the discursive spaces
of the environmental justice movement and the theses of
ecological modernisation are to be conjoined in a
programme of radical political action.*
—David Harvey (1996, 401)

The Lesotho Highlands Water Project (LHWP) is an $8 billion, multi-phase water supply infrastructure project designed to divert rain water and runoff from the Senqu/Orange River through a series of five dams and tunnels, across the mountains of Lesotho, to the urban and industrial heartland of South Africa hundreds of kilometers to the north. In addition to providing water, the LHWP also generates a small amount of hydropower and it is anticipated that it will ultimately provide $50 million in annual revenues to the government of Lesotho. The LHWP is Africa's largest single construction project, and Katse Dam is the continent's highest dam at 185 meters. That dam and 70 kilometers of diversion tunnels (together constituting "Phase 1A") were completed in January 1998 at a cost of $2.5 billion, and the $1.5 billion construction of the Mohale Dam (Phase 1B) proceeded almost immediately.

After considering the bulk of evidence associated with debates over the dam, this chapter concludes that the LHWP is a costly, corrupt, poorly designed, badly implemented, economically damaging, ecologically disastrous, and distributionally regressive megaproject. Yet the project is still advertised as critical to South Africa's development, and even as a symbol of a new and improved mode of regional cooperation.

To illustrate, the Katse Dam's distorted importance to the South African government was reflected, in September 1998, in the route the South African National Defence Force took during the controversial invasion aimed at propping up an unpopular government which had effectively been overthrown a few days before. Rather than deploy troops to patrol the capital city, Maseru, which was soon burned to the ground by looters (apparently because Botswana-based troops dawdled on their way to protect the city), a platoon from the Bloemfontein-based 44 Parachute Brigade moved rapidly far up into the Lesotho mountains (Southall 1998). A *Sunday Independent* journalist (14 February 1999) later reported from Maseru:

> The common perception here is that two South African helicopters flew to the site of the dam which was being guarded by Lesotho Defense Force (LDF) troops. From the air, they opened fire on the sleeping soldiers. South African special forces troops were then landed and massacred any LDF man they could find alive. The only dispute, especially in the highland villages near the dam, is the numbers killed. Some say 16, which is the official figure; others say 27. A serving South African officer, on condition of anonymity, maintained that "a certain captain" had perhaps been "rather overzealous" in securing the Katse dam. But he insisted that the context should be understood. When the South African troops entered Lesotho, they were aware that some opposition politicians had threatened to blow up the dam and there was a real fear that troops at the dam might damage the installation. . . . The anger apparently triggered the rioting, directed initially at the many South African businesses in Maseru, but which soon spread to all foreign businesses. Once the rioting started, indiscriminate looting began and spread rapidly. "Nobody stopped them. South African soldiers just laughed and Basotho soldiers were looting too," said an Indian shopkeeper whose store was burned to the ground and who now works as a casual shop assistant. "They brought trucks and took away furniture on the top of cars." In the aftermath, Lesotho has

had to deal with the loss of as many as 20,000 jobs in central Maseru and a massive dent in already badly battered investor confidence. It also faces ongoing bickering among the three major and nine minor political parties, widespread disillusionment with the entire political process and considerable anger and resentment about the events of recent months. All in all, an extremely volatile mix. But the water has begun to flow to South Africa from the multi-billion rand investment in the mountains and millions in royalties have begun to flow into the coffers of Lesotho. Given that the financial stakes are so high and the local political fabric so fragile, *Pax South Africanus* seems here to stay.

For South Africa, the damage included not only two South African troops and two medics killed in the Katse firefight, but the souring of longer-term bilateral relations and the first appearance in Pretoria of a vigorous sub-imperialist strain of regional geopolitics. According to a March 2000 report by *Mail & Guardian* journalists (*Mail & Guardian*, 20–26 March 2000):

Some Basotho are crying "cover-up" after Lesotho authorities who invited the SA National Defence Force in the first place moved to keep the matter out of the courts. And a senior Lesotho royal charges that the South African government and Nelson Mandela, president at the time, have ignored repeated requests for an explanation. . . . Meanwhile, Prince Seeiso, brother of King Letsie III, this week said relations with South Africa remained strained by the Katse incident. The Lesotho royal family is known to have opposed the SADC intervention and is seen as loosely allied to the democratic opposition. Seeiso, emphasising he spoke not on behalf of Letsie but as an individual and a principal chief, said he has been asking South African ministers to explain the Katse killings, but without success. His understanding was that LDF soldiers did not provoke the attack. "The helicopters came and circled the area. As soon as people came out to see what was happening, they were done for."

How sensible was South Africa's military prioritization of Katse, not to mention the billions of rands pumped into the LHWP, plus many more billions in the future? For critics, the LHWP represents the worst traditions of Western development 'solutions' to what in reality are problems associated with irrational apartheid-capitalist resource utilization, particularly South Africa's extraordinarily unequal distribution of water. The LHWP exacerbates these underlying problems by the way it merely 'bandaids' a symptom: future water shortages in the Johannesburg metropolis. At the same time, the LHWP worsens an enduring development crisis—unavailability of water—by increasing costs to impoverished urban users without reference to their needs.

This chapter reflects arguments and advocacy in favor of a wholly different approach ("demand-side management"), and in doing so, unveils divergent discursive approaches to environmental justice associated with the LHWP. In short, say activists from Alexandra township, rather than flowing through Johannesburg townships' water and sewerage pipes, which are riddled with apartheid-era leaks that drain some 40 percent of the incoming water, at a retail price far higher (the World Bank recommends five times higher, Roome 1995) than existing water sources, Lesotho's water should flow along its natural course through the Free State and Northern Cape to the Atlantic Ocean. Township pipes and taps should be repaired forthwith and Johannesburg's hedonistic corporate and high-income residential water consumers, as well as inefficient Vaal River catchment area farmers, should pay much more for water in the interests both of conservation and of social justice. Lesotho's own development options should be dramatically widened in the process, with the aim of ending the bizarre residues of neocolonial dependency associated with migrant labor bondage to South Africa, foreign debt-peonage, and the legacy of myriad misguided development projects (Ferguson 1990).

This was the essence of the argument of civic leaders in Alexandra and Soweto in late 1997 and early 1998. It was even endorsed by the neoliberal *Business Day* newspaper's environmental reporter (*Business Day*, 19 March 1998), as well as by a variety of environmental pressure groups. The critique was then taken to the World Bank's Inspection Panel (a kind of auditor-general) in April 1998 by three Alexandra residents (the relevant documentation, including official reaction, can be found in Letsie and Bond [2000]).

But such arguments have their costs, and a political backlash suddenly hit the Alexandra residents. A subset of key civic movement leaders changed position in the wake of intense political intimidation (in the form of a threatening letter from Water Affairs Minister Kader Asmal, and ANC branch-level pressure on them). Likewise, water sector professionals associated with the National Water Conservation Campaign and Rand Water (the catchment area water board serving greater Johannesburg) reversed their previous public opposition to LHWP expansion. An important Lesotho church group also retreated from what appeared to be a certain legal confrontation with the Bank over compensation for displaced residents. The argument against LHWP was publicly, and vociferously, rejected by Bank staff and by Asmal, who had just been named chair of the World Commission on Dams, and his Director-General, Mike Muller, largely on grounds of the threat of drought (*Mail & Guardian*, 8–14 May 1998). In July 1998, the U.S. executive director to the World Bank, Jan Piercy, refused even to meet the Alexandra residents, though they were a five-minute drive away from her five-star Sandton hotel. In August, the Inspection Panel also rejected the critique, following a visit and questionable analysis by James MacNeill. Matters seemed to have subsided, even as *Business Day*'s Simon Barber (9 September 1998) celebrated the defeat of the redistributive argument.

Over the next two years, the protesters' proposed alternative strategy—demand-side management partly through higher tariffs for luxury consumption and partly through fixing water system leaks—took a back seat to supply enhancement. The vast majority of national water project financing was directed towards supply enhancement—especially major dams in the Tugela and Mkomazi basins, the Mzimvubu basin, the Orange River, and the Western Cape—notwithstanding the fact that such new sources of water would be physically exhausted within three decades (*Saturday Star*, 3 November 1998). When a major new aquifer was discovered in the Western Cape in late 2000, water bureaucrats had even less reason to impose conservation measures on the most hedonistic households, such as those in Constantia, Cape Town, whose consumption was measured at 1,800 liters each day.

At that point other factors began to emerge that warranted a fresh look at the debate over dams and water access. Further government studies of downstream flow reduction in the Orange River confirmed the potential for an LHWP-initiated ecological catastrophe, as environmentalists had long predicted (Hoover 2000). Moreover, the overriding logic of the LHWP critique based on socioeconomic justice issues was quite sound, as recognized, ironically, throughout the final report of the World Commission on Dams in November 2000. (Residents of both the Lesotho highlands and Alexandra township celebrated the report by jointly calling for a moratorium on further dam construction.)

Simultaneously, the need for dramatic expansion of clean water access was amplified by a cholera outbreak caused by cutoffs of free water supplies, affecting low-income rural households in KwaZulu-Natal province. By mid-2001, over 100,000 people had been infected and over 200 had died. Soon after the outbreak began, a Constitutional Court case brought by Cape Town shack settlement leader Irene Grootboom finally guaranteed socioeconomic rights (such as water) to low-income citizens.

All this occurred during the run-up to a crucial round of municipal elections (December 2000), so President Thabo Mbeki conceded to demands being made by trade unionists and NGOs for a lifeline supply of water (and electricity), placing "free services" in prime position amongst ANC electoral campaign promises. But no one really anticipated that the election promises—which in any case had already been made in the 1994 Reconstruction and Development Programme—would be kept. Instead, unaffordable retail tariffs associated with water supply in Johannesburg (indeed in all of Gauteng province) would continue to hamper water access well into the twenty-first century. Moreover, the planned "iGoli 2002" corporatization of metro Johannesburg's water supply (via a consortium led by a French firm involved in LHWP construction and corruption) implied yet further upward pricing pressure regardless of ANC promises.

These water-related complications have generated challenges to the so-called 'brown' agenda—*urban ecology,* particularly as it relates to (black) residents with low incomes—for decades to come. The problems were particularly poignant and indeed ironic in January 1998, when a predicted El Nino drought failed to materialize and the first flow of LHWP water to Gauteng was turned back from the already-overflowing Vaal River. But the price increases on low-income consumer bills were not similarly redirected.

In all these respects, the LHWP has become an important symbol of the extent to which the post-apartheid South African government is willing to listen and respond to socioenvironmental-justice critiques of its policies and pet projects. The LHWP story provides, too, a measure of whether arguments involving both technical and moral claims can be taken seriously within the World Bank. Throughout, the Bank was the central organizer of technical, financial, social, and ecological information about the LHWP, and will continue in this vein in future. Hence its involvement raises interesting questions about the professional competence and participatory orientation of the world's single-largest institutional investor in infrastructure, questions that Alexandra Township residents put to the Inspection Panel and that deserve further consideration below. After a review of the political context for the LHWP, the social, environmental, and economic critiques can be considered. These critiques are appropriate for all bulk infrastructure projects, and pose doubts about the Bank's commitment to distributional justice and accountability—doubts also reflected in other settings across the world (Fox and Brown 1998).

Ultimately, this chapter also considers the merits of different ecological discourses emerging from particular social struggles, or as Raymond Williams termed them, "militant particularisms." Contrasting discourses are intrinsic to the diverse politics of localities, but some political-ecological themes may have more universal discursive undertones. As leading U.S. antitoxics activist Lois Gibbs (cited in Harvey 1996, 389) has argued, the growing environmental justice movement takes the position "what is morally correct?" instead of "what is legally, scientifically, and pragmatically possible?" This position, insists David Harvey (1996, 389), "permits, through the medium of social protest, the articulation of ideas about a moral economy of collective provision and collective responsibility as opposed to a set of distributive relations within the political economy of profit."

In order to track the debate over the LHWP it is important to explore the difference between environmental justice rhetoric and an ecological modernization discourse locked within "the political economy of profit." The clearest statement of ecological modernization objectives is found in the United Nations *Declaration on Environment and Development* signed in Rio in June 1992 (Principle 16): "to promote the internalisation of environmental costs and the use of economic instruments, taking into account the approach that the polluter should, in principle, bear the cost of pollution, with due regard to the public interest and without distorting international trade and investment."

What the LHWP's green and brown critics have mainly done thus far is argue on legal, scientific, and economic grounds that environmental and human damage in Lesotho has *not* been internalized (and often not even recognized), and in particular, that Phase 1B should not be built for at least another couple of decades so that more attention can be paid to improving water delivery systems from the demand side. As we shall see, this argument was not successful, at least initially, with the World Bank Inspection Panel, although it won the blessing of the World Commission Dams' final report.

But even though the Commission report gave both the green and brown critics' case more credibility, it still remains for public anger to build in Johannesburg as water tariffs increase, as water continues to be shut off notwithstanding extraordinary public health risks, and as the logic of water commodification and even privatization continues to crowd out the public interest. Then, as has happened there and elsewhere so many times before, major social movements could mobilize around demands for water that have not been met even though access to water is codified as a human right in South Africa's 1996 Constitutional Bill of Rights.

The Political Context

The political background to the five-stage LHWP is long and convoluted. The boundaries of Lesotho were drawn in the mid-nineteenth century, when invading European settlers of Dutch and British ancestry forced the Basotho people off the rich farming area now known as South Africa's Free State province, into the neighboring mountains. Under subsequent British colonial rule, the LHWP was conceived in 1954, twelve years before Lesotho's independence. Formal government planning began in the mid-1970s, and by the early 1980s, with protest in South Africa reemerging and international sanctions beginning to gather momentum, violence broke out within Lesotho over the potential water sales to the apartheid government. Lesotho's Prime Minister, Leabua Jonathan, reacted by agreeing to the LHWP only on condition that he would control the outflow of water to South Africa. A coup, backed by South Africa, followed in 1985 and Lesotho's new military regime pressed ahead with the alliance (Southall 1998).

In the mid-1980s the South African government was at the height of its pariah status, and welcomed the international legitimacy that a cross-border project, catalyzed by the World Bank, would bring the apartheid regime. In October 1986, as harsh repression and states of emergency—as well as the foreign debt repayment "standstill" of September 1985—foreclosed any chances of South African access to foreign funds, the LHWP Treaty was announced and given controversial financial support by the Bank. This is worth considering in some detail in view of the late 1990s campaign for cancellation of (and reparation of lending profits associated with) apartheid-era debt (Horter 1996; Bond 1997).

Although the World Bank's sister organization, the International Monetary Fund, had granted apartheid South Africa a $1.1 billion loan as late as 1982 (following which it was banned by most Western governments from ever doing so again), the Bank's last lending relations with Pretoria were during the late 1960s. But the Bank lent Lesotho—with its $450 per capita income—$110 million for the LHWP because of South Africa's ability to stand surety, and indeed the only financial risk analysis in the Bank's initial report concerned whether Pretoria would default. At a conference on the LHWP sponsored by the Johannesburg NGO, Group for Environmental Monitoring, in August 1996, Michael Potts (1996, 1) of the Development Bank of Southern Africa (DBSA, an LHWP funder) conceded, "Given the limited access to foreign funds by the South African government and the limitations on contractors' funding proposals—export credit was not available to South Africa—a very complex treaty was negotiated to bypass [anti-apartheid financial] sanctions." In order to arrange the financing package, the World Bank also lent Lesotho $8 million at concessionary rates through its International Development Association, in order to disguise what Asmal himself has referred to as "sanctions busting" (*Business Report,* 1 December 1997, 1). Recounts environmental activist Korinna Horter (1996, 16):

> According to the Bank's project report, preparations for project financing were so complex that it required "the amount of staff work that would normally go into about 10 projects." That was because Lesotho did not have the credit-worthiness needed to obtain the major international funding

required for Phase 1A, and giving the money directly to apart-heid South Africa was politically unacceptable. World Bank documents show that the Bank was concerned about "the project being perceived as being in the Republic of South Africa's interest" and about other possible co-financiers' "political sensitivities" about aiding the apartheid regime. To assuage the other lenders' "sensitivities," the World Bank helped set up a trust fund in Britain through which South Africa could service its debt.

In August 1996, Asmal (1996, 2) told the NGO conference of his own later reversal on support for the LHWP:

Ten years ago I was opposing the LHWP Treaty on political grounds and now I am called on to ensure its implementa-tion. In the intervening years many things have changed, including, crucially, the relationship between Lesotho and South Africa, from a relationship of client-state and pariah Big Broeder to that of democratic equals.

This assessment of power relations was thrown into question a couple of weeks later, when a construction subsidiary of Anglo American Cor-poration experienced labor problems at the Buthe Buthe construction site and called on the local police to intervene; at least five workers were killed before peace was restored (Bond 1997). And just over two years after Asmal expressed his sense of restructured regional geopolitics came the controversial post-coup invasion.

Indeed, throughout the 1990s the capital of Maseru was rocked by popular protests and occasionally violent infighting between military factions. Conflict between three nationalist political parties intensified in the late 1990s over the spoils of a shrinking state, in part because the steady demise of South African mining employment during the 1990s meant that Lesotho's economy had even fewer resources to share among a desperately poor population.

Under such stressful economic conditions, Lesotho politics were profoundly affected by transnational construction corporations angling for a share of the enormous project. In August 1999, a court case was heard against the Basothu chief executive officer of the Lesotho Highlands Development Authority (LHDA), Masupha Sole. Prosecutors with access to Sole's Swiss bank accounts argued that between 1988 and 1998 he had successfully extracted at least $2 million in bribes from some of the largest construction firms in the world, including ABB of Switzerland, Impregilo of Italy, and Dumez of France (which is owned by Lyonnais des Eaux, a regular subject of corruption charges) (*Business Day,* 5 August 1999; *Washington Post,* 13 August 1999). According to the charge sheet, the firms allegedly paid the following into Sole's personal accounts:

- ABB, $40,410;
- Impregilo, $250,000;
- Sogreah, $13,578;
- Lahmeyer International, $8,674;
- Highlands Water Venture consortium (Impregilo, the German firm Hochtief, the French firm Bouygues, UK firms Keir International and Stirling International, and South African firms Concor and Group Five), $733,404;
- Lesotho Highlands Project Contractors consortium (Balfour Beatty, Spie Batignolles, LTA, and ED Zublin), $57,269;
- Acres International (Canada), $185,002;
- Spie Batignolles (France), $119,393;
- Dumez International (France), $82,422;
- ED Zublin (Germany), $444,466;
- Diwi Consulting (Germany), $2,439; and
- LHPC Chantiers, $63,959.

Denials followed, including the important rebuttal by the World Bank that a letter from a key Bank official (Patel 1994) to the Lesotho government more than six years after the corruption began, demanding that Sole *not* be fired—so as not to "seriously jeopardize the progress of the project," on the grounds that Lesotho "shall consult with the Bank prior to making changes to its senior staff appointments" and threatening "legal action"—was drafted without knowledge that Sole was corrupt. The Bank subsequently stated, in a letter to the International Rivers Network, that it only learned of the corruption in June 1999 (cited in Environmental Defense Fund and International Rivers Network 1999, 3).

Was the LHWP yet another Third World case of a white elephant project inappropriately financed with hard currency and replete with documented evidence of corruption and winks/nods from the World Bank? If so, should the people of Lesotho and South Africa be responsible for repaying the loans associated with the LHWP? Jubilee 2000, a global network of social movements that emerged in the late 1990s with the explicit objective of questioning the legitimacy of Third World debt believes the answer is no. Jubilee 2000 South Africa launched a campaign to repudiate—and to demand reimbursement of earlier payments of—what was termed "apartheid-caused debt" as a component of more general "odious debt" (which by international precedent did not have to be repaid if it was shown that the original debtor was illegitimate) (Ashley 1997; World Development Movement and Action for Southern Africa 1998).

Jubilee's main opponents were a much more powerful bloc of apartheid-era creditors for LHWP Phase 1A, including the World Bank ($110 million), European export credit agencies ($304 million), South Africa's export credit agency ($107 million), Banque Nationale de Paris ($19.7 million), Crédit Lyonnais ($17 million), Dresdner Bank ($15.8 million), Hill Samuel ($14.5 million), Commonwealth Development Corporation ($36 million), European Investment Bank, African Development Bank, and Pretoria's Development Bank of Southern Africa.

In view of the prevailing balance of forces, the post-apartheid South African government adopted a posture of active hostility to, and misinformation about, the apartheid debt campaign (*Sowetan,* 24 June 1998; *Sunday Independent Business Report,* 8 November 1998; for rebuttals see *Sowetan,* 30 June 1998; *Sunday Independent,* 15 November 1998; and *Sunday Independent Business Report,* 15 November 1998). But failing to locate allies within the South African state did not prevent Jubilee 2000 SA from promoting, in Harvey's words, "through the medium of social protest, the articulation of ideas about a moral economy of collective provision and collective responsibility." The immediate political challenge, however, remains the strengthening of links between such abstract campaigning for economic justice and concrete campaigns already established by (green) advocates of social and environmental justice in Lesotho and (brown) advocates of socioenvironmental justice in Johannesburg's townships.

The Green Critique

What were the criticisms of the LHWP? In the Highlands, socioeconomic and environmental problems associated with the LHWP should have been ameliorated by World Bank staff and allied planners through the Lesotho government's Rural Development Programme and fund. The fund, however, was soon embroiled in corruption scandals (as was the Muela hydropower scheme), and royalty through-flows were scaled back to better match "absorptive capacity."

But even had the fund been properly allocated, amelioration of the socioecological problems was never as straightforward as planners had expected. Phase 1A directly displaced 2,000 people—approximately 300 households—but indirectly affected at least 20,000 more who lost the use of common resources or income through the submersion of 925 hectares of arable and 3,000 hectares of grazing land. Ancestral burial grounds were also flooded. In the relatively barren Maluti Mountains, tiny woodlots and fields for cultivation and grazing are guarded carefully by local peasants. But sufficient numbers and quality of replacement trees were not provided once the water began to rise. For those peasants who lost their fuel wood, cash compensation—as little as R1 per square meter, even for thickets of full-grown poplar—was inadequate to pay for alternative fuels.

LHWP authorities initially provided the peasants with inadequate replacement fodder for cattle, and failed in some cases to give local people access to construction jobs. Moreover, valuable topsoil inundated by the Phase 1A water was either never recovered or was diverted to the gardens of European and South African consultants living in the area rather than to those displaced by the rising waters. Many of the latter were given low-quality replacement housing that amounted to little more than uninsulated storage shedding. Women, children, and the elderly were particularly hard hit. According to Mathato Khitsane of the Highlands Church Action Group, "The project shows no sensitivity to the impact on gender issues and roles of women" (Bond 1997). In 1997, church surveys indicated widespread dissatisfaction on the part of many residents with resettlement schemes and provisions for reimbursement (Lori Pottinger personal communication).

Notwithstanding Asmal's periodic commitments to increase levels of compensation (Asmal 1998a, 1998b), the disputes continued (*Business*

Report, 26 November 1998). According to Hoover (2000), studies showed that "Household income figures for the LHWP northeastern mountain region fell 65 percent faster than the national average during the LHWP's initial years."

In November 1999 people from the Makotoko, Matala, and Ha Nkokana communities displaced by the Katse and Mohale dams testified at NGO hearings about their experiences, as part of the World Commission on Dams process (Environmental Monitoring Group et al. 1999, 6.6.1–6.6.3):

> MALISEMELO TAU: The LHDA project told us . . . if we move away there, and the project builds a dam there, that water can save many people's lives. We agreed to move away to save many people's lives with our water and we hoped that the project will be trusted to satisfy us with all that it promised to do for us because we save many people's lives. . . . When we did research at our destination, we found that there is no water until now. We have a great problem of water at the new village. We get water from the river by wheelbarrows. We drink water from the river and the river is very far from us. . . . The owners of that place resettled by LHDA have tears running on down their cheeks every day.

> ANNA MOEPI: Ladies and Gentlemen, our lives before the Lesotho Highlands Water Project was a nice one. We were living in peace and harmony. . . . Our lives in the new location leave a lot to be desired. . . . You see our lives as deteriorating day by day. We are worse off. . . . The project had initially promised that we would be trained on self-reliant projects that would include income-generating activities. Nothing is happening.

> BENEDICT LEUTA: The roads that they have built are the only good thing I can think of about the Lesotho Highlands Water Project. . . . But the roads also destroyed a lot. The road culverts cause erosion in our fields. And in my village we had some wells that were covered by the road. . . . After the road covered them, we received no compensation. We

had to pay the government to come help us bring water down from high in the mountains. . . . We are less healthy after the dam has been built. . . . Also the chiefs gained because they were sub-contracted to LHDA and also received bribes from many people. . . . The affected people were the losers. Some people lost their land and received no compensation or employment.

Compensation for lost land, social goods, and livelihoods was not the only social challenge. In addition, the LHWP's role in the socioeconomic modernization of Lesotho villages brought with it a dramatic increase in AIDS. Already by 1992, 5 percent of construction workers were HIV positive, and high rates of transmission to local villagers were observed in one major study (Kravitz et al. 1995). As Asmal (1996, 4) conceded, "Social problems such as increased alcohol abuse, increased sexually-transmitted disease and increased stock theft have all been reported in villages along the new Katse Road." However, he continued:

These negative impacts must be weighted against the benefits arising from the project, including access to improved health and educational facilities, water supply to communities, sanitation at schools, and, at villages close to the sites, the construction of community halls, community offices, creches, open markets and road access. One must also weigh in the benefit of employment opportunities for local people, both in the construction phase and in the considerable long-term maintenance tasks.

Indeed, 157 latrines were installed in eight schools, and in seven villages trenches were dug for water supplies, the former with nearly ninety kilometers of unrelated feeder roads to be constructed by 1999. But this was relatively small consolation when considered in the context of the $2.5 billion cost of Phase 1A. And while the introduction of tarred roads into the area brought increased trade, it also resulted in the closure of the major local store. The effect of more than a decade of road building in the Lesotho Highlands, anthropologist James Ferguson (1990) has shown, was to impoverish peasants further, as markets undermined local food production and officials milked more taxes and fees from the now accessible peasants.

Likewise, Phase 1B inundated 550 hectares of extremely good crop-land and forced the resettlement of four hundred families. This, added to the fact that much of Lesotho's arable land had been eroded over the past three decades, means that less than 9 percent of the country's soil is available for cultivation. Phase 1B not only exacerbated land hunger, but destroyed crucial habitats of the Maluti Minnow (an endangered species), bearded vulture, and four other species considered "globally threatened" (Horter 1995, 1996; Pottinger 1996).

Other potential ecological problems associated with the LHWP have also emerged. The early feasibility studies—conducted by a British-German consortium—failed to include an Environmental Impact Assessment, which resulted in cost overruns of 15 percent caused by an unanticipated need to line the Katse tunnels with cement. Moreover, soil erosion and sedimentation—which typically lowers dam capacity by 1 percent per year and silts intake areas—were not initially taken into consideration. In two similar cases, elsewhere, after sedimentation was finally factored into India's infamous Sardar Sarovar Dam it tipped the balance towards cancellation of the Bank's involvement; and reservoir-induced earthquakes in the Highlands village of Mapeleng generated a crack 1.5 kilometers long, damaging nearly seventy houses and diverting an important water spring from the surface (Bond 1997).

Moreover, there is also a chance that the LHWP's environmental flaws will backlash against South Africa itself. According to Snaddon, Wishart, and Davies (1996, 7):

> The LHWP will eventually divert 2.2 $H10^9m^3y-1$ from the Headwaters of the Orange River in Lesotho, into the Ash/ Liebenbergsvlei tributary of the Vaal River in the Free State. This will be the largest Inter-Basin Transfer in southern Africa, and it will result in considerable alterations of the rivers concerned. These systems will remain unstable for a very long time. The overall environmental effects of the LHWP have not adequately been assessed, and assessments of the instream flow requirements of the rivers involved in the scheme have focussed only on the donor systems.

The South African Department of Water Affairs and Forestry's (DWAF) original *Orange River Project Replanning Study* made very superficial estimates of downstream irrigation needs (ignoring, for instance, any new requirements for emergent black farmers). DWAF (1996, 4) admitted that even in 1996 it could not "yet claim that it has conclusively determined the present and future irrigation water requirements in the study area."

Free State University Zoology Professor Maitland Seaman (1996, 6) warned that "The [Orange] river might even dry up in exceptional years" because of the LHWP.

A 1999 *Orange River Development Project Replanning Study* by consultants BKS and Ninham Shand evaded most of the thorny issues, continuing, for example, to assume that there would be no increase in water available for irrigation. The study found that when the Mohale Dam "starts to impound water, the excess water available for hydropower generation will be significantly reduced" (DWAF 1999, 7–8). The study suggested that further LHWP dams beyond Mohale would be inefficient for diversion, compared to the potential for pumping more than four times as much water from the Orange River into the Vaal River from a large new proposed dam further downstream from Lesotho (at Boskraai).

Indeed, Lesotho's own access to water is also a matter of great concern, notwithstanding that the BKS/Ninham Shand study incorrectly assumed that "formal water use along the Senqu River and its tributaries is very small and was taken to be accounted for by the compensation and environmental releases for the dams" and hence "no further allowance was made" for Lesotho's water needs (DWAF 1999, 7–6). In reality, virtually all other experts and commentators argue that there is insufficient water in the country to share with South Africa beyond the LHWP's Phase 2. Even up to Phase 2, "critically severe" biophysical and social impacts of water diversion can be anticipated, according to an official 1999 Instream Flow Requirement study of the Senqu within Lesotho. At $51m^3s^{-1}$, the extraction of water along the lines anticipated in the LHWP Treaty would have mitigation and compensation implications of 20 million maluti per year (with still "moderate to severe" impacts under the lowest-extraction scenario of $44m^3s^{-1}$) (Metsi Consultants 1999, x). As things stood, predicted one senior Southern African Development Community official (Lengolo Monyake), within ten to thirty years Lesotho would face severe water scarcity (*Saturday Star*, 3 November 1998).

The social and ecological problems within Lesotho associated with the LHWP not only led to local criticism, they gained the attention of international activist/advocacy NGOs like Christian Aid, the Environmental Defense Fund (EDF), and the International Rivers Network (IRN). LHWP opponents began badgering the World Bank to provide more compensation to displaced people and address the ecological damage. The activists represented, according to the *Saturday Star* (3 November 1998):

> a loose coalition of environmental lobbyists, NGOs and churches. Leadership essentially comes from the California-based International Rivers Network, whose Africa coordinator, Lori Pottinger, has visited Lesotho to collect the views of villagers and has been tireless in her criticisms of the scheme, over the Internet and at conferences. The coalition also includes South African bodies such as the Group for Environmental Monitoring and the Southern African Rivers Association. Increasingly, the media in South Africa and Lesotho are carrying letters and articles questioning the high social and environmental costs and the political ramifications of the scheme.

In light of these concerns, it is revealing to consider Bank LHWP Task-manager John Roome's (World Bank 1998, 18) own assessment of "possible controversial aspects" of the LHWP:

> The project has been in the spotlight from international NGOs. Although a detailed study of meetings and consultations have been undertaken, some International NGOs (e.g., EDF, IRN) may not support the Bank's decision to proceed with the funding of Phase 1B at this time—partly related to the issues set out below (basically judgment calls on whether progress in Phase 1A has been satisfactory and whether the economics of delays to Phase 1B are acceptable), but partly on principle as part of the larger "big dams" debate. This has taken further importance with the appointment of Prof. Asmal (the SA minister concerned) as Chair of the recently established World Commission on Dams. The argument

against large dams contends that they: are not economically viable; are not socially acceptable; are environmentally disastrous; can be a major cause of impoverishment, and can result in unacceptably high international debt. For this project however, the economics show that this is lowest cost supply, has a good Economic Rate of Return and demand management is being put in place; Socially the numbers involved are low, there has been "good planning" but implementation is key; Environmentally the impact is limited and has been well managed; Poverty-wise the project supports poverty reduction activities and does not squeeze out other activities; and fiscally SA bears the debt, not Lesotho and users pay—not tax payers. . . . Local NGOs have been critical of the Lesotho Highlands Development Authority's level of performance on the social aspects of the project. The Lesotho Council of NGOs has however recently signed a declaration endorsing the implementation of the project. They agree that LHDA's performance has improved in recent years, but they argue that there is still room for further improvement. One local NGO (Highlands Church Solidarity and Action Centre) has from time to time taken a more aggressive stance against the project—supporting calls for Phase 1B to be delayed. As of mid-March 1998 they seemed to support the Lesotho Council of NGOs' position and have no objection to the project proceeding to Phase 1B.

On the one hand, a senior bank official acknowledged that Christian AID, IRN, and EDF "created space for greater Bank and government attention to mitigation measures," which in turn, concluded Fox and Brown (1998, 511), "reflects a broader pattern in which public pressure from Northern NGOs encourages World Bank officials to grant more legitimacy to local NGOs as alternative interlocutors." On the other hand, this was also a recipe for co-optation, even temporarily, and not only of Lesotho's NGOs (which Roome recorded above). As discussed below, there also arose an urgent need for the Bank and the South African government to co-opt (or failing that, intimidate) local organizations on the other side of the border, once the green critics were joined by critics from Soweto and

Alexandra. For in 1998 the stakes suddenly rose when Johannesburg township organizations began to argue for a long delay in Phase 1B.

The Brown Critique

The LHWP is, in the discourse of the South African state, a developmental project. The statements from Mandela and Asmal cited above indicate this. The reality, though, appears to be different: the LHWP makes the provision of water to low-income, black Johannesburg residents more, not less, difficult. The LHWP water will primarily be used by Vaal-area farmers (who will pay a small, highly subsidized share of the cost once DWAF's National Water Pricing Policy is implemented), by wealthy domestic users, and by industry (Roome 1995; Archer 1996). Certainly foreign investors would be potential beneficiaries (were it not for the unfortunate fact that South Africa has suffered a dramatic net outflow of foreign direct investment since 1994).

Only 25 percent of the water sold in Gauteng in 1995 by Rand Water—comprising 41 percent of the Vaal River System's supply—was bought by low-income consumers, while 36 percent went to middle- and upper-income consumers, 24 percent to industry, and 15 percent to large mines. In 1995, approximately 1.5 million residents of Gauteng did not have direct access to water, and to supply them with 50 liters per person per day would have required only 22 million cubic meters (kiloliters, or "kl") of additional supply annually, representing a small fraction of the water that middle- and upper-income Gauteng consumers use to water their gardens and fill their swimming pools (Archer 1996, 58–59). The first two dams (Phases 1A and 1B) of the LHWP will together provide about a billion extra kiloliters of water per year to Gauteng when operating at full capacity.

And yet the irony of the LHWP was that by 1998 an enormous additional cost burden was already being borne by impoverished township dwellers. Asmal insisted (1996, 2) that "The debt related to the water transfer part of this project will be redeemed by South Africa through income generated by the project. In other words, the end users will pay for the project, at tariffs well within the capabilities of the beneficiaries, making it economically viable." Yet the data below throw this assessment into question.

From the mid-1990s, Christian Aid, EDF, and the Group for Environmental Monitoring were drawing attention to demand-side issues—especially consumption and conservation—associated with the LHWP water (Archer 1996; Horter 1996). But it was only when thousands of Soweto residents marched to the Johannesburg city council in July 1996 to protest a 30 percent increase in their water tariffs that the Soweto Civic Association learned from municipal officials of the LHWP's cost implications.

The rising cost of both bulk and retail water was soon to become an important debating point, as two joint workshops with the Alexandra Civic Organisation in 1997 established that because of rising bulk water costs, the LHWP would make it harder for Gauteng municipalities to (a) keep water prices down; (b) desist from water cut-offs; and (c) repair leaking pipes in the townships. This realization catalyzed a temporary brown-green, cross-border alliance and ultimately, as explored in more detail below, an April 1998 challenge to the World Bank Inspection Panel by three civic leaders. By delaying Phase 1B for an estimated seventeen years, the Alexandra residents insisted, resources could be spent on conservation and maintenance, as well as on redistributing water to township households. The residents cited a Rand Water official who argued that the annual savings of a Phase 1B delay at current interest rates would be R800 million, which, in a single year, would easily have been sufficient to repair existing systems.

Ultimately, the cost of Vaal River water following the construction of LHWP Phases 1A and 1B would increase by a factor of five—from R0.30/kl (largely repayment of several other previous dam loans) to R1.50/kl (Roome 1995). This huge cost translated between July 1995 and July 1998 into Rand Water price increases to municipalities of 35 percent to pay for Phase 1A alone. In turn, Johannesburg passed these costs on to consumers, of whom the poor paid a higher proportion (a 55 percent price increase for the first block of the Johannesburg block tariff) (World Bank Inspection Panel 1998, para 81, fn). As water prices rose more people failed to pay and municipal water cutoffs intensified.

The conditions in which Johannesburg township residents live reflect systemic apartheid-capitalist underdevelopment. As historical sites merely of labor reproduction—with virtually no commerce allowed and very few educational and community amenities provided—black townships played a major role in maintaining South Africa's very poorly paid proletariat. Alexandra was a classic example, with the Southern Hemisphere's wealthiest neighborhood—Sandton—just two kilometers over a hill (Mayekiso 1996). Inadequate municipal services were integral to township underdevelopment (McDonald 1998, and chap. 11 in this volume), notwithstanding the oft-documented net benefits for public health, the urban environment, gender equality, productivity, local economic development and the like (Bond 2000a, chap. 3) of the provision to low-income people of adequate supplies of water and electricity. Little of that mattered in a setting that at its core was designed to squeeze as much unskilled, poorly remunerated labor time out of working-age black men as possible (women were typically forced to remain behind in rural areas, providing an enormous "social wage" subsidy to urban capital in the form of free child-rearing for workers too young yet to go to the mines and factories, health care for sick workers, and old-age care for old workers).

Hence the apartheid-capitalist municipal services legacy is shocking. As expressed in the community leaders' (Alexandra Residents 1998, para 1.9) complaint to the World Bank Inspection Panel:

> By consuming less than 2% of all South Africa's water, the country's black township residents together use less than a third of the amount used in middle- and upper-income swimming pools and gardens, not to mention white domestic (in-house) consumption or massive water wastage by white farmers who have had enormous irrigation subsidies over the years and who use 50% of South Africa's water.

Reflections of the miserable state of apartheid-era infrastructure include the following (Alexandra Residents 1998, para 1.9):

> Out of every 100 drops that flow through Gauteng pipes, 24 quickly leak into the ground through faulty bulk infrastructure. Still more waste occurs in leaky communal, yard, and house taps. In the higher elevations of Alexandra township, these problems are witnessed in the perpetual lack of water pressure. Hundreds of thousands of low-income people in Alexandra and other townships have no immediate house or yard access

to reticulated water supplied by our Johannesburg municipality, and instead receive at best only communal access, with all the public health problems that this implies. Indeed, the lack of available water on a universal basis means that public health conditions are worse; geographical segregation of low-income Gauteng residents (from wealthier residents) is more extreme; women are particularly inconvenienced, and their income-generation and caregiving capacities are reduced; and the environment is threatened (in part because of the shortage of water-borne sanitation).

Most importantly from an economic standpoint, a large proportion of the LHWP costs were being passed from the TransCaledon Tunnel Authority (TCTA) to DWAF, and then on to municipalities, and, in turn, to retail consumers, disproportionately to those customers who had been historically oppressed by lack of access to water. The LHWP costs began to be reflected as the primary basis for retail water price increases that began in 1994. As the Inspection Panel (1998, para 77) found:

> Since April 1994, the bulk water tariff that TCTA charges DWAF has slightly more than tripled, rising from R0.242/kl to R0.751/kl. During the same period, April 1994 to April 1998, the tariff that DWAF charges its large consumers, including Rand Water, has slightly more than doubled, rising from R0.457/kl to R0.945/kl. This of course includes the amount that DWAF pays to TCTA for LHWP water. . . . Rand Water's charges to the municipalities have also increased during this period. From April 1994 to April 1998, the bulk water tariff that Rand Water charges the municipalities increased . . . from R1.201/kl to R1.685/kl.

While bulk water charges to municipalities rose by 35 percent between mid-1995 and mid-1998, in large part due to the LHWP, the levy for the first (lowest) block of the Johannesburg block tariff increased by 55 percent (World Bank Inspection Panel 1998, para 81, fn), indicating that relatively speaking, first-block consumers paid a higher proportion of the increase than did consumers who used more water.

Yet such price increases were not sufficient evidence for the Panel to declare that paying for the LHWP would be a burden on low-income township residents. The Panel (1998, para 80) went on to ask:

How have the municipalities responded? At this point the linkages back to LHWP become very tenuous. At the municipal retail level in Gauteng, a host of factors impact on water charges, and on their collection, and it is simply not possible to isolate one factor against the others.

This represents, one might argue, an *incomplete* (or even incompetent) ecological modernization discourse, because indeed factor analysis of the component costs of municipal water should have been feasible. Because "the Panel is not satisfied that there is *prima facie* evidence linking this situation to the [LHWP], nor to the Bank's decision to proceed with financing 1B," the Panel (1998, para 99) recommended that a full investigation *not* be carried out. Such an investigation would have followed the Alexandra residents' (1998, para 2.10) allegation that:

Municipalities have borne the costs of rising water prices and limited retail affordability in recent months, and are passing them on to workers, who are increasingly suffering wage and retrenchment pressure, and to communities, in the form of increased levels of water cut-offs. This reflects both overall municipal fiscal stress (as central to local grants declined by 85% in real terms from 1991/92 to 1997/98) as well as higher priced bulk water costs. Debts by Gauteng municipalities for bulk sewerage and bulk water supplies that are more than 60 days overdue amounted to R69,000,000 at the end of 1997, and another R20,000,000 in water-related debts were between 30 and 60 days overdue. The 24 Gauteng municipalities raised total income of R968,000,000 from water bills to all classes of consumers in 1997 and spent R1,019,000,000 on water services (a deficit of R51, 000,000). In contrast, of the 236 municipalities that report across South Africa, water bills raised R2,414,000,000 in 1997, and expenditures were just R2,388,000,000 (a surplus of R26,000,000). This is surprising given that Gauteng is South Africa's wealthiest province. The fiscal stress caused by deficits on the water account are part of the reason that the following Gauteng municipalities were declared, in December 1997, to be in default of government "viability" criteria (sufficient cash and investments to meet one month's personnel bill): Johannesburg, Pretoria, Alberton, Brakpan, Randfontein, Bronkhorstpruit, Walkerville and Vereeniging Koponong.

In turn, the Alexandra residents (1998, para 2.11) continued, this fiscal crisis was being transferred to communities:

The direct consequence of rising indebtedness has been intensified municipal "credit control" against those households who cannot afford to pay for increasingly costly water. Rand Water price increases announced in February 1998—which were more than 50% above the inflation rate, because 75% of the increase is from the LHWP—will affect the claimants at a time that unemployment is increasing, overall municipal bills are being increased and some wealthy ratepayers are offering stiff resistance to paying their fair share. The implications of rising water prices and the lack of a "lifeline tariff"—a basic water service available to even to the very poor—include not only switching of funds in household budgets away from other necessities, but also a dramatic increase in residential water cut-offs in Gauteng since early 1997. According to the Department of Constitutional Development's "Project Viability," 24 out of the 30 Gauteng local authorities (representing a population of more than 12 million people) that replied to an official questionnaire, engaged in water cut-offs. These cut-offs affected 512 households in the first quarter of 1997, 932 households in the second quarter, 1 210 households in the third quarter and 5 472 households in the fourth quarter. The ability of many of these households to afford their bills was limited, as witnessed by the fact that only 252 449 613 and 1 064 Gauteng households were reconnected in those four quarters of 1997, respectively. There are many other potential indicators of the costs of increasing water tariffs associated with the LHWP, including public health costs and ecological problems (as excessive water-borne sanitation costs lead to informal sanitation arrangements), most of which generate a bias against low-income women, which should also be researched and factored into the water pricing and access policies. However, these are at present not being adequately considered, due to the intensive pressure municipalities face to balance their books in the very short term.

The cutoffs intensified in 1998. (There have been no detailed statistics of municipal "credit control" since early 1998, because the Project Viability reports were so depressing that the series was cancelled by Pretoria.) In the black township of Leandra in neighboring Mpumalanga province, for instance, the water supplies of 70,000 residents were cut by 70 percent by Rand Water for several months. These figures *included residents who had paid their bills* but suffered because the official mains were cut (*Reconstruct, Sunday Independent,* 20 December 1998). The Inspection Panel (1998, para 86) appeared entirely unsympathetic, invoking democratic political authority:

> Non-payment for services began as a strategy in the struggle against apartheid. It has continued as a habit of non-payment if not a culture of entitlement. . . . The Inspector was informed that the Government of South Africa, DWAF, Rand Water and the municipalities have taken a firm position on payment for services, including water and sanitation services. Failure to pay is resulting in cut-offs. Given the many factors at play, however, it is clearly difficult, perhaps impossible, to determine the extent to which non-payment and hence cut-offs stem from this habit of non-payment or from a simple inability to pay.

At issue here was whether LHWP expansion would exacerbate rather than ameliorate the affordability problems. The matter was urgent, for Gauteng municipalities would continue to react to extremely serious financial difficulties by dramatically increasing both the retail price of water and the pace of water cutoffs to low-income consumers as well as the retail price of water. The Inspection Panel did not *deny* the possibility of a direct link, but its tools of ecological modernization were not sophisticated enough for it to measure that link.

An even larger innovation associated with the ecological modernization thesis now came into play: the strategy of demand-side management. The adoption of this strategy was also not disputed in any of the discourses, although the Bank would not accept claims (e.g., by the director of DWAF's "Working for Water" program) that water savings as high as 40 percent could be achieved through conservation strategies. More important than the absolute amount of water savings was whether the additional costs associated with the LHWP would act as a disincentive to conservation (since in order to pay for the LHWP construction, its downstream buyers would have to sell the LHWP water, hence conservation would make full cost-recovery of the LHWP construction costs that much harder). The Bank claimed not, and the Inspection Panel was neutral but placed its faith in DWAF's stated commitment to conservation.

There was, however, an additional problem that very directly related to the Alexandra residents' agenda for redistribution. The residents maintained that demand-side management entailed a variety of reforms (1998, para 5.3.5):

> repairing our townships' leaky connector pipes and leaky water taps, modernising and fixing meters, changing water usage patterns through progressive block tariffs, promoting water-sensitive gardening and food production, intensifying water conservation education, regulating or prohibiting excessive watering of suburban gardens, implementing other water use regulation, clearing invasive alien trees, promoting school water audits, billing consumers with more informative material, and installing low-flow showerheads, dual-flush toilets and similar mechanical interventions.

Progressive block tariffs—through which a free lifeline is available for all lowest-tier consumption but much higher prices are charged subsequently—are the most important feature, particularly if distributive justice and conservation are to be achieved. Interestingly, the World Bank itself, in its 1994 *World Development Report* on infrastructure, endorsed a lifeline supply and progressive block tariffs:

> Subsidized provision of infrastructure is often proposed as a means of redistributing resources from higher-income households to the poor. Yet its effectiveness depends on whether subsidies actually reach the poor. . . . There are, however, ways in which infrastructure subsidies can be structured to improve their effectiveness in reaching the poor. For example, for water, increasing-block tariffs can be used—charging a particularly low "lifeline" rate for the first part of consumption (for example, 25 to 50 litres per person per day) and higher rates for additional "blocks" of water. This block tariff links price to volume, and it is more efficient at reaching the poor than a general subsidy because it limits subsidized consumption. Increasing-block tariffs also encourage water conservation and efficient use by increasing charges at higher use. (World Bank 1994, 80–81)

Yet as the Alexandra residents (1998, para 1.10) complained, "The possibility for changing water usage patterns through progressive block tariffs was never factored in to LHWP demand calculations, in part because key Bank staff (though not the Bank's Washington headquarters) explicitly opposed differential pricing of water." Here the residents referred to Roome's (1995, 50–51) October 1995 presentation to Asmal, which argued against sliding tariffs, citing in particular the case of Johannesburg (which had a moderately progressive tariff structure) (see Bond 2000a, chap. 4 for a critique). Roome's only sustainable criticism was that block tariffs "may limit options with respect to tertiary providers—in particular private concessions much harder to establish." This is understandable in view of the World Bank goal of privatizing municipal water: private bidders would indeed be deterred if they encountered an obligation to consider redistribution (a lifeline water supply) when pricing water to maximize profit, since the firm's marginal cost and revenue curves necessarily depart from a redistributive water pricing structure.

Most South African cities moved in this direction prior to the ANC's

October 2000 promise of a free lifeline water supply and rising block tariff. Tellingly, instead of raising the slope of Johannesburg's near-flat block tariff to levels that would have achieved social justice and conservation, the city managers hired World Bank consultants as part of the iGoli 2002 corporatization program and instead provided only a small water grant (of R30 per month) to a meager 24,000 "indigent" households whose poverty status could be confirmed through stigma-inducing "means-testing." (The main city manager, Ketso Gordhan, turned down a World Bank job offer in late 2000 to become deputy chief executive of FirstRand, which included South Africa's most aggressively pro-privatization merchant bank.)

Asmal, meanwhile, finally endorsed progressive block pricing in principle. But he never overrode a White Paper on "Water and Sanitation" which as early as 1994 had insisted that the first "lifeline" block of water should *not* be free of charge (as did the Inspection Panel 1998, para 83). Inexplicably, Asmal's neoliberal bureaucrats and advisors Mike Muller, Len Abrams, and Piers Cross convinced the new minister to define "lifeline" as the equivalent of "operating and maintenance" costs (i.e., marginal cost) (Department of Water Affairs and Forestry 1994; for a critique, see Bond and Ruiters 2000). Although his 1998 National Water Pricing Policy contained a provision for a bulk "free" lifeline reserve of 25 liters per person per day for all South Africans, Asmal made no effort to ensure that once that water was provided to the water boards and municipalities it would be purified and supplied to residents at less than operating and maintenance costs. Given the vast increases in the overall recurrent costs of bulk water supply because of the LHWP, this abstract lifeline proposal in the water pricing structure would offer no relief. Again, in rejecting a more thorough investigation of the merits of a free lifeline water supply to offset the LHWP cost/price increases, the Inspection Panel endorsed the status quo.

The World Commission on Dams, however, benefited from a more critical group of researchers and commissioners who, in November 2000, explicitly recommended that a "priority should be to improve existing systems before building new supply, [and] that demand-side options should be given the same significance as supply options" (cited in Hoover 2000). On a variety of other brown and green issues, the Commission backed the LHWP critics' perspectives, but Asmal brought ex-president Nelson Mandela to introduce the report at its London launch, and effectively sidelined these criticisms (*Interpress Service,* 18 November 2000):

> We knew the controversy and complexities of such an under-
> taking [the LHWP] and had to carefully negotiate the political
> minefields and legal challenges, taking into consideration
> environmental, financial, social and economic impacts. A
> dam—a means to an end—which was one option among oth-
> ers, emerged as our best option under the circumstances.

This statement, without reflection or justification, suggests some of
the limits to ecological modernization discourse, and demonstrates why
recourse to technical arguments and process alone were not sufficient to
serve the interests of Johannesburg's low-income township residents.

The Limits of the Ecological Modernization Discourse

The disappointing official reactions to the brown critique of the LHWP
raise the question of whether ecological modernization was the appropriate discursive tactic for the Alexandra critics to use. This approach, as Harvey (1996, 377) describes it, is based on the use of rational scientific
(including socioeconomic) enquiry in order "to configure what would be
a good strategy for sustainable economic growth and economic development in the long run. The key word in this formulation is 'sustainability.'"

Ecological modernization is, without question, an improvement on
a purely orthodox (neoclassical economic) approach to environmental
management, as reflected in the infamous remark in a 1991 memo signed
by the World Bank's chief economist, Lawrence Summers: "I think the
economic logic behind dumping a load of toxic waste in the lowest-wage
country is impeccable and we should face up to that" (*The Economist*, 8
September 1992). A deeper consideration of costs and benefits that incorporate ecological values was welcome in the otherwise barren (if "impeccable") context of 1990s neoliberal economic hegemony. Scientific
studies in the spirit of ecological modernization, Harvey (1996, 378)
points out, generated a better understanding of:

> acid rain, global warming and ozone holes demanding wide-
> ranging collective action beyond nation-state borders, thereby
> posing a challenge (legal, institutional, and cultural) to the

closed bureaucratic rationality of the nation state. . . . This kind of science provided crucial support to many environmental pressure groups, many of whom initially viewed scientific rationality with skepticism and distrust. The thesis of ecological modernization has now become deeply entrenched within many segments of the environmental movement. The effects, as we shall see, have been somewhat contradictory. On the one hand, ecological modernization provides a common discursive basis for a contested rapprochement between them and dominant forms of political-economic power. But on the other, it presumes a certain kind of rationality that lessens the force of more purely moral arguments . . . and exposes much of the environmental movement to the dangers of political cooptation.

Here the LHWP Phase 1B controversy reflects a broader phenomenon, not least because the World Bank and its Inspection Panel have moved onto turf traditionally associated with the "bureaucratic rationality"—and especially the social control functions—of the nation-state (in Lesotho, Ferguson's study of the Highlands is seminal, while Foucauldian analysis of the South African developmental state is still wanting). Thus, if in reality the LHWP was initially in part a sanctions-busting, prestige project, with crucial geopolitical overtones, and later a scheme to assure water access to some of the least deserving companies and upper-class households anywhere in the world, nevertheless, its socio-ecological critics had to be treated by project sponsors with extreme ideological care. At stake, after all, were the reputations of the World Bank, of big dam projects in general (as the opening quote from Roome suggests), and of the ecologically modernized World Commission on Dams and its chairperson.

Thus, as Harvey (1996, 379) remarks, "some sort of configuration has to be envisaged in which ecological modernization contributes both to growth and global distributive justice simultaneously. This was a central proposition in the Brundtland Report for example." (By coincidence the main LHWP investigator of the Inspection Panel was MacNeill who, a decade earlier, had been secretary-general of the Brundtland World Commission on Environment and Development.) It is therefore easy to understand the significant and perhaps unprecedented (certainly in Southern African terms) attention paid to the LHWP's social implications (poverty, displacement, livelihood, and downstream consumption) as well as its ecological challenges, by skilled technocrats associated with the Bank (as witnessed in the World Bank's *Project Appraisal Document*) and Inspection Panel (MacNeill's report). Asmal (1998b, 4) himself articulated the ecological modernization thesis quite eloquently:

> As we move into the new millennium, as we move forward into the 21st century, there is ever less and less money available for building dams; there are ever fewer and fewer rivers left undammed; there is ever more and more resistance to the enormous social and environmental impacts of large dams. In the international field this tension has been recognised both by environmental groups and by those who fund major water infrastructure development. The World Commission on Dams has been established by the World Bank and the International Union for the Conservation of Nature to investigate a way to preserve the balance between the need for the development of water infrastructure, the protection of the environment and the recognition of the rights of rural populations, especially in developing countries, those people, as in Lesotho, who may lose their land, livelihoods and way of life as a result of the building of a dam.

Yet was the brand of ecological modernization claimed by Asmal, the Bank, the Inspection Panel, and the World Commission on Dams up to the challenge posed by the green-brown critique? Hoover's (2000) comparison of the Commission report and what has actually transpired in relation to the LHWP demonstrates the vast gap between Asmal's ecological-modernization rhetoric and the terrible reality.

Thus the WCD recommended that "Special attention is necessary to ensure that compensation and development measures are in place well in advance" of resettlement and that "a clear agreement with the affected people on the sequence and stages of resettlement will be required before construction on any project preparatory work begins" (Hoover 2000). Despite all the controversy over the LHWP resettlement, such compensation had not been worked out even for Phase 1B when work began in 1998.

Similarly, the Commission recommended negotiations "in which stakeholders have an equal opportunity to influence decisions from the outset of the planning process" (Hoover 2000). In reality, noted Hoover:

> Participation by affected communities has been minimal at best. Affected people have had no forum to effectively negotiate how the project's dams would impact them, let alone influence the decision to build them. In late 1999 agents of Lesotho's National Security Service confiscated materials about the WCD from a man affected by the LHWP after he returned from NGO-sponsored regional hearings for the WCD. In Lesotho, security agents routinely attend community meetings on the LHWP, inhibiting meaningful participation.

Lesotho's heavy-handed actions recall Asmal's (1998c) own intimidation of the Alexandra and Soweto civic leaders in a letter that accused them of "politically-mischievous activities" that were "guided by priorities and processes outside South Africa," and culminated in the threat that:

> since this deals with a matter of national interest, I will now take the necessary steps to establish whether you have a mandate from your national organization or are indeed merely posturing. I do not raise this as a threat. . . . Should you wish to proceed with any dialogue on this issue, I must therefore insist that you formally withdraw your request for an Inspection Panel investigation.

Repressive politics thus intervene periodically where ecological modernization discourses do not do the trick. However, even without intimidation, there remain extensive technical questions about the Bank's and Panel's justification of Phase 1B (Letsie and Bond 2000). For example, in relation to the Gauteng municipalities' comprehensive failure to implement demand-side management measures, "The Panel did not consider this because it does not relate to Bank Management acts or omissions in compliance or non-compliance with the OD" (Inspection Panel 1998, para 65). In fact, a reasonable interpretation of Bank Operational Directive 4.00 (para 5) ("Design of investment programs for supplying water or energy should consider demand management . . .") would lead to an investigation of the ultimate municipal end-users of Bank-financed water, particularly given the well-documented bias in consumption patterns.

Or as another example, the Panel's (1998, para 81) finding that there are (very small) graduations in Johannesburg's block tariffs (rising by a factor of just four from lowest to highest consumption block)—which "does not appear to bear out the assertions made by the [Alexandra residents] concerning block rates"—does not contradict the argument that if *far greater* progressions in block rates were imposed (as was the case in Hermanus, in the Western Cape and as the "Working for Water" program unsuccessfully proposed elsewhere) there would be far greater success in water conservation and redistribution.

The Panel's (1998, para 86) concern about non-payment for services could easily be addressed by applying a universal (free) lifeline policy that would allow cutoffs (or trickle flow) after consumption of the first block, entirely consistent with a "culture of entitlement" (disparaged by the Panel) that in turn is entirely consistent with the inclusion of the right to water in the Bill of Rights of the South African Constitution.

It is, therefore, entirely within the spirit of ecological modernization —while also consistent with environmental justice discourses—to criticize the Panel for failing to respond to the following quite reasonable questions:

- given the bias of access—and wastefulness—in water use toward wealthier, predominantly white, consumers, *should redistributive measures become a much higher priority than they are at present?*
- given the perennial shortages of water in South Africa and the threat of drought, *should DWAF, the water boards, and the municipalities give demand-side management much higher priority both on redistributive and conservation grounds than they do at present?*
- given not only that township infrastructure is continually plagued by systemic physical failure—and given, too, the fact that of three million (mainly rural) households who have benefited from taps installed within 1/2 km of their residence

since 1994 an estimated 90 percent now no longer have access to water because of systemic breakdown based often on lack of affordability—*should DWAF, water boards, and municipalities use their resources to improve installation and maintenance on a more generously subsidized basis?*

■ given that "lifeline" rates may be unaffordable for the poorest urban and rural residents, *should both national, water board, and municipal government policy shift to more decisively commit to defining lifeline as "free"?*

■ given that from 1994 to 1998, LHWP bulk water prices trebled due to dam construction costs, DWAF bulk prices to Rand Water also doubled, and Rand Water prices to Gauteng municipalities rose by 40 percent (with low-income Johannesburg residents facing a 55 percent increase in the price of the first block of water from 1995 to 1998), and given that many municipalities continue to suffer severe fiscal crisis, *should urgent steps be taken to ensure that bulk water prices are frozen (as was promised by the TCTA and DWAF) and, most importantly, that Rand Water desists from cutting off water services to entire towns, and that municipalities desist from engaging in mass water cutoffs to large sections of townships (as often happens even when individual households pay their bills)?*

Alexandra's brown critics of the LHWP would answer these questions firmly in the affirmative (Letsie and Bond 2000) while the various official defenders of the LHWP endorse, on the grounds of ecological modernization, the status quo. A radicalization of the discursive space of environmental justice is clearly called for, as are practical radical actions that transcend even the positive reforms (such as affirmative answers to the above questions) associated with the brown critique.

Challenges for Environmental Justice Politics

Using the LHWP case study, Harvey's (1996, 400) perspective on the politics of environmentalism can now be considered in more depth:

At this conjuncture, therefore, all of those militant particularist movements around the world that loosely come together under the umbrella of environmental justice and the environmentalism of the poor are faced with a critical choice. They can either ignore the contradictions, remain with the confines of their own particularist militancies— fighting an incinerator here, a toxic waste dump there, a World Bank dam project somewhere else, and commercial logging in yet another place—or they can treat the contradictions as a fecund nexus to create a more transcendent and universal politics. If they take the latter path, they have to find a discourse of universality and generality that unites the emancipatory quest for social justice with a strong recognition that social justice is impossible without environmental justice (and vice versa). But any such discourse has to transcend the narrow solidarities and particular affinities shaped in particular places—the preferred milieu of most grassroots environmental activism—and adopt a politics of abstraction capable of reaching out across space, across the multiple environmental and social conditions that constitute the geography of difference in a contemporary world that capitalism has intensely shaped to its own purposes. And it has to do this without abandoning its militant particularist base.

Can the green and brown critiques of the LHWP meet, and in the process generate a more substantial socialist environmentalism? A joint press statement in late January 1998—signed by the Group for Environmental Monitoring, the Alexandra and Soweto civics, Earthlife Africa, the Environmental Justice Networking Forum, the Lesotho Highlands Church Action Group, and the IRN—criticized Phase 1B in early 1998 (*Business Day,* 22 January 1998), and in February of that year, Moshe Tsehlo, acting coordinator of the Highlands Church Solidarity and Action Centre ("the only NGO operating on a full-time basis to serve the affected communities"), wrote to Roome that, "We will now support steps being taken by sister NGOs in South Africa to bring a case to the World Bank's Inspection Panel, claiming that the Bank has not followed its own policies."

The critiques were, however, not synthesized, partly because of geographical distance between the grassroots bases, and partly because extremely effective divide-and-conquer strategies were deployed by government officials to counter the growing opposition. In the course of a February 1998 meeting between Lesotho and South African NGOs, facilitated by Lesotho officials, the Lesotho solidarity eroded, and tensions arose between the more conservative Lesotho NGOs and their South African visitors. Even the Church Solidarity and Action Centre was forced to retreat, and withdrew its intention to support the Inspection Panel case.

This was telling, not because it suggests that militant particularisms in two different—rural and urban, green and brown—contexts cannot be fused, but rather the opposite: militancy can too easily wane under conditions of official pressure in countries that have had recent experience of deep repression. The same waning of militancy was evident when, in the wake of a funded trip to the dam for a few Soweto and Alexandra leaders and under pressure of explicit intimidation by Asmal, leaders of the two civic associations withdrew a draft (6 March 1998) claim to the Inspection Panel on 20 April, leaving the three residents to carry on independently (with their less-vulnerable NGO supporters) a few days later. After Roome filed a rebuttal to the Alexandra residents in May, several World Bank Executive Directors visited the site in June (although despite invitations and their presence in a hotel a few kilometers from Alexandra they did not make time to meet the three residents) and then approved the $45 million Phase 1B loan. In July, the Panel's MacNeill visited Alexandra and conducted a preliminary investigation into the residents' case. When in late August the Inspection Panel rejected the brown critique, and when a green critique did not immediately emerge, it appeared—momentarily—that all was well (*Business Day*, 9 September 1998).

But just over two years later, an explosion of criticism of the LHWP emerged, and the elusive green-brown coalition was suddenly reconfigured. The occasion was the multiple launch of the World Commission on Dams final report, which Kader Asmal presided over in several regions of the world during November 2000. After considering the overlap between their own socioenvironmental concerns and the Commission's analysis, a "Southern African Preparatory Meeting" of environment NGOs and community organizations (including Alexandra and Lesotho activist groups) immediately issued a statement calling for the World Bank, regional development banks, export credit agencies, bilateral agencies, governments, and other relevant authorities to:

immediately establish independent, transparent and participatory reviews of all their planned and ongoing dam projects. Whilst such reviews are taking place, project preparation and construction should be halted. Such reviews should establish whether the respective dams comply, as a minimum, with the recommendations of the WCD. If they do not, projects should be modified accordingly or be stopped altogether. All institutions which share in the responsibility for unresolved negative impacts of dams should immediately initiate a process to establish and fund mechanisms to provide reparations to affected communities that have suffered social, cultural and economic harm as a result of dam projects. All public financial institutions should place a moratorium on funding the planning or construction of new dams until they can demonstrate that they have complied with the above measures. (Southern African Preparatory Meeting 2000)

The Alexandra leaders were joined by groups from Lesotho, amongst which were some that had earlier endorsed Phase 1B: the Council of NGOs, Federation of Women's Lawyers, Rural Self Help Development Association, Transformation Resource Centre, Lesotho Durhata Link, Red Cross Society, Blue Cross Society, Lesotho Youth Federation, Highlands Church Action Group, Community Legal Resource and Advice Centre, Young Christian Students, and the Lesotho NGO Credit Centre.

In a taped television interview (Cashdan 2000), Alexandra leader Johnny Mpho was ecstatic that the dispute about the merits of the Mohale Dam was over: "This is very very wonderful. Our colleagues from Lesotho agree with our problem about what is happening in our poor community in Alexandra." In the same interview, Mpho's comrade, Sam Moiloa, criticized Asmal's uncaring attitude at the Commission report launch to the LHWP's problems:

I am not satisfied with the answer from Kader Asmal. In the first place, the Inspection Panel which he claims answers us, did not answer us, because they said there is no link between the Lesotho problems and the South African problems. So I'm wondering, because the link I know, is water. What do these well-educated people think, that there is no link, what do they mean? We are going to go on with the battle to make sure that the poorest of the poor are catered for. The World Bank and the South African government must stop this LHWP and concentrate on uplifting the standard of living of the people. So we are going to network more with the NGOs and community organisations of Lesotho and Gauteng, and we are going to proceed with this battle, and we are going to win it. We are not going to stop the engagement with the World Bank. We are going to pursue the battle together with the people of Lesotho, as we have gathered from them that they do not benefit. They say it point blank to us that they do not have access to water, which is the same thing as with us. Together with them we're going to forge ahead.

It is impossible to say whether such an informal popular alliance can hold over time. Ultimately, the green and brown critiques of the LHWP have to come together not merely through such demands for moratoria, but in a fully functional and durable manner, if we are to follow Harvey's political argument. This is how William Cronon (1991, 385) concluded his famous study of Chicago's ecological footprint:

> To do right by nature and people in the country, one has to do right by them in the city as well for the two seem always to find in each other their mirror image. In that sense, every city is nature's metropolis, and every piece of countryside is its rural hinterland. We fool ourselves if we think we can choose between them, for the green lake and the orange cloud are creatures of the same landscape. Each is our responsibility. We can only take them together and, in making the journey between them, find a way of life that does justice to them both.

But the questionable and expensive extension of Johannesburg's footprint up the mountains of Lesotho, when Gauteng township residents still suffered from a lack of access to water, is not the end of the matter. Environmental politics, Harvey (1996, 400–401) insists, must also:

deal in the material and institutional issues of how to organise production and distribution in general, how to confront the realities of global power politics and how to displace the hegemonic powers of capitalism not simply with dispersed, autonomous, localised, and essentially communitarian solutions (apologists for which can be found on both right and left ends of the political spectrum), but with a rather more complex politics that recognises how environmental and social justice must be sought by a rational ordering of activities at different scales. The reinsertion of "rational ordering" indicates that such a movement will have no option, as it broadens out from its militant particularist base, but to reclaim for itself a noncoopted and nonperverted version of the theses of ecological modernisation. On the one hand that means subsuming the highly geographically differentiated desire for cultural autonomy and dispersion, for the proliferation of tradition and difference within a more global politics, but on the other hand making the quest for environmental and social justice central rather than peripheral concerns. For that to happen, the environmental justice movement has to radicalise the ecological modernisation discourse.

This radicalization does not only entail the kinds of technical critiques of World Bank cost-benefit analyses and Inspection Panel mandates established in the LHWP case. The rational ordering of South Africa's space economy must also be considered as one of the starting points for future attacks on the irrational expansion of bulk water mainly for the benefit of Gauteng's large-scale farmers, corporations, and wealthy consumers. Harvey (1996, 392) remarks:

> If biocentric thinking is correct and the boundary between human activity and ecosystemic activities must be collapsed, then this means not only that ecological processes have to be incorporated into our understanding of social life: it also means that flows of money and of commodities and the transformative actions of human beings (in the building of urban

systems, for example) have to be understood as fundamentally ecological processes. The environmental justice movement, with its emphasis upon marginalised and impoverished populations exposed to hazardous ecological circumstances, freely acknowledges these connections. Many of the issues with which it is confronted are specifically urban in character. Consequently, the principles it has enunciated include the mandate to address environmental justice in the city by the cleaning up and rebuilding of urban environments.

This line of thinking takes us further than debates over new supplies of Lesotho water to Gauteng versus demand-side management. We have arrived at a position where it is only honest to address the urban ecological discourse established a century and a half ago in Marx and Engels's *Communist Manifesto,* particularly the call there for a "gradual abolition of all the distinction between town and country by a more equable distribution of the populace over the country." This does not mean forced ruralization, of course, nor a return to the discredited Bantustan decentralization schemes attempted by the apartheid regime during the 1970s and 1980s (Bond 2000a, chap. 1). Instead, it suggests the need for a more reasonable approach to long-term geographic planning, based not on historical accidents associated with mineral discoveries but on more sustainable ecological and socioeconomic rationales.

Johannesburg was born, after all, in 1886, merely because of the discovery of gold, that centuries-old relic of faithlessness in the value of money. With more industrial substitutes for gold and—in the wake of dramatic financial market turbulence since the mid-1990s—a declining luxury consumption market for gold jewelry, not to mention the difficulties of achieving profitable yields from deep mining operations or the offensive ecological (especially water despoliation) and labor-related circumstances (health, safety, and migrancy) associated with South African gold mining, there should be no reason for Johannesburg to continue as South Africa's economic heartland over coming decades and centuries. The overcapacity that characterizes uncompetitive Gauteng manufacturing sectors offers little basis for economic strength in a more flexible era based increasingly on the South African government's strategy (albeit a failure thus far) for promoting export-oriented growth. It should be logical for Johannesburg to decline gradually, much like a Detroit or other rust belt towns.

If Johannesburg's decline is to be accompanied by the construction of a more humane system of production, it will require not only transcending the near-exhausted (but politically still excessively potent) "Minerals-Energy Complex" (Fine and Rustomjee 1996) that has proved so ecologically and economically self-destructive (for a case study of the residual power of big mining-metals capital and the consequences for environmental injustice in Port Elizabeth, see Hosking and Bond 2000). Instead, advise Fine and Rustomjee (1996, 252), "We place considerable emphasis upon a state programme of public expenditure to provide social and economic infrastructure. This forms part of a strategy to provide for basic needs. The problem of how to finance such a programme is less acute than the formation of the political, social and institutional capacity to carry it out."

At one point recently, South Africa promised a far greater degree of political capacity to shift production systems not only sectorally into more 'sustainable,' redistributive structures (such as using a relatively decommodified, basic-needs infrastructure as the basis for kick-starting more balanced economic development) (Bond 2000a, chaps. 3–5), but also geographically. As the African National Congress Reconstruction and Development Programme mandated in 1994, "Macro-economic policies must take into consideration their effect upon the geographic distribution of economic activity. Additional strategies must address the excessive growth of the largest urban centres, the skewed distribution of population within rural areas, the role of small and medium-sized towns, and the future of declining towns and regions, and the apartheid dumping grounds" (ANC 1994, Section 4.3.4). Like many other RDP promises, this one was immediately broken in government's 1995 *Draft Urban Development Strategy* (Ministry of Reconstruction and Development 1995, 9; see Bond 2000a, chap. 13, for a detailed critique):

> The country's largest cities are not excessively large by international standards, and the rates of growth of the various tiers also appear to be normal. Hence there appears to be little reason to favour policies which may artificially induce or restrain growth in a particular centre, region or tier. . . . The

growth rate is sufficiently normal to suggest that effective urban management is possible and there is, therefore, no justification for interventionist policies which attempt to prevent urbanisation.

Indeed, because "South Africa's cities are more than ever strategic sites in a transnationalised production system" (Ministry of Reconstruction and Development 1995, 41), the debate has to be joined by a wider questioning of South Africa's insertion in the international division of labor (Marais 2000; Bond 2000b).

Harvey (1996, 402) concludes his analysis of environmental justice discourses by noting that "There is a long and arduous road to travel to take the environmental justice movement beyond the phase of rhetorical flourishes, media successes, and symbolic politics, into a world of strong coherent political organising and practical revolutionary action." That too might be the key lesson to be learnt from the experience of the protest of the Alexandra residents against the neoliberal South African state's prioritization of "development" and its distributional bias toward big corporations and wealthy (mainly white) consumers demonstrated in its token strategies thus far to redirect water use. The reformist, technicist critiques of the LHWP advanced to date via the World Bank Inspection Panel are clearly insufficient to foster real momentum for change, or to generate more decisively the alliances required for a broader (brown-green, urban-rural) critique of environmental injustice. In view of this, the only options that remain are practical but no less revolutionary anti-capitalist analysis, demands, and organization.

References

African National Congress. 1994. *Reconstruction and Development Programme*. Johannesburg: Umanyamo Publications.

Alexandra residents. 1998. "Inspection Panel Claim Regarding World Bank Involvement in the Lesotho Highlands Water Project." Alexandra, 23 April.

Archer, R. 1996. *Trust in Construction? The Lesotho Highlands Water Project*. London and Maseru: Christian Aid and Christian Council of Lesotho.

Ashley, B. 1997. "Challenging Apartheid Debt: Cancellation a Real Option." *Debate* 3.

Asmal, K. 1996. "Speech to GEM Workshop on Lesotho Highlands Water Project." In Group for Environmental Monitoring, ed. "Record of Proceedings: Lesotho Highlands Water Workshop." Johannesburg, 29–30 August.
——. 1998a. "Lesotho Highlands Water Project: Success Story." Address to Meula press conference, 21 January.
——. 1998b. "Opening of the Lesotho Highlands Water Project." Speech, 22 January.
——. 1998c. *Lesotho Highlands Water Project, Ref 4/9/3/1.* Pretoria: Ministry of Water Affairs and Forestry.
Bond, P. 1997. "Lesotho Dammed." *Multinational Monitor,* January–February.
——. 2000a. *Cities of Gold, Townships of Coal: Essays on South Africa's New Urban Crisis.* Trenton, N.J.: Africa World Press.
——. 2000b. *Elite Transition: From Apartheid to Neoliberalism in South Africa.* London and Pietermaritzburg: Pluto Press and University of Natal Press.
Bond, P., and G. Ruiters. 2000. "Droughts and Floods." In M. Khosa, ed. *Economic Transformation.* Pretoria: Human Sciences Research Council Press.
Cashdan, B. 2000. "Lesotho Highlands Water Project." Interview tapes.
Cronon, W. 1991. *Nature's Metropolis: Chicago and the Great West.* New York: Norton.
DWAF (Department of Water Affairs and Forestry). 1994. "Water Supply and Sanitation." White Paper. Cape Town: Government Printers.
——. 1996. *The Orange River Project Replanning Study.* Pretoria: Government Printers.
——. 1999. *Orange River Development Project Replanning Study.* Pretoria: Government Printers.
Environmental Defense Fund and International Rivers Network. 1999. "Groups Call on World Bank to Ban Companies in African Bribery Scandal." Press Release. Washington, D.C., and Berkeley, Calif., 24 September.
Environmental Monitoring Group, International Rivers Network and Group for Environmental Monitoring. 1999. "Once There was a Community: Southern African Hearings for Communities Affected by Large Dams." Final Report, Cape Town, 11–12 November.
Ferguson, J. 1990. *The Anti-Politics Machine: "Development," Depoliticization, and Bureaucratic Power in Lesotho.* Cambridge: Cambridge University Press.
Fine, B., and Z. Rustomjee. 1996. *The Political Economy of South Africa.* Johannesburg: Witwatersrand University Press.
Fox, J., and L. D. Brown. 1998. *The Struggle for Accountability: The World Bank, NGOs and Grassroots Movements.* Cambridge, Mass,: MIT Press.
Harvey, D. 1996. *Justice, Nature and the Geography of Difference.* Oxford: Blackwell
Hoover, R. 2000. "Evaluating the LHWP Against WCD Guidelines." Unpublished report. San Francisco: International Rivers Network.
Horter, K. 1995. "The Mountain Kingdom's White Oil: The Lesotho Highlands Water Project." *The Ecologist* 25 (6).

————. 1996. "Making the Earth Rumble: The Lesotho-South Africa Water Connection." *Multinational Monitor,* May.

Hosking, S., and P. Bond. 2000. "Infrastructure for Spatial Development Initiatives or for Basic Needs? Port Elizabeth's Prioritisation of the Coega Port/IDZ over Municipal Services." In M. Khosa and Y. Muthien, eds. *Infrastructure for Reconstruction in South Africa.* Pretoria and London: Human Sciences Research Council and Ashgate Press.

Kravitz, J. D. 1995. "Human Immunodifficiency Virus Seroprevalence in an Occupational Cohort in a South African Community." *Archives of Internal Medicine* 155 (15).

Letsie, D., and P. Bond. 2000. "Social, Ecological and Economic Characteristics of Bulk Water Infrastructure: Debating the Financial and Service Delivery Implications of the Lesotho Highlands Water Project." In M. Khosa and Y. Muthien, eds. *Infrastructure for Reconstruction in South Africa.* Pretoria and London: Human Sciences Research Council and Ashgate Press.

Marais, H. 2000. *South Africa: The Political Economy of Transformation.* London and Cape Town: Zed and University of Cape Town Press.

Mayekiso, M. 1996. *Township Politics: Civic Struggles for a New South Africa.* New York: Monthly Review Press.

McDonald, D. 1998. "Three Steps Forward, Two Steps Back: Ideology and Urban Ecology in South Africa." *Review of African Political Economy* 75.

Metsi Consultants 1999. "The Establishment and Monitoring of Instream Flow Requirements for River Courses Downstream of LHWP Dams." Lesotho Highlands Development Authority Contract 648, Maseru.

Ministry of Reconstruction and Development. 1995. *Urban Infrastructure Investment Framework.* Pretoria: Government Printers.

Patel, P. 1994. "Lesotho: Highlands Water Project (Ln.3393–LSO)." Washington, D.C., 2 December.

Pottinger, L. 1996. "The Environmental Impacts of Large Dams." In Group for Environmental Monitoring, ed. "Record of Proceedings: Lesotho Highlands Water Workshop." Johannesburg, 29–30 August.

Potts, M. 1996. "Presentation by the DBSA to the Lesotho Highlands Water Workshop." In Group for Environmental Monitoring, ed. "Record of Proceedings: Lesotho Highlands Water Workshop." Johannesburg, 29–30 August.

Roome, J. 1995. "Water Pricing and Management: World Bank Presentation to the SA Water Conservation Conference." Unpublished paper, South Africa, 2 October.

Seaman, M. 1996. "Questions." In Group for Environmental Monitoring, ed. "Record of Proceedings: Lesotho Highlands Water Workshop." Johannesburg, 29–30 August.

Snaddon, C. D., M. J. Wishart, and B. R. Davies. 1996. "Some Implications of Inter-Basin Water Transfers for River Functioning and Water Resources

Management in South Africa." In Group for Environmental Monitoring, ed. "Record of Proceedings: Lesotho Highlands Water Workshop." Johannesburg, 29–30 August.

Southall, R. 1998. "Is Lesotho South Africa's Tenth Province?" *Indicator SA* 15 (4).

Southern African Preparatory Meeting. 2000. "Southern African Call to Action." Pretoria, 23 November.

World Bank. 1994. *World Development Report 1994: Infrastructure for Development.* New York: Oxford University Press.

———. 1998. "Lesotho: Lesotho Highlands Water Project-Phase 1B: Project Appraisal Document (17727–LSO), R98–106(PAD), Water and Urban 1, Africa Region." Washington, D.C., 30 April.

World Bank Inspection Panel. 1998. "Lesotho/South Africa: Phase 1B of Lesotho Highlands Water Project: Panel Report and Recommendation." Washington, D.C., 19 August.

World Development Movement and Action for Southern Africa. 1998. *Paying for Apartheid Twice: The Cost of Apartheid Debt for the People of Southern Africa.* London: WDM and Actsa.

I Used to Get Water from a River

Mpume Nyandu

"**I** used to get water from a river which was situated where the dam is today. Now I have to go to KwaSikhosana and it takes about two hours to get there. The dam robbed us of our forefathers' fields which were our source of food and the worst part of it is that many of us received nothing in return," laments one of the very old people of Rooikop, near Driefontein.

The dam referred to is the Heyshope dam built in Driefontein in the mid-1980s. The arrival of the dam inconvenienced a lot of people in many ways and is still doing so more than a decade later.

Driefontein is a rural settlement situated in the North Western part of Piet Retief in the Wakkerstroom district of the Mpumalanga Province. It is estimated that 14,000 families had to move off their land, unwillingly, to make way for the dam. According to the Transvaal Rural Action Committee (TRAC), plans for the removal of the Driefontein and the neighboring settlements of Daggakraal and KwaNgema were already being discussed by government as early as 1965. But the real problems started in 1983 when the government decided to forcibly remove people living in Driefontein and the surrounding areas. There was major conflict and strong resistance from the communities. People were determined to stay on their land.

Sitha Gama, who still lives in Driefontein, vividly remembers one dam official, a white man, speaking in Zulu saying, "Noma hgabe ninenkani kanjani ayeza amanzi" (It doesn't matter how stubborn you get but the water is coming).

Residents were simply told that the area had been earmarked for a dam. No explanation was given as to why the dam had to be positioned in their community or who was going to benefit from it.

When asked about this more recently, a Department of Water Affairs consultant based in Mpumalanga said "the Heyshope dam water is mainly for industrial purposes. It's mostly used by ESKOM [Electricity Supply Commission] and SASOL [a parastatal company involved in the conversion of coal to oil]." This explanation has never been formally communicated to the people of Driefontein and its neighboring communities.

After the dam was built people were faced with a variety of problems. Grazing land for livestock was submerged as was the clean river water from which the animals drank. Initially, part of the dam was fenced off but members of the community removed the fence so their cattle could drink from the dam. This resulted in a number of animals falling into the dam and drowning.

For the people of Driefontein, the irony is that despite the fact that there is much water in the dam, there is a severe shortage of clean drinking water in the area. The few taps available often dry up and break down and a long time elapses before they are fixed.

Another effect of the dam, which occupies an area of 5,024 hectares and has a storage capacity of 452 million cubic meters, was to separate the people of KwaNgema and Driefontein, who once formed a closeknit community. According to Sitha Gama of Driefontein, the possibility of building a bridge to help bring these communities closer had been discussed, but the Department of Water Affairs dismissed the idea, saying it was dangerous. This means that people have to pay a steep taxi fare of R8 for a single trip to visit friends and relatives on the other side. William Ngema of the KwaNgema section complains bitterly: "I want my kids to go to school, but we have no school this side. When the dam divided up the area the school remained on the Driefontein side. Our children go to a shack school which gets blown away by the wind."

The area also has no proper roads. When it rains, the dam overflows making the only miserable dirt road muddy and slippery. "Once it's muddy it's very dangerous and very difficult to drive through without almost skidding into the dam. There are no rails protecting vehicles from skidding into the dam. When the dam is full it's impossible to get to the other side," says Mr. Wilson Kunene, a resident of the KwaNgema section.

The Heyshope dam is not the only problem for Driefontein, KwaNgema, and Rooikop. In the mid-1990s, the establishment of the Maquasa coal mine added to their frustrations. Mining activities affect the three communities at various levels.

Rooikop residents are currently living in constant fear of being moved off their land as the mine moves closer and closer to their houses. The mine owners are threatening to move them to another piece of land so that more coal can be extracted from the land they are currently occupying. Many of the Rooikop residents are very old people whose family histories in the area date back more than three generations. They know no other home; their forefathers were born there and died there.

Mrs. Mnisi, a Rooikop resident in her late sixties, says: "The mine said they are going to compensate us for our land and take us to a new place. They took us to see the new place and I said no I don't want to be far away from my family graves. We have to keep visiting the graves of our forefathers. The mine said they were going to move us with the graves but I have not heard a word about graves in our recent talks with them. The digging of graves really hurts me. It hurts a lot to know that our forefathers will be disturbed from their peaceful sleep. I was also already looking forward to my last day on earth when I'd be taken to rest next to my parents, grandparents, and great grandparents. If they move us now my dream won't come true. I feel very sad."

The mine officials are reported to have said that they will not be held responsible for any injuries to any person or damage to any property as result of mine blasting if people refuse to move to the land offered to them.

The Driefontein community, meanwhile, has to deal with the noise and dust pollution caused by huge trucks traveling to and from the coal mine. The community has complained time and time again to no avail. Jane Khumalo of the Driefontein Advice Centre says: "We have to deal with the noise and dust from the mine trucks every day of the week, night and day. We spoke to the mine about this pollution and they promised to use dust suppression which is a liquid that is supposed to suppress dust. But they only spray part of the road." The residents say that sometimes when the road is sprayed it gets very muddy.

On the other side of the dam, the KwaNgema community is left with a vacant and damaged piece of land that was formerly another coal mine for which people had been moved off their land. When mining started in KwaNgema, promises were made that there would be development and job opportunities in the area. It appeared that the community would benefit from the mine. But the promised benefits never materialized. The people of KwaNgema say they have been told by the mining company that the land will not be usable for many years to come; that it has to be rehabilitated before anyone can settle on it.

Faced with two major industrial problems, the dam and the mine, the people of Driefontein and the surrounding areas are not quite sure where their future lies. Sitha Gama says the community would like government officials to come out and see all the problems. "As the KwaNgema community, we see ourselves as neglected people. White people come in and do what they like with our land and our lives. We don't know what to do about it, we feel very insecure. We don't know what's coming next."

In Rooikop Baba Khanyi says: "We think God is the only one who can help us out of this situation. I don't think anyone else can."

Chapter 10

Workplace Environmental Justice

Trade Unions and the Struggle for an Ecological Platform

Peter Lukey

> *Business is delighted to bask in the publicity given to its campaigns against crime [in South Africa]. However, it plays another role in law and order that receives (virtually) no mention. And it is not unhappy about this lack of publicity, for what is being kept in the shadows is its role as a leading lawbreaker. . . . Most health and safety accidents at work are caused by employers' breaches of the law. The silence surrounding this is all the more surprising given that the problem of accidents at work is both enormous and well documented.*
> —*Mail & Guardian*, 19–25 June 1998

Organized labor has immense political power in South Africa—not least of which is its ability to mobilize millions of South Africans in public protest and to bring the wheels of industry to a grinding halt. This power, multiplied through solidarity in union associations, was particularly strong during the anti-apartheid struggle in the 1980s and remains a force in the post-apartheid era.

Trade unions have also played a critical role in the environmental justice movement in South Africa. It could be argued, in fact, that organized labor supplied the first environmental justice activists in the country, through its struggle since the turn of the century for improvements in the "work environment." The miners' strike of 1913, for example, in which twenty-one strikers were killed in clashes with police, was called in part to protest poor working conditions.

As David Pepper (1993, 63) has pointed out in the European context, environmental struggles are neither new nor foreign to the union movement:

> In nineteenth- and early twentieth-century Britain . . . the trades union movement was essentially an *environmental* protest movement. Its struggle for health and safety at work was a struggle for quality of environment at the point of production. Its struggles for decent wages were struggles for environment in the social sphere of reproduction. Few other campaigns have had such impact on the quality of people's environment and lives in the West as these [emphasis in the original].

Workers are also most likely to feel the effects of workplace environmental hazards *outside* of the factory. As Friedrich Engels noted in his observations of the urban layout of mid-nineteenth-century Manchester, England: "The east and north-east sides [of the city] . . . are the only ones which the bourgeoisie has not built [and do not live in], because ten or eleven months of the year the west and south-west wind drives the smoke of all the factories hither, and that, the working-people alone may breath" (cited in Markham 1994, 66).

South Africa's apartheid history gives Engels's observations of early environmental injustice a further twist. Not only were workers forced to live downwind of their polluting workplaces, these workers were, more often than not, black. Thus, they bore (and indeed most still bear) a double burden, facing environmental hazards in their workplaces and environmental hazards where they live.

Despite the earlier actions on workplace health and safety, it was not until the 1990s that these issues began to be articulated as "environmental" concerns and connected with broader environmental issues outside of the factory. However, given the highly politicized nature of the union movement in South Africa it did not take long for environmental justice to become part of the movement's lexicon. As Rod Crompton and Alec Erwin (1991, 80) noted in their seminal piece on labor and the environment more than ten years ago, "If workers must wear protective equipment then by definition environmental contamination is taking place. . . . Trade union struggles for health and safety in the workplace constitute the first line of defence for an embattled environment."

The purpose of this chapter is to review the first decade of trade union struggles for environmental justice in South Africa and to highlight the kinds of obstacles unions face as they attempt to move beyond the issue-specific campaigns that characterized their environmental activities in the 1990s. The chapter begins with a brief history of union involvement in the environmental movement in South Africa and describes the current state of health and safety and environmental policy as it relates to workers. It then outlines a number of organizational and, more importantly, philosophical constraints to developing more comprehensive red-green alliances in South Africa, and proposes a pragmatic, short- to medium-term strategy for overcoming some of these hurdles under the banner of "workplace environmental justice."

A History of Environmental Struggles

In the closing years of the 1980s there was arguably only one broad-based environmental group involved in high-profile environmental activism in South Africa; namely Earthlife Africa (ELA). ELA was, and remains, a loose, nationwide alliance of volunteer activists, grouped into local branches. ELA's "Statement of Belief" is based on that of the German Green Party, with a strong environmental justice agenda. However, given the legacies of racial segregation in South Africa, and notwithstanding the organization's progressive political outlook, ELA's membership remained overwhelmingly white and middle-class—a situation akin to that described by Robert Bullard (as cited in Alston 1993, 188) in the United States context: "although concern about the environment cuts across racial and class lines, environmental activism has been most pronounced among individuals who have above average education, greater access to economic resources, and a greater sense of personal efficiency."

At the time of ELA's formation and early activities the apartheid regime was clamping down with increasing vigor on dissenting voices. Available avenues for protest against the regime were being systematically closed down and the anti-apartheid movement was attempting to explore alternative ways of challenging it. Environmental concern, and environmental justice in particular, was seen as one possible avenue.

With the unbanning of anti-apartheid political groups in 1990 additional space was created for environmental activism and in 1992 a conference under the banner "What Does It Mean to Be Green?" was organized by ELA. Seventeen countries were represented at the conference and, according to David Hallowes (1993, 1–7), South Africa was represented by people from rural communities, civic associations, trade unions, NGOs from almost every sector, government institutions, business, universities, religious bodies, and conservation organizations. The conference effectively launched the Environmental Justice Networking Forum (EJNF) with a resolution that stated that a national body should be established to coordinate the work of NGOs concerned with the environment and that membership should be as broad as possible but should subscribe to a set of values embodied in a mission statement reflecting the values which found support at the Earthlife Conference (Hallowes 1993, 323) (see the introduction in this volume for more details on EJNF). Specifically, there were calls for solidarity between workers and environmentalists, both nationally and internationally (Thorpe 1993; Harris 1993), and for workers' rights to information about, and participation in, environment and development issues (Miller 1993, 96–100).

The main trade union umbrella organization in the country—the Congress of South African Trade Unions (Cosatu)—is a member of the EJNF, as are many of its affiliate organizations. Several of these trade unions (notably the Chemical Workers Industrial Union [CWIU] and the National Union of Mineworkers [NUM]) have been actively involved in national government environmental policy development in the post-apartheid era. Trade unions are also dealing more seriously with health and safety issues and trying to integrate these ideas into broader pollution and waste management issues (Magane et al. 1997). The South African Municipal Workers' Union has even begun to challenge government plans to privatize municipal services, partly on environmental grounds.

In terms of concrete action, trade unions in South Africa have been involved in numerous high profile environmental campaigns. It is widely acknowledged, in fact, that the joint union-environmental group protest outside the gates of Thor Chemicals in KwaZulu-Natal on 14 April 1990 was the catalyst to the development of an environmental justice movement in South Africa in general, and to red-green alliances in particular (see chap. 1 and narrative "Crippled for Life by Mercury Exposure" in this volume). Greenpeace described the situation at Thor Chemicals as the "most horrifying case of international waste trade" and the worst "abuse of an economically dependent" workforce that they had ever seen (Kockott 1994, 1).

In August 1991 Thor workers became unionized with the Chemical Workers Industrial Union (CWIU). In the same year, tests done by the Industrial Health Unit showed that 87 percent of Thor workers had mercury levels in their blood that were four times the accepted limit (Butler 1997, 199). The union and a host of other environmental and health organizations then began a series of investigations into the situation (both locally and internationally) and after three years of enquiries, protests, and legal and political action, Thor Chemicals finally announced in February 1994 that it would halt the import of toxic wastes and get out of the mercury business altogether (although it continued to handle local toxic waste from within South Africa) (Kockott 1994, 3–4). In the interim, two workers died from mercury poisoning and an unknown number of other workers were mentally and physically impaired.

Legal wrangling over the Thor situation continued for several years afterwards, and protest groups were ultimately disappointed that charges of culpable homicide against Thor managers were dropped by the state, but the case did represent an important victory for the labor and environmental movements. As Mark Butler (1997, 206) concludes in his assessment of the alliances formed in this particular struggle, "Although this potential [for red-green alliances] is yet to be more generally realized, there can be little doubt that in the case of Thor Chemicals, the overall campaign has drawn strength from the alliance between Earthlife Africa, the Environmental Justice Networking Forum and the CWIU. This alliance has also facilitated supportive networking with international organizations such as Greenpeace."

Other notable instances of red-green alliances include the mid-1990 campaign by ELA, the Food and Allied Workers' Union (FAWU), the Dolphin Action and Protection Group, and the Cape Town Ecology Group to protest illegal gill-netting by Taiwanese fishing trawlers (Koch 1991, 26), and the August 1992 protest, involving ELA and the Transport and General Workers' Union (TGWU), against a waste shipment docking in Durban. The latter also involved cooperation on the part of Greenpeace and the International Transport Workers Federation (Harris 1993, 89).

Not all union-environmental group coalitions have been successful, however, and the majority of such partnerships and actions have been issue-specific and focused on a single enterprise or sector. Once a particular issue has been resolved, partnerships tend to dissolve along with them. As a result, there have been few long-term associations between unions and environmental organizations. The anticipated potential for strong red-green alliances in the early 1990s (Koch 1991; Crompton and Erwin 1991) does not appear to have materialized beyond short-term issue-specific campaign partnerships, and there appears to be little discussion on the broader dialectics of red-green politics in the country.

A case in point was the landmark 1995 Cosatu conference on health, safety, and environment policy, and the subsequent workshop in 1996, which put environmental justice issues firmly onto Cosatu's agenda, though environmental issues are still not seen as an inherent component of the federation's political agenda. This is confirmed by the then General Secretary's statement that: "In our 10 years as Cosatu we have given enough attention to politics . . . but not enough to social issues such as health, safety and the environment" (cited in Magane et al. 1997, 182).

Further evidence of the limited success of unions in addressing workplace health and safety issues is the sheer number of accidents in the industrial workplace. In 1997 alone, 863 workers were killed in workplace accidents (*not* including mining), an average of more than three deaths per working day (*Mail & Guardian,* 19–25 June 1998). These figures could be seen as a marginal reduction on those reported for 1995 (942 deaths in industry and a further 533 deaths in the mining sector [Magane et al. 1997]), but it is not clear whether this is due to the reporting problems or whether there has, in fact, been an actual decrease in workplace related deaths. As the report in the *Mail & Guardian* argues, the data on workplace safety are of questionable value with employers taking an average of 107 days to report incidents that are required by law to be reported within seven days. Of equal concern is the fact that employers are allowed to report (serious) incidents telephonically. Telephonic reporting means there is unlikely to be any written evidence/confirmation of the incident at the factory for possible follow-up—that is, statistics, investigations, court cases, and so on—leaving no "paper-trail" for possible follow-up activities. Furthermore, the vast majority of deaths are attributed to accidents and do not include data for those workers who have died as a result of occupational disease (e.g., asbestosis).

These gruesome figures give some indication of the real dangers associated with the South African workplace. Gloomier still is the fact that 70 percent of contraventions of health and safety laws in 1997 resulted from employers' failures to meet their statutory obligations, validating Paul Benjamin's argument that "the health and safety system [in South Africa] is really one of the last surviving bastions of apartheid" (cited in Magane et al. 1997, 189).

It can be argued that unions have only been dealing with environmental health and safety issues for the last ten years and, as such, one must accept that any potential red-green movement must walk before it can run. Nevertheless, the development of an environmental discourse amongst trade unionists and the development of union-environmental alliances have been uneven and impermanent. Most protest actions have focused on discrete instances where the environmental, health, and safety impacts are readily acknowledged or have become impossible to ignore. Most importantly, there would appear to be some real constraints, both practical and philosophical, on the building of more broad-based and permanent union-environmental alliances in the country, and these are described in the following section of the chapter.

Possible Constraints to Further Red-Green Alliances

Perhaps the single most important barrier to more effective, broad-based alliances between trade unions and environmental groups in South Africa is the capacity of unions to manage these relationships and their own internal policy debates on where environmental issues fit in with other union concerns. Magane et al. (1997, 176–93) describe these difficulties in detail.

First, there is the issue of a lack of specialist capacity within unions. Where unions do have the capacity to address workplace safety, health, and environment issues, these are generally handled by someone with a wide range of other union responsibilities and therefore do not receive the attention or resources they require. There are a few exceptions to this—the CWIU and the NUM have had dedicated health, safety, and environment officers for some time, and the National Union of Metalworkers (NUMSA) and the South African Municipal Workers' Union (SAMWU) have more recently created similar posts—but for the most part these issues fall on the shoulders of groups and individuals who are too busy to deal with them adequately. There is also an unresolved debate within the trade union movement about whether these issues should in fact be dealt with by specialists or simply made part and parcel of the work of all union officials.

Second, there is a perceived lack of general awareness at the shop floor level about health, safety, and environmental issues. Whether these issues are dealt with by a specialist committee or by all union officials, there must be broad knowledge amongst workers about their health and safety rights in order for individual workers to trigger a response from union officials. Thus, there is a great need for centralized training courses for shop stewards and union officials.

Third, there is a lack of coordination amongst union federation affiliates about the issues. In order to address workplace environmental issues in an integrated and holistic fashion, there is a need to address both geographically specific and workplace-specific issues. This requires the coordination of efforts between unions organizing in different industrial sectors as well as those organizing in specific environmental "hot-spots."

Finally, there is an unresolved debate about whether unions should encourage and support the participation of the non-union-based joint employee-employer structures prescribed by the Occupational Health and Safety Act of 1993. Some unionists see this to be participation in "illegitimate" structures.

The Pursuance of a Reactionary Agenda

For the most part, employers have taken a knee-jerk, reactionary approach to new workplace health and safety legislation and view workers rather than the production systems as the problem. The reaction from employers has been to take the "protective" route—better protective clothing and respiratory devices, better emergency plans, better worker and "safety officer" training, and so on. The level of protection supplied to workers is usually inversely proportional to the ergonomic comfort of the worker—the more dangerous the workplace, the more unwieldy and uncomfortable the protective devices. The result is that for relatively little cost, industry can say that it has addressed workplace health and safety issues and workers themselves may indeed experience a decline in occupationally related health and safety problems.

The reality is that the measures employed to address the supposed "shortcomings" of the human body's capacity to deal with dangerous environments places the health and safety burden on the shoulders of the worker, rather than addressing the dangerous workplace itself. Thus, even in situations were workers have been fully informed about the hazards of their workplace and the importance of shielding their bodies against these dangers, they often take the risk of exposure because it is less onerous than wearing uncomfortable protective devices like breathing apparatuses.

This reactionary approach to workplace health and safety may have extremely negative implications with regard to worker perceptions of safety, health, and environment. One of the implications of this approach could be that workers avoid campaigns to improve working conditions because the outcome is likely to mean personal discomfort created by "protective" solutions. If this is indeed the case, strong, shop floor based campaigns are unlikely until such time as the reactionary approach to unsafe working environments is systematically challenged.

Jobs versus Environment—The Unresolved Debate

One of the biggest philosophical barriers to better union-environmental group alliance building in South Africa is the long-standing "jobs versus the environment" debate. Capital and management often use the argument that higher environmental standards automatically lead to job losses as a way of avoiding expensive regulations and creating friction between environmentalists and unionists. Unionists will use the same argument when faced with what they perceive to be a threat to existing jobs and/or the potential for new job creation.

There are, of course, arguments that debunk the simplistic "job loss" scenario. These arguments include (Renner 1991; Thorpe 1993; Lukey 1995):

- seeing potential job losses due to environmental pressures as part of the general struggle for job security at a time of major structural change in the economy;
- the argument that companies that survive purely by externalizing their environmental costs can never guarantee job security anyway;
- the environmental service sector (e.g., recycling, solar energy) is one of the fastest-growing industries in the world and, as a result, the job-losses versus job-gains balance sheet may not necessarily be negative;
- implied moral arguments that a single job cannot be protected at the expense of the health and safety of fellow workers and the surrounding community;
- implied arguments that the jobs versus environment debate is based on spurious "facts" invented by management as a means to further exploit both workers and environment.

Although union leadership and workers in South Africa may accept some of these arguments it appears that the jobs versus environment debate still colors union thinking. This is illustrated in Magane et al. (1997, 177) where the "relationship between jobs, on the one hand, and health, safety and environment, on the other" is held to be a "key difficulty" within unions in taking up the issue of workplace environmental safety.

The St Lucia mining debate (see also chap. 1 in this volume) is often used to illustrate this perceived difficulty. Here the debate focused on the extension of mining operations into an ecologically important area in northern KwaZulu-Natal. Unions sided with management in their calls for the extension of mining activities because of the potential to sustain existing jobs and possibly create new ones. Environmentalists argued that mining would seriously compromise an important ecosystem and would seriously degrade the long-term sustainable development of the area. Using this example, Magane et al. (1997, 178) state that "there *is*, in fact, an absolute conflict" between jobs and the environment [emphasis in the original].

In South Africa's present economic climate and development status it is hardly surprising that this debate continues—a point that is forcibly brought home by the fact that even when work-related deaths at Thor Chemicals were common knowledge, there was never a shortage of new job recruits.

This tension between the more traditional, conservation-oriented environmental groups—those who see themselves giving a voice to our voiceless life support systems—and trade unionists who see themselves giving a voice to the more immediate and concrete concerns of the working class will be difficult to resolve. Environmental justice organizations like Earthlife Africa, with their inherently anthropocentric focus, are in a better philosophical position to address the tensions, but an uneasy relationship still exists between environmental justice activists and trade unionists. As an example, it appears that some unions, in their efforts to train their members in general environmental issues, have chosen to employ industrial consultants rather than to use the services of environmental NGOs. Although this may be indicative of the capacity constraints of environmental NGOs, it could also imply that these NGOs present an ideology or value-base that unions are uncomfortable with.

As with any form of social change, what will be required to effectively address safety, health, and environment in the workplace in South Africa is a concerted campaign driven from the shop floor. But for this kind of grassroots initiative workers must be convinced that higher safety/environmental standards are not going to lead to job losses or significantly slower job growth. Unfortunately, the debate in South Africa has failed to move beyond this "crude polarization" of jobs versus the environment, and "it appears as if South Africa is going to have to reexamine many of these questions for itself" (Magane et al. 1997, 178).

One possible way around this apparent impasse is to think in terms of "workplace environmental justice." The last section of this chapter proposes a working definition of this concept for South Africa and discusses how it might be conceptualized and implemented.

Workplace Environmental Justice

Subsection 24(a) of the new Bill of Rights grants everyone in the country "the right to an environment that is not harmful to their health or wellbeing." A natural extension of this clause is that workers should have the right to a *workplace environment* that is not harmful. But "rights," without legal tools and resources to ensure that they are effectively enforced, are of little use. The following definition of workplace environmental justice is therefore proposed: Workplace environmental justice is the effective exercising of workers' rights to a working environment that is not harmful to health and well-being. This definition is intrinsically anthropocentric, focusing as it does on the rights of workers—their safety, livelihoods, and future job prospects. As such, workplace environmental justice is fundamentally about workers' quality of life and livelihoods.

But workplace health and safety must push the boundaries of traditional trade union activism in a number of key areas. First, it must go beyond the reactionary "protective clothing" model discussed above. In order to do this, workers and unions will need to see health and safety within the context of production processes, choices of raw materials, and even the final products produced. Central to this broader critique would be a critical analysis of so-called clean technologies (e.g., more efficient boilers, more benign solvents). Although clean technologies can improve the immediate working environment, these initiatives are often driven by management for reasons that have little (if anything) to do with the health and safety of workers. As the following quote from an executive at a South African chemical company illustrates, many South African managers would appear to be more interested in competitive pressures and the demands of the international market than they are in the health and safety of their workers and other South Africans:

> We are looking to cleaner technologies, waste minimisation and utilisation of by-products. We don't want to be at a disadvantage in the international market as a result of environmental issues. . . . We are also concerned to avoid accidents or other problems which, aside from anything else, would be a major problem in international markets. We don't want to be seen as irresponsible. (quoted in Bethlehem 1997, 77)

Trade unions need to engage critically in these clean technology debates and insert local pressures on companies for change while at the same time challenging the more revisionist elements of this clean technology agenda.

It is also important that trade unions recognize the obligations that workplace environmental justice entails *outside* of the factory. The right of a worker to a safe and healthy place to work is bound by the constitutional rights of all South Africans to a clean and healthy environment. In other words, workplace environmental problems cannot simply be transferred from the shop floor to the broader environment by venting pollutants outside—a point made all the more important by the fact that industrial areas are generally adjacent to the poor black communities in which most of the workers live.

Finally, workplace environmental justice could add some badly needed objectivity to debates on land and resource use. Decisions on this subject often get bogged down in (ultimately unresolvable) debates about their aesthetic/ecological value as compared to their economic value. Worker environmental justice would introduce an additional cost-benefit analysis by looking specifically at the job trade-offs associated with different land and resource use options. If, for example, there were a debate over whether to build a chemical plant on prime agricultural land, union leaders representing both agricultural and chemical workers could meet to discuss the job and health and safety trade-offs. These discussions would have to weigh up issues which, amongst others, could include: (i) the balance between the number of jobs created and jobs lost; (ii) judgments about the quality of jobs and skill requirements of the jobs associated with the land use; (iii) the upstream and downstream knock-on impacts of land use choice on jobs along the product life cycle; and (iv) the sustainability and security of jobs in relation to the land use.

An example of this is the debate that took place over the location of the Iscor steel plant in an ecologically sensitive area in Saldhana Bay, north of Cape Town, in the mid-1990s. Steelworkers fought for the development because it meant the creation of new jobs, while fishing industry workers fought for the protection of the marine resources that would be jeopardized by the plant. The process allowed for the introduction of a more objective and worker-centered dialogue while at the same time dealing with broader questions of resource use and sustainability (see also chap. 1 in this volume).

Conclusion

As noted above, environmental justice in the workplace will only come about as part of a mass movement for social change. Reactive programs in individual workplaces are insufficient. With this in mind, the following "shopping list" (phrased as desired outcomes) of possible intermediate objectives for progressive unions and their federations may be useful:

- a recognition of workplace environmental justice as part and parcel of trade union political agendas through increased discussion and debate within the movement and alliance partners;
- broad-based awareness on the shop floor about workplace environmental justice through education and training;
- broad-based general awareness of improvements in the working environment through means other than protective devices, including production and product alternatives;
- active union/environmental NGO dialogue on red-green politics through open discussion and formal debate.

Workplace environmental justice is seen here as a pragmatic means of getting unions to think about environmental issues in a more strategic and coordinated way that would benefit both their membership and the communities they live in. It does not presume to resolve the broader philosophical debates over anthro- versus ecocentric environmental positions or the value of cost-benefit analysis. What it does is to provide a short- to medium-term framework that will resonate with workers for whom "the value of life cannot easily be separated from the value of a livelihood" (Magane et al. 1997, 179).

The urgency of this issue is demonstrated by the fact that in the time it has taken you to read this chapter it is possible that another South African worker has been killed or disabled by what is probably a completely avoidable incident.

References

Alston, D. 1993. "Environment and Development: An Issue of Justice." In D. Hallowes, ed. *Hidden Faces: Environment, Development, Justice: South Africa and the Global Context*. Pietermaritzburg: Earthlife Africa.

Bethlehem, L. 1997. "Catalysing Change: International Environmental Pressure on South African Exporters." In L. Bethlehem and M. Goldblatt, eds. *The Bottom Line: Industry and the Environment in South Africa*. Cape Town: University of Cape Town Press.

Butler, M. 1997. "Lessons From Thor Chemicals: The Links between Health,

Safety and Environmental Protection." In L. Bethlehem and M. Gold-blatt, eds. *The Bottom Line: Industry and the Environment in South Africa*. Cape Town: University of Cape Town Press.

Kockott, F. 1994. *Wasted Lives: Mercury Recycling at Thor Chemicals*. Johannesburg: Earthlife Africa and Greenpeace International.

Koch, E. 1991. "Rainbow Alliances: Community Struggles around Ecological Problems." In J. Cock and E. Koch, eds. *Going Green: People, Politics and the Environment in South Africa*. Cape Town: Oxford University Press.

Crompton, R., and A. Erwin, 1991. "Reds and Greens: Labour and the Environment." In J. Cock and E. Koch, eds. *Going Green: People, Politics and the Environment in South Africa*. Cape Town: Oxford University Press.

Hallowes, D., ed. 1993. *Hidden Faces: Environment, Development, Justice: South Africa and the Global Context*. Pietermaritzburg: Earthlife Africa.

Harris, A. 1993. "Greenpeace, Environmentalism and Labour." In D. Hallowes, ed. *Hidden Faces: Environment, Development, Justice: South Africa and the Global Context*. Pietermaritzburg: Earthlife Africa.

Lukey, P. 1995. *Health Before Profits: An Access Guide to Trade Unions and Environmental Justice in South Africa*. Pietermaritzburg: Environmental Justice Networking Forum and Frederich Ebert Stiftung.

Magane, P., S. Miller, M. Goldblatt, and L. Bethlehem. 1997. "Unions and Environment: Life, Health and the Pursuit of Employment." In L. Bethlehem and M. Goldblatt, eds. *The Bottom Line: Industry and the Environment in South Africa*. Cape Town: University of Cape Town Press.

Markham, A. 1994. *A Brief History of Pollution*. London: Earthscan Publications.

Miller, S. 1993. "Health, Safety and Environment." In D. Hallowes, ed. *Hidden Faces: Environment, Development, Justice: South Africa and the Global Context*. Pietermaritzburg: Earthlife Africa.

Pepper, D. 1993. *Eco-Socialism: From Deep Ecology to Social Justice*. London: Routledge.

Renner, M. 1991. *Jobs in a Sustainable Economy*. Washington, D.C.: Worldwatch Institute.

Thorpe, V. 1993. "Solidarity First: Environmental Priorities for Labour Internationalism." In D. Hallowes, ed. *Hidden Faces: Environment, Development, Justice: South Africa and the Global Context*. Pietermaritzburg: Earthlife Africa.

Crippled for Life by Mercury Exposure

Mpume Nyandu

Loss of memory, headaches, aching joints, and loss of sexual desire are just some of the problems common to many people who work or have worked for Thor Chemicals, a British company based in Cato Ridge, KwaZulu-Natal. The company imported thousands of toxic mercury waste barrels from the United States and other countries for "recycling" but failed to warn workers about the dangers of working with the waste. The result was that two workers died of mercury exposure and many others have been badly affected by the toxic material.

Johannes Nxumalo, a former Thor worker, says he was aware of what was happening to his colleagues and of the fact that he was beginning to be affected physically, but because "I was hungry and I needed money, I was forced to work." He continues: "My colleagues and I used to jog to and from work every morning and afternoon, as a way of getting rid of the poison in our bodies."

Thor workers and former workers recount their experience with great pain and anger. Baba Zakwe (55) tells how he was retrenched from Thor Chemicals. "I started working at Thor as a temp, in 1989, and I was retrenched six years later. I have no idea why I was retrenched but what I know is that the doctor said the mercury level in my blood was always high. When I got retrenched I got R11,000. That's all I got and I don't think that was compensation for my illness."

When Zakwe was retrenched in 1995 he was living with his wife and four children. His wife, who was also unemployed at the time, made a little money by selling chips and sweets to schoolchildren. She has since died. Zakwe, who goes to the Wentworth hospital regularly for check-ups for mental illness, says, "Right now we have nothing, no money." "I have a huge bill at the hospital and they keep pestering me to pay. I always tell them I do not have money, I am unemployed. My children are also unemployed. We rely on people donating food to us. People give beans, maize meal, and stuff like that. My son who is still at school is doing Standard Nine, my two daughters had to leave school at Standard Eight and Standard Six because I could not afford the fees. My son's fees are paid by my eldest daughter who is now married."

Zakwe does not get a disability grant because "I did not know I could apply for a disability grant." Such an application would be complicated by the fact that he would have to furnish proof that he was crippled by his work environment. Thor denies that workers are affected by the chemicals they handle at work. According to a current employee, "as Thor workers we all suffer from more or less the same problems, the leading one being forgetfulness." He says the company doctor has told the workers that it is normal to forget. The management, for their part, has never complained about the workers suffering from loss of memory.

Workers also allege that once they have worked for Thor it is almost impossible for them to find a job elsewhere. Gideon Nkala of Inchanga says: "When you go looking for a job, they look at your employment card, and when they see that you have worked for Thor Chemicals they tell you to come back another day and they do not say why."

Nkala, who worked at Thor from 1990 to 1992, is one of many workers retrenched after their health started deteriorating. He says when he started with the company he was able to walk the ten kilometers to work and also played soccer. He was basically fit and active. Today he is sickly and constantly exhausted, he sweats excessively, his feet have ringworm-like sores and, as a result, he cannot wear shoes. He often loses his appetite. He believes that "The previous government placed Thor where it is because they knew black people did not know about the dangers of mercury. They knew that what people wanted was employment."

It seems the Thor mercury problem does not only affect those who handle the toxic material directly but also the environment of the Inchanga community which is below the plant. Thor is situated less than three kilometers from Inchanga. According to one worker, "There are two big ponds at the Thor plant which are always full of water with chemicals. When it rains these ponds often overflow and the contaminated waters from these ponds go down a stream called Umngcweni, where people's cattle drink." Johannes Nxumalo adds: "What is sad is that people slaughter these animals and eat the meat, and I think the chances of the mercury being transmitted from the meat to people are great."

Johannes believes that the fumes emitted by the Thor chimneys might constitute a further health hazard. Some members of the community believe that the increased violence in the Inchanga area in recent times may be linked to mercury exposure. Some of the violence follows accusations of witchcraft which are rife as otherwise healthy people begin to suffer from headaches, mental illness, and exhaustion.

Countries with stricter and firmer health standards in the workplace have refused to accept toxic mercury waste and, according to Richard Meeran, an English lawyer working on the Thor case, there is "evidence which shows Thor moved part of its British plant to South Africa in the 1980s after the country's health and safety executive, which monitors health standards in local firms, expressed concern about the high levels of mercury in blood and urine of workers in England."

Although Thor Chemicals has been forced to shut down the mercury recycling plant, they have not said what will happen to the many barrels of mercury which have not yet been recycled. According to one worker: "They keep saying they have closed the section that produces the poison [mercury] but there's always smoke coming from that side. So we are not really safe with the huge amounts of waste waiting in the warehouses. Even if the company was to close down today, they still need to deal with the toxic waste." Most Thor workers and former workers agree that the mercury waste should be shipped back to the countries from which it originated, or generations and generations to come will have their lives ruined by it.

Chapter 11

Up Against the (Crumbling) Wall

The Privatization of Urban Services and Environmental Justice

David A. McDonald

The shiny new hotels of the Waterfront in Cape Town and the building cranes of Sandton in Johannesburg belie the bigger reality of post-apartheid South Africa: crumbling or nonexistent infrastructure and poor quality municipal services for the majority of the country's urban population. In the early 1990s it was estimated that 7 million people (out of a total population of approximately 40 million) were living in densely populated informal settlements in urban areas with few, if any, basic services (IDRC 1992). Crime and violence in these areas were rife, unemployment was as high as 80 percent, and easily preventable diseases like tuberculosis and diarrhea were major causes of illness and death (Wilson and Ramphele 1989). According to the African National Congress (ANC), there were more than 12 million South Africans without access to clean drinking water in 1994 and 21 million people without adequate sanitation (ANC 1994, 28). An additional ten percent of the population did not have access to a toilet of any kind, one-third relied on pit latrines, and 14 percent had no form of refuse removal whatsoever (RSA 1995, 10).

The post-apartheid government has made the provision of these services a key part of their reconstruction and development mandate and has made important strides in this regard. By the end of its first term of office in 1999, the ANC claimed to have provided three million people with access to potable water, to have connected two million households to the electricity grid, to have built new homes (along with relevant service infrastructure) for three million people, and to have built five hundred new health clinics (Khosa 2000).

The number of South Africans without adequate services still remains in the millions, however, and many new infrastructure schemes have fallen into disuse because of a lack of operating funds, technical problems, and/or cutoffs for non-payment. According to the Rural Development Services Network as many as 90 percent of the water delivery schemes provided by government since 1994 are no longer operational (RDSN 2000). Rural areas are worse off than cities in terms of the absolute number of people who do not have services, but high population densities in urban areas and the heightened potential for the spread of infectious diseases, shack fires, and related social violence make the quality of life in urban areas in South Africa among the worst in the world today.

Infrastructure in many of the older urban townships of the country is on the verge of collapse. Townships like Langa, built on what was then the outskirts of Cape Town in the 1920s, are in desperate need of bulk infrastructure refits, and although most of its residents are technically receiving services like in-house water and sewerage, the reality is that these services are constantly failing: sewerage mains back up; water pipes burst; stormwater drains clog with sand, refuse, and other debris.

The environmental implications of these infrastructure and service delivery deficits are serious. The lack of toilets and refuse collection means that people have to defecate in rivers and streams and dump their refuse in open spaces, creating disease vectors for malaria, cholera, and tuberculosis, and contributing to ground and surface water contamination. A lack of electricity (and other sources of safe energy) forces people to cut down trees and burn coal and kerosene, contributing to deforestation, soil erosion, localized air pollution, and house fires. The lack of these services is arguably the most serious environmental problem in the country today—if for no other reason than the sheer number of people who are directly affected by its consequences.

The story of how urban poverty and poor service provision leads to environmental degradation is now well documented in South Africa (Khan 1991; Lawson 1991; IDRC 1995; McDonald 1996, 1998; Bond 1999) as it is in other countries around the world with similar problems (Stren et al. 1992; Hardoy, Mitlin, and Sutterthwaite 1993; Bartone et al. 1994; World Bank 1992, 1994a). More importantly, the environmental justice movement in South Africa—most notably through the work of the Environmental Justice Networking Forum (EJNF) and some of its member organizations—has placed this issue of service delivery squarely on the national environmental agenda. Virtually every piece of environmental (or environmentally related) post-apartheid legislation makes reference to the need for better services and municipal infrastructure, as well as the need to address the environmental injustices resulting from years of apartheid neglect and discriminatory placement of environmentally noxious disposal facilities like sewerage treatment plants and dump sites (see for example RSA 1998a, b, c). The term *environmental justice* has even found its way into the lexicon of government documents on the issue, with concerns about environmental racism and the distribution of environmental "bads" dominating the discourse.

But rather than repeat this story, this chapter explores one aspect of the service delivery–environmental justice link that has been underinvestigated in South Africa: the environmental implications of privatizing municipal services like water and refuse collection. Policy documents on the environment in South Africa are silent on the issue, as are policy documents on privatization. Environmental justice groups in the country, for their part, remain largely focused on the environmental implications of the absence of adequate services rather than the implications of who delivers these services. There has been some discussion of the environment in academic debates over the role of the private sector in municipal services in the country, but these contributions have not been systematic or comprehensive in their coverage of the issue and tend not to deal with the underlying theoretical rationale for privatization.

Privatization (in its various forms) is still in its infancy in South Africa, but all indications are that it will become an increasingly important factor in the service delivery equation, with cities throughout the country implementing wide-ranging privatization strategies in the late 1990s and early 2000s (McDonald 1998; Bond 2000a, b; McDonald and Smith 2001).[1] It is essential therefore to better understand the environmental implications of privatizing municipal services in the country, particularly as they relate to the living and working environments of the urban poor.

The chapter begins with a brief discussion of what is meant by the term "privatization" and describes its various manifestations. It then provides a summary of the environmental arguments for and against the privatization of municipal services and situates these debates in the South African context. Privatization, it must be noted, is touted by organizations like the World Bank as something of an environmental panacea for poverty-ridden cities, and the Bank and other international institutions like the Urban Management Programme (UMP), the United Nations Development Programme (UNDP), and the United Nations Centre for Human Settlements (UNCHS) have dedicated enormous resources to promoting private sector participation as the best way to address urban service provision and environmental degradation (World Bank 1992, 1994a, b; Cointreau-Levine 1994; Leitmann 1994; Serageldin, Cohen, and Sivaramakrishnan 1994; Serageldin and Steer 1994; Gidman et al. 1995; Shin et al. 1997; UNDP–World Bank 1998; Hoornweg and Thomas 1999; World Bank–UNCHS 1999). This chapter looks specifically at the claims that these organizations make about private sector efficiency, accountability, innovation, capital expenditure, and resource conservation, and why they believe that privatization is the best way to improve the living environments of the urban poor as well as the sustainability of cities as a whole.

The chapter then critically evaluates these claims and highlights the environmental flaws and contradictions in the pro-privatization arguments. Evidence from South Africa is used to support these positions, as is material from a wider range of privatization experiences elsewhere in the world. Equally important are the more theoretically grounded criticisms of privatization. Private sector participation in urban service delivery cannot be disaggregated from the interests of national and international capital or from the micro social, political, and spatial realities of post-apartheid cities. Municipal resources remain highly skewed along racial lines, bureaucratic decision making remains largely in the hands of a few (predominantly white and apartheid-era) engineers, and fiscal restraints at the national level have made it difficult for cities to expand their infrastructure, all of which must be taken into account when evaluating the privatization option. It is this conjunctural analysis of service delivery that is perhaps the most important of all, bringing into question some of the fundamental principles behind privatization as well as the ecological modernization paradigm behind it.

The central argument of the chapter is that privatization may provide temporary relief for the urban poor in South Africa desperate to improve the environmental quality of their lives, but this relief is likely to be short-lived (or never realized at all) because of the red-lining of poor communities, corruption in the private sector, price increases for the urban poor, cutoffs of basic services, and violations of environmental, safety, and health regulations. Not all these problems happen in every instance, but the empirical and theoretical evidence is that privatization worsens access to core services for the urban poor and ultimately exacerbates environmental degradation.

My objective here is twofold: first, to contribute to the ongoing debates over the privatization of municipal services in South Africa with an overview of its implications for environmental justice; and second, to bring the privatization debate to the closer attention of the environmental justice movement. The demand for the upgrading and extension of municipal services is important , but the "who" and the "why" of service delivery is at the heart of environmental equity and sustainability and must be taken up by the environmental justice movement if we are effectively to address the service delivery question.

What Is Privatization?

Private sector participation in the delivery of municipal services can take a variety of forms—from one person collecting refuse and fixing water pipes in a small section of a township to a large multinational corporation providing bulk water supply. The size and types of contracts can vary considerably as well, from a one-year, fee-for-service, renewable contract to a thirty-year license. Ownership of assets also varies, with the state retaining ownership in some cases and the private company in others. Table 1 provides a breakdown of these different options.

Table 1: Different Forms of Privatization

Service Contract	The public authority retains responsibility for operation and maintenance of service, but specific components of the service (for example billing and metering) are contracted out to the private sector. Service contracts usually have a duration of one to two years.
Management Contract	The management contractor takes responsibility for the operation and maintenance of the service or parts of the service. The public authority retains ownership of the assets and responsibility for new investments. The public authority also remains responsible for tariff collection. Management contracts tend to cover a timespan of two to five years.
Lease or Affermage	The lessee rents the facility from the public authority and becomes responsible for operating, maintaining, and managing the system and for collecting the tariffs. The public authority remains responsible for new investments in the service. Leases generally have a duration of eight to fifteen years.
Concession	An arrangement by which the concessionaire has overall responsibility for the services, including operation, maintenance, and management, as well as capital investments during the concession period. The concessionaire is also responsible for tariff collection. The ownership of fixed assets remains with the public authority, however. Concession contracts tend to cover a period of twenty-five to thirty years.
BOT, BOOT	Build (Own) Operate Transfer contracts are generally used when large new parts of a service system such as water treatment plants and wastewater treatment plants are constructed. The private operator builds the plant and assumes responsibility for its operation and maintenance. After a predetermined time the facility is transferred to the public authority. The length of a B(O)OT contract is usually twenty-five to thirty years.
Full Divestiture	Full divestiture pertains to a situation where the utility has been fully privatized. Ownership of the utility rests with the private operator. The private operator is responsible for operation and maintenance, investments, and tariff collection. The private utilities operate under supervision of a (public) regulatory regime.

(Adapted from Schuttenbelt and Lorentzen 1994)

It should be evident from table 1 that most "privatization" schemes do not actually involve the sale of municipal assets and are in fact public-private partnerships (PPPs). Only the outright sale of state assets constitutes privatization per se. This is a point that the World Bank is at pains to emphasize in its own push for private sector involvement, arguing that

PPPs do not mean an abdication of public control or ownership. Just how equal and accurate this notion of a "partnership" is in the real world of PPPs is something that will be discussed at length in this chapter. For the moment it is sufficient to underscore the point that much of the private sector involvement in South Africa and other parts of the world is in fact a public-private partnership, with continued government involvement and oversight in service delivery.

The term "privatization" is therefore something of a misnomer, but will be used in this chapter as a generic expression for private sector involvement in service delivery for purposes of convenience and because the term is widely acknowledged in popular discourse. The term is also used here, however, because each of the different forms of privatization outlined in table 1 operates within generally accepted private sector principles—principles which are very different from those that have traditionally driven public sector service delivery. Running a service "like a business" requires the introduction of a new set of management philosophies and economic guidelines and it is the relationship between these private sector principles and environmental justice that this chapter attempts to illuminate in the South African context.

Arguments For and Against Privatization

The environmental arguments in favor of privatization fall into four categories: the need for capital and expertise to alleviate environmental degradation; the need for efficiency gains to provide better and more affordable services to the poor; better accountability for environmental monitoring; and the introduction of better environmental technologies through innovative management and research. A summary of each of these arguments is provided below, followed by a rebuttal.

These characterizations of the pro-privatization arguments are drawn primarily from the work of the World Bank and its affiliates (as per the citations provided earlier). The characterizations are necessarily brief because of space restrictions but they do capture the central tenets behind the privatization arguments as they apply to the environment. The writings of these organizations have been selected because they have been central to the development and articulation of theoretical positions on the environmental benefits of privatization, and because the organiza-tions have been very influential in the shaping of urban policy in South Africa.[2]

Capital and Expertise

Perhaps the most fundamental argument in favor of privatization is that the public sector simply does not have the necessary resources or expertise to provide services on the scale that they are required in cities like Johan-nesburg and Cape Town. Limited state budgets combined with the sheer enormity of the task make rapid public sector service expansion unlikely, if not impossible. Moreover, the public sector is considered to lack the necessary engineering, accounting, and other trade and professional skills to provide the required services timeously and satisfactorily.

The private sector, on the other hand, is considered to have the capi-tal and expertise required for service delivery and expansion and, most importantly, is able to invest and operate at very short notice. In Britain, for example, the privatization of the water industry is said to have pro-vided over £30 billion for new infrastructure investment in the 1980s alone (Manson 1994, 11). Rather than wait for scarce public resources to materialize the private sector can provide quality services quickly, and begin to address the environmental degradation caused by inadequate service delivery much faster than the public sector could hope to do.

The problem with this line of argument is that it takes as a given that public resources are not available for large infrastructure and service expansion. In reality, of course, the amount of public funding available for infrastructure development is a political choice. In what has become something of a self-fulfilling prophesy, local and national governments around the world have introduced conservative macro-economic poli-cies and severe fiscal restraints and then turned to their constituents and announced that "the state does not have sufficient funds for infrastruc-ture investments." The growing hegemony of this neoliberal discourse in the 1980s and 1990s has stifled debate on public investment and led to a form of institutional amnesia where bureaucrats and policymakers appear to have forgotten that there has historically been a very different approach to public sector investment in urban services and infrastruc-ture. The image of the state as insolvent becomes "common sense" and the Thatcherite adage of "there is no alternative" (TINA) becomes a popular acronym for privatization advocates.

The same sequence of events applies to South Africa where the state invested very heavily in urban infrastructure under apartheid (albeit along highly skewed racial lines) and where, more recently, the ANC, prior to coming to office in 1994, called for major state investments in urban services. However, with the introduction in 1996 of Growth Employment and Redistribution (GEAR), a fiscally conservative macroeconomic policy framework brought in by the ANC without consultation with its labor partner, the Congress of South African Trade Unions, there was a dramatic shift away from public sector spending.

GEAR has had far-reaching effects on investments in service delivery. First, fiscal restraint at the national level has meant severe cutbacks in intergovernmental transfers to local government—the level of government responsible for the majority of urban infrastructure development and service delivery in South Africa (RSA 1994b). Between 1991 and 1998 these intergovernmental transfers were reduced by 85 percent in real terms (Barchiesi 2000), with some cities experiencing additional decreases of as much as 55 percent between 1997 and 2000 (Unicity Commission 2000). Not all these cuts are the responsibility of the ANC, but GEAR has had a significant impact on the capacity of local governments to fulfill their constitutionally mandated service expansion requirements.

To put these figures in perspective, in fiscal 2000 intergovernmental transfers to local governments across South Africa were in the order of R3 billion per year, with a possible increase of only 15 percent over the next few years. Meanwhile, projections of the capital costs of addressing service backlogs are in the order of R45 to R89 billion (depending on the level of services provided), with government-sponsored operating costs (e.g., free lifeline services) adding billions more per year (RSA 1995, 2000a). It is not surprising, therefore, that local governments have begun to explore private sector options for generating capital.[3]

To make matters worse, national government has put caps on the rates increases that local governments are able to levy on (wealthy) property owners. The Draft Local Government Property Rates Bill of 2000, for example, makes it clear that national government will not allow local governments to apply taxes at the local level which threaten its macroeconomic strategy: "A municipality may not . . . exercise its power to levy

rates on property in a way that would materially and unreasonably prejudice national economic policies, economic activities across its boundaries, or the national mobility of goods, services, capital or labor" (RSA
2000b, chap. 2, s4). With approximately 90 percent of all local government revenues generated locally (of which approximately 25 percent
come from property rates), these caps make it difficult to increase revenue
streams, once again opening the door to private sector participation.

Perhaps as a result of the dominant TINA mentality, there has been
no sustained or systematic effort in South Africa to explore ways of better utilizing existing public resources (before trying to raise new private
sector resources), despite the enormous potential for a more equitable
and efficient use of municipal assets, personnel, and equipment. Because
of the racialized and highly fragmented nature of municipal government in the country apartheid cities were amongst the most inequitable
and inefficient in the world and it was anticipated that there would be a
"substantial amount of financial and human resources" available for "re-
direction" into poor neighborhoods when these municipalities were
forced to amalgamate into single, non-racial units after 1994 (RSA
1994a, 15). White municipalities were extremely well resourced during
apartheid (and still are for the most part) with per capita infrastructure
investment rates that equaled or exceeded those of most European and
North American cities in the 1970s and 1980s (Ahmad 1995).

Since 1994 little has been done to track and monitor these municipal resource inequalities. There have never been full-scale audits of municipal resources in any of the metropolitan areas and there are very few
metropolitan-wide statistics for resource distribution. Partly as a result of
this information deficit, redistributive efforts have also been weak. One
recent survey found that public sector resources in historically white
areas of Cape Town were as much as 100 times greater per capita than
those in historically black areas.[4] Although anecdotal, these findings are
indicative of what is thought to be a widespread problem in the country.

It would appear, as well, that there is little political commitment to
finding ways of improving public sector efficiency. Although the ANC
promised during its campaign for the local government elections in October 2000 that "national and provincial governments will keep the public
sector as the preferred provider of municipal services, to ensure adequate
service for all communities," ANC national government policy papers

and official legislation fail to make the same commitment. One example of this lack of commitment is found in the Department of Local and Provincial Government's White Paper on "Municipal Service Partnerships" (the ANC's term for "public-private partnerships"). Released in early 2000, the paper attempts to clarify the government's position on "preferred options," but succeeds merely in establishing the downgrading of the public option to one that is no more important than private sector initiatives: "While the Government is committed to facilitating the use of MSP [municipal service partnership] arrangements, this does not mean that MSPs are the preferred option for improving service delivery. It is rather that MSPs should enjoy equal status among a range of possible service delivery options available to municipal councils" (RSA 2000c, 14).

The formation of the Municipal Infrastructure Investment Unit (MIIU) is another important development in this regard. Established as a five-year program in 1997 with funding from foreign donors, the MIIU's stated Mission is "to encourage and optimize private sector investment in local authority services." Activities to be undertaken involve "assistance to local authorities in the process of hiring private sector consultants and the management of contracts with the private sector" and "developing project proposals involving private sector investment" (MIIU 2000).

The MIIU has been extremely active in promoting and financing the privatization and corporatization of municipal services (with the help of foreign donors) and has provided advice and funding to dozens of municipalities in the country along these lines, including the controversial thirty-year contracting of water in Nelspruit. The fact that no parallel organization has been set up at a national level to promote and conduct research on how best to improve and extend public sector service delivery is perhaps the most telling indication of the ideological impulses driving urban policy in central government. In fact, a request in 1997 to the Department of Water Affairs and Forestry by the South African Municipal Workers' Union (SAMWU) for a mere R150,000 to run pilot tests on improving public-sector water delivery options in Cape Town was turned down.[5]

The privatization of municipal services in South Africa is neither inevitable nor necessary. The reliance on private capital to upgrade and expand services in the country is largely a political decision driven by an ideological commitment to fiscal restraint. It is not a policy based on a thorough analysis of public sector resources (particularly at the level of local government) or the potential for public sector reform. The environmental consequences of these political decisions are potentially disastrous, as we discover in the following sections.

Efficiency

The second environmental argument of the World Bank and others in favor of privatization is that private firms are more efficient than the public sector. Competition for contracts and the need to make a profit for the company motivates managers to cut costs and constantly find more efficient ways of providing services. This entrepreneurial spirit, it is argued, is missing from city workers and managers, who are portrayed as lazy and unmotivated.

These efficiency gains, it is claimed, are then translated into lower service costs for the end user, particularly for the urban poor, making services more accessible to a wider range of people (and therefore reducing pressures on the urban environment). In addition, money saved by the state can be directed into further service extensions/upgrades, targeted subsidies for the poor, and/or a range of other environmentally enhancing investments (e.g., parks).

International experience with private contractors, however, has shown that anticipated cost savings for end users, and for the state, often do not materialize. One reason is that private companies regularly win contracts with what is called a "low ball" bid and then ratchet-up prices once they have established themselves in a monopoly or near-monopoly position (CUPE 2000). These price increases are often justified in terms of "unanticipated" or "extra-contractual" costs, with the end result being consumer prices that are significantly higher than those under public sector delivery, resulting in problems of inaccessibility for the poor, service cutoffs for people unable to pay the price increases, and price gouging.

Nor are private firms necessarily more efficient than the public sector. One of the biggest myths in the pro-privatization literature is that of the super-efficient private-sector worker. "American folk wisdom," comments Elliott Sclar (2000, 21) in the United States context, "holds that public service is uncaring, unbending, bureaucratic and expensive, whereas competitively supplied private services . . . are efficient and responsive." The empirical evidence, he goes on to say, suggests that there is in fact very little difference between the two. If anything, public sector employees are more productive than their private sector counterparts because most public sector work is labor intensive and the public sector usually has "state-of-the-art techniques" when it comes to labor utilization (Sclar 2000, 60–8).

There is also evidence of government officials in various countries artificially raising the price of publicly provided services just prior to privatization in an attempt to make private sector bids appear lower than prices charged by the public sector and to convince the general public that the private sector is more efficient. In Buenos Aires, Argentina, for example, there were five price increases just prior to the privatization of the water and sanitation system in 1993—all of which were highly suspect from an economic point of view—allowing the private firm that was awarded the contract to introduce a (much heralded) 27 percent price decrease immediately after taking over the water system (Ferro 2000).

A similar strategy is reported on (and recommended to other governments) by Mark Dumol, a Filipino government official, in a World Bank publication on the Manila water concession. Dumol (2000, 42) writes, in a chapter entitled "Need to Have Bids Lower than the Existing Water Tariff," that "In August 1996, about five months before the bid submission, the water tariffs were increased by about 38 percent. This tariff increase was actually long overdue and would have been implemented regardless of privatization. . . . Nevertheless, it gave us a substantially greater chance that the bids would be lower." Dumol goes on to cite the Buenos Aires water concession as the inspiration for the price hike strategy in Manila.

Most importantly, there are the "hidden costs" of privatization to consider, particularly as they apply to the environment. Violations of environmental regulations by private firms are widespread, with toxic spills, illegal dumping, and other bylaw infringements costing governments significant amounts of money to rectify while at the same time placing the health and safety of the public at risk. One example of this in the South African context occurred in 1999 when eight trucks of dangerous medical waste were found to have been dumped illegally by Enviroserv, a private waste company, in Bloemfontein. The waste consisted of syringes, blood products, body parts, and other medical waste. In this case the perpetrators were caught and the firm bore the costs of clean up, but the municipal dump where the waste was left was used by scavengers, putting them at risk of infection as well as leading to the possible spread of water-borne diseases (*Mail & Guardian*, 9–15 September 1999).

This is far from being an isolated incident. Private service providers are notorious for violating health and environmental regulations, as the following brief list of firms that have been caught and fined in other countries illustrates:

■ In 1998, Thames Water in the UK was taken to court over the release of five million gallons of a cocktail of raw sewage and industrial chemicals into the River Thames at Erith. Residents were required to move out of their homes and were unable to return for up to one year after the incident. The accident is thought to have been caused by negligence on the part of the company but Thames Water was reportedly uncooperative throughout the investigation and the cause of the leaks remains unknown. This was the twenty-fourth time the UK Environment Agency had prosecuted Thames Water since 1995 (Cook 2000).

■ AEP, Southern Co., and Cinergy, were charged in the autumn of 1999 with evading the Clean Air Act in the United States by modifying coal-fired generating plants in order to significantly extend their lifespan without having been granted permission to make the modifications. At the end of June 2000 the charges were extended by the Environmental Protection Agency (EPA) to include several more power generation plants (PSIRU 2000).

■ Waste Management Incorporated (WMI), the largest waste disposal firm in the world, whose major shareholders have included George Soros and Vivendi's waste management subsidiary Onyx, is responsible for a long string of environmental violations. WMI has paid more than $370 million in fines over the past twenty years in the United States alone for environmental infractions and other offences, including price-fixing schemes, investor fraud, and shareholder deception. Some of the more recent sanctions against WMI and its affiliates are:

  • October 15, 1992—Chemical Waste pleaded guilty and paid a record $11.6 million fine for six violations of environmental laws at a Superfund site it was cleaning up in Pennsylvania;

- October 1997—it was revealed that three workers had died in separate accidents in 1996 at a Waste Management facility in Brooklyn, New York;

- November 1998—WMI agreed to pay a $125,000 fine to the state of Virginia for improperly disposing of medical waste. The company allegedly shipped medical waste from New York City to Virginia in trucks not approved to carry hazardous materials and then illegally disposed of the waste in a landfill in Virginia (EBIC 2000).

It is also worth noting that a 1993 report by the Criminal Intelligence Service of Ontario (Canada) entitled "Organized Crime and the Environment" singled out WMI for possible influence peddling and a slew of environmental infractions: "The list of WMI's environmental violations is extensive. Violations include falsifying records, violating inventory limits, mislabelling of drums containing hazardous waste to mislead inspectors, mishandling of hazardous wastes . . . selling home heating oil contaminated with PCBs and dioxin, bribing mayors to obtain municipal waste hauling contracts, and so on" (CISO 1993).

These are only a few of the instances where private firms have been caught violating regulations. There are no doubt many more cases where private firms *have not* been caught, with the total number of unreported environmental infractions, and the associated costs to the public fiscus and public health, remaining unknown. Suffice it to say that these hidden costs are significant and may outweigh any savings garnered by privatizing in the first place.

This is not to suggest that private firms are the only organizations to violate environmental and other legislation. Public service providers in South Africa have also been a problem in this regard, particularly when it comes to dumping waste in or near black townships and informal settlements. Environmental racism is still very much alive in the South African public service (McDonald 1997) and there are lazy and corrupt officials at all levels of government. Nevertheless, there are fundamental differences in the way that public sector institutions approach questions of efficiency and these differences can have a significant influence on environmental management. For one, the public sector is not driven by the need to make a profit or undercut its competitors at all costs. The public sector can accept certain "inefficiencies" in the name of public safety, and thereby provide a deeper level of insurance that the public good—rather than private gain—will be the primary motivation for service delivery. Private sector firms, on the other hand, operate in their own closed environment and are concerned solely with efficiency gains and losses within the firm. They have little interest in the financial health of other firms or other sectors, let alone the less tangible gains and losses like gender equity, aesthetics, and spatial desegregation associated with service delivery. Private firms are unable to think in terms of the broader public good because they are bound by the immediacy of shareholder demands and profitability.

And what of those communities that are red-lined by private sector service providers because they fear that residents cannot pay, or that the effort to collect revenue will prove too costly despite possible government subsidies? Here efficiency issues must also be considered. One of these relates to the social, environmental, and health implications, especially for women and children, of exclusion, and the societal costs this implies, once again eating into any gains in monetary efficiency made through privatization. The second relates to the costs of having the public sector pick up the pieces left unattended. Any effort to service the patchwork of areas deemed undesirable by the private sector is bound to be rendered "inefficient" by spatial irregularities, lack of economies of scale, and inevitable morale problems with employees working in "problem areas." These public providers are then held up, in turn, as an illustration of the "inherent inefficiencies" of the public sector, while private service providers enjoy the benefits of "cherry picking" the easiest and most profitable areas to service. In those areas deemed problematic, a vicious cycle of decay ensues as the public sector finds it increasingly difficult to muster the resources to provide good services.

The health and safety of workers can also be compromised by privatization because private service delivery firms are seldom unionized (this is true of South Africa as well). Municipal work can be dangerous and unpleasant: picking dead animals off the street; cleaning broken sewerage lines; collecting buckets of "nightsoil" (urine and feces) from informal settlements; handling chemical defoliants; repairing potholes on busy roads. These health and safety factors are particularly acute in underserviced urban areas in South Africa where refuse piles can harbor rats and toxic waste, backed-up sewage lines can contain disease, and workers can be the victims of social and political violence simply by being in the wrong place at the wrong time. Given the history of labor relations generally in South Africa, it is not surprising that working conditions for (black) municipal workers have been very bad in the past. A lack of adequate safety equipment, poor or nonexistent training, and the use of archaic systems like nightsoil buckets has meant that municipal workers there have faced dangerous and unhealthy working conditions for decades (McDonald 1994). The formation of SAMWU in 1987 led to some important improvements in this regard, but most concessions have been hard fought on a municipality-by-municipality basis and SAMWU members still regularly face dangerous health and safety situations.

The question then arises: What happens to a private sector workforce that is not unionized? Although there has been no comparative research on this issue in South Africa to date, anecdotal evidence from public sector union representatives suggest that private sector employees are generally worse off than their public sector counterparts in terms of wages, benefits, health, and safety. This is particularly true of micro-enterprise operations in the townships, where working conditions are the most dangerous, and where it is most difficult to monitor private firms because they are small and have a large number of operators. There may be some scope for unionization or labor negotiations in some of the larger private sector service companies (where working conditions are more easily monitored by the state and labor unions), but how and if these arrangements unfold in the micro-enterprise sector in South Africa remains to be seen.

The point being made here is that the "working environment" must be seen as an integral part of the larger efficiency equation. Saving money while putting workers at risk is an unacceptable way to achieve efficiency gains. Moreover, if the immediate working environment is made worse by privatization there is something wrong with the overall environmental vision. Any attempt to improve the environmental living conditions of the urban poor must take into account the impact this will have on those doing the actual labor.

Accountability

A third environmental argument in favor of privatization is that the public sector is inherently corrupt and unaccountable to the public, and cannot, therefore, be relied upon to monitor its own environmental activities when it comes to waste management, water treatment, and so on. Nepotism and incompetence, combined with what is deemed to be an unwillingness on the part of public sector employees to accuse their colleagues of wrongdoing, are seen to be the main source of weakness when it comes to environmental monitoring by governments. In other words, governments cannot be trusted to monitor themselves.

The solution, it is argued, is to have the private sector provide services and have an independent regulator (run by a wide range of stakeholders, including government) monitor what they do. In this way there is no conflict of interest between employees of the state, and the independent regulator has the right to fine, and even fire, the private company that has violated an environmental regulation. Private firms are deemed to be more accountable because they must abide by a transparent set of rules outlined in their contract and monitored by the independent regulator.

Once again, however, international experience suggests this is not necessarily the case, with private firms tending to be *less* accountable than their public sector counterparts (Mulgan 1997a, 1997b, 2000; Roberts 2000). As Richard Mulgan (1997a, 110) observes, the contracting out and privatization of public services leads to a "considerable diminution of public accountability" because the degree of political responsibility generally declines and various information-seeking tools like "freedom of information" legislation, which apply to the public sector, are either significantly weaker in or entirely absent from the private sector. One reason for this is active avoidance on the part of private firms of independent scrutiny because they do not want to "expose [themselves] to public embarrassment." In particular, private sector directors or managers do not want to "open themselves to the same degree of media interrogation that politicians must accept, even on matters of clear public interest" (Mulgan 2000, 94).

Another reason that privatization reduces accountability is that accountability is expensive. It takes time and money to be accountable to the public, and these costs "have the potential to undermine the efficiency gains from contracting out" (Mulgan 1997a, 113). It has even been argued that it is precisely because of the reduction in public accountability that private sector firms are able to secure some efficiency gains over the public sector (Roberts 2000).

There is also growing evidence of corruption on the part of private service providers, particularly large multinationals, with independent regulators being bribed, or threatened, to "turn a blind eye" to environmental and other contract violations. The waste industry is particularly notorious for this kind of activity, with allegations of significant organized crime linkages (Cray 1991; Crooks 1993; CISO 1993), but there is evidence of corruption across a wide range of service sectors. Most importantly, it is multinational firms, not local bureaucrats and politicians, as the mainstream press would have us believe, which are largely responsible for driving this culture of bribery and corruption (Hawley 2000).

Accountability is also a problem when it comes to the relationship between server and client. Households and industry often violate environmental codes—sometimes unwittingly—and it is up to the service provider to monitor these consumption and waste flows to ensure that the end user is complying with environmental, health, and safety regulations. A household may, for example, leave several half-empty paint cans to be collected for disposal in the regular municipal dumpsite which should technically go to a hazardous waste site. What should happen in this case is that the private supplier should not collect the paint cans and should inform the resident of the proper procedures for disposal. The likelihood of this happening with a private sector provider is arguably much lower than it is with a public sector provider given the amount of time (and money) required to educate clients on a regular basis. There is also the risk of annoying a client and possibly losing a contract as a result of customer dissatisfaction. The latter is particularly true of large industrial clients who may be able to seek alternative (and less pesky) private service providers.

Even if private service providers are always trustworthy and state regulators always vigilant, budget cuts mean that local and provincial governments are finding themselves less and less capable of enforcing accountability. Environmental monitoring is often one of the first items to go in the rush to reduce government spending. In the province of Ontario, Canada, for example, the budget of the Ministry of the Environment was slashed by 44 percent between 1996 and 1998 and one-third of the staff (including nine hundred scientists) was laid off after a fiscally conservative government was elected. When the Ministry was forced to close its regional environmental testing laboratories as a result of these budget cuts, it had to cancel 400,000 tests done each year to check potable water quality. These responsibilities were downloaded in 1996 to municipalities that were given only eight weeks notice. Unable to cope with the deluge of new responsibilities, many municipalities farmed out water testing to private companies. Others were unable to deal effectively with the lack of provincial government support and their new monitoring responsibilities, with particularly tragic consequences for the town of Walkerton where *E. coli* bacteria killed seven people and infected more than two thousand in May 2000 (McDonald 2000). It is important to note that it was not the private company that was at fault here—they appear to have conducted the tests properly—it was the confusion that surrounded the downloading of responsibilities and lines of accountability and the lack of adequate training of public sector employees.

In South Africa, responsibilities such as water and sanitation have been downloaded to municipalities with equal rapidity and confusion has been exacerbated by municipal amalgamation and an often intransigent apartheid-era bureaucracy. Moreover, cash-strapped municipalities are now expected to manage new workloads and extend services to millions of urban and rural poor with an 85 percent reduction in intergovernmental financial transfers. Some South African municipalities have been able to cope better than others, but the capacity of local government to monitor the activities of private sector service providers is limited in part by insufficient resources.

This lack of capacity is all the more disconcerting when one considers the incredible fragmentation of municipal services in South African cities as a result of apartheid urban planning. The currently amalgamated City of Cape Town, for example, comprised more than twenty-five separate municipalities and some sixty-nine local decision-making bodies as recently as 1996. Each of these municipalities had its own service delivery infrastructure and decision-making units. There has been some rationalization of these service entities but for the most part there is still enormous fragmentation. To add a collection of private sector players to the mix at this stage will make environmental monitoring an even more chaotic (and inefficient) exercise.

This latter point is all the more pertinent when one considers the large numbers of micro-enterprise activities being promoted for service delivery in the townships. It may be feasible to monitor the delivery of bulk water by a multinational company for an entire municipality (although the British apparently failed to do even this effectively [Manson 1994, 12]). It is much less feasible to expect a municipality to effectively monitor the countless number of small private service providers sprouting up in poor urban areas. Corruption and bribery, in turn, find fertile ground in this kind of underfunded and scattered supervisory environment.

Matters are aggravated by the fact that South Africa has weak and fragmented pollution and waste legislation. A Draft White Paper on "Integrated Pollution and Waste Management for South Africa" was produced in 1998 in an attempt to deal with the problem, but according to Jan Glazewski (chap. 7 of this volume) "the draft remains a draft. . . . [and is too] general and lacking of any rigorous analysis of the legal system regulating and administering pollution control" to be of much use. The potential for the private sector to take advantage of loopholes in this legislation must be taken into account.

And finally, there are asymmetries of power between private sector providers and public service regulators that can distort the "independent" monitoring relationship of a private sector service provider. In Buenos Aires, for example, the independent regulator assigned to monitor a thirty-year contract to supply water and sanitation to the city has been largely marginalized. According to sources within the regulatory agency, the private firm that won the contract (Aguas Argentinas—a consortium of firms led by multinational giant Suez Lyonnaise des Eaux) has repeatedly ignored the regulator's requests for information, has allegedly bribed senior government officials to obtain extra-contractual price increases, and has continually postponed contractually committed investments in a new sewerage plant, leading to serious environmental problems with ground and surface water contamination (Loftus and McDonald 2001).

This Buenos Aires example is important because it is the largest water concession in the world, servicing more than nine million people, with considerable national and international attention being paid to it. There is also strong representation on the regulatory body by all three levels of government. If a regulatory agency fails to make a private company accountable under these circumstances, what can be expected to happen to the independence of regulatory agencies that operate outside the international spotlight and with much weaker government representation?[6]

Innovation

A final environmental argument in favor of privatization is that private firms are more innovative when it comes to the introduction and development of new, environmentally friendly technologies and systems. The reason firms are seen to be more innovative is that competition forces companies to search continuously for new technologies and new methods of service delivery that will give them a competitive advantage. The public sector, on the other hand, is deemed to be missing this innovative drive because of the lack of competition and incentive in the public system. Public service delivery, it is argued, will always lag several steps behind the private sector in terms of introducing new environmental technologies and systems (e.g., wet/dry refuse collection; hazardous waste treatment facilities; energy efficient generators).

While there are no empirical studies to back up or refute this claim, the track record in South Africa has hardly been encouraging. The provision of housing and services like waste management by private contractors in the country has been anything but creative, following well-trodden patterns of investment in energy-dependent and resource-inefficient systems of service delivery. Despite significant advances in areas of natural sewage treatment, low-flow toilets and showers, waste diversion systems, solar heating and power, better housing insulation, and so on, and despite the well-known problems associated with traditional service systems like landfill sites and waste incinerators, private contractors in South Africa have entrenched rather than challenged energy intensive and environmentally damaging systems. Overcapacity and overproduction of building materials no doubt plays a major part in the maintenance of these environmentally unsustainable practices in the housing market, but there would appear to be a more deep-seated problem with a lack of private sector innovation in the country with no notable environmental advances in any of the core services it delivers.

There has been some success in other countries with private firms developing environmentally friendly technologies and systems, but there is no reason to believe that profit is the only incentive for innovation. To the contrary, history and contemporary experience have shown that public institutions have been at the cutting edge of innovation in a wide range of fields, from the arts to the sciences, with no direct monetary incentives for their inventors. One need only think of the enormous creativity stemming from public universities and hospitals to acknowledge the potential for innovation in the public sector.

But it is the less celebrated, day-to-day public sector inventiveness that is important for our discussion here: the sewerage manager who develops a method of using fewer chemicals in the treatment process; the refuse collector who identifies more efficient ways of organizing collection routes; the urban planner who creates innovative and accessible open spaces. For every example of a lazy, unimaginative public employee, one can think of a counter-example of a public servant who has gone out of his or her way to provide a better service. (That World Bank officials, as public employees who pride themselves on innovation, should not recognize this incongruity in their own line of argument is ironic.)

Admittedly, the public sector in South Africa has not historically been renowned for its innovative tendencies. Apartheid-era municipal bureaucrats in particular tend to act more as obstacles to reform than as agents of change. But the civil service is changing demographically and in terms of skills and ideologies, and many new local government councilors in the country bring with them a deep sense of civic responsibility as spokespersons for the poor and marginalized and are committed to creating change.

There are also important sources of public sector innovation that have gone largely unexplored in South Africa—most notably among front-line workers. Municipal workers are at the coalface of service delivery and are arguably the most knowledgeable people in the country about the potential for efficiency and other innovative change. They are also keenly aware of the environmental impacts of the jobs that they do (McDonald 1994).

However, poor management-labor relations in municipalities (see for example MSP 2000), and an apparent unwillingness on the part of all three levels of government in South Africa to fund worker- or union-driven alternatives to privatization, have stifled the potential for workers and their union representatives to help develop creative public sector options. This is not for lack of trying. The South African Municipal Workers' Union has been extremely active in promoting environmentally sustainable and socially equitable public sector alternatives to privatization but these efforts have been marginalized politically or severely underfunded (for an example of the latter see Pape 2001).

This potential for public sector workers to think creatively about service delivery is all the more relevant in South Africa given that most workers, and many lower level managers and supervisors, go home at night to the squalor and danger of underserviced townships and informal settlements. They have a vested interest in improving service delivery that is not driven by monetary compensation.

The issue of "institutional memory" is also a factor here. With private firms regularly leaving service delivery networks as a result of competitive bidding, there is a potential loss of long-term institutional memory of service systems—knowledge that can be critical in terms of developing new and innovative ways of dealing with environmental "hot spots," the environmental expectations of the communities serviced, and an understanding of environmental trends and irregularities. This kind of information can be particularly useful in environmental emergencies, where it is critical to have workers and managers with an intimate knowledge of the areas they service. Private firms are unlikely to invest in this kind of institutional knowledge and innovation on a long-term basis given the relatively short duration of many service contracts.

How Much Is Enough?

One final question that we must ask ourselves is whether private sector service providers can deal effectively with issues of resource conservation. The primary focus of this chapter has been issues of *underconsumption* and the environmental implications associated with a lack of adequate services and infrastructure, but it is equally important to discuss the longer-term implications of privatization on the *overconsumption* of scarce resources like water and electricity.

Middle- and upper-income South African households are amongst the most profligate users of resources in the world. Per capita consumption of water, electricity, and other basic resources in historically white suburbs is as high or higher than that in any country in Europe and North America. It has been estimated, for example, that middle-class South Africans are responsible for up to two percent of global greenhouse gas emissions worldwide despite constituting an imperceptible fraction of world population (Eberhard and van Horen 1995). Similar resource abuses arise with water and refuse collection. While millions of poor South Africans go without adequate access to either of these services, middle-class suburbanites water their gardens, fill their swimming pools, wash their cars, and are responsible for the overwhelming proportion of solid waste going to landfill. Can privatization be expected to deal adequately with this issue? More importantly, how much is enough of a particular service and at what point does household consumption (and waste production) become environmentally problematic?

This question of "how much is enough" is, of course, an age-old environmental debate, and I do not intend to resolve it here. What I would like to do is suggest that the privatization of municipal services removes much of the political and moral leverage required to deal with this question effectively, based as it is on a demand-led approach to service delivery where the "customer is always right" and where the incentive to sell (or collect) as much of a product as possible is what motivates the private firm.

Under a demand-led service delivery system if you can afford the service you can have it. Private companies have no incentive to limit the amount of resources consumed or wastes produced (they profit from both) and they have no incentive to redirect resource/waste distribution in a more equitable manner (there is no money to be made from this). The ANC can ask, as Jay Naidoo (1995, 6), the former Minister responsible for the Reconstruction and Development Programme (RDP), did in the mid-1990s whether it is right to be watering gardens in white suburbs while homes in the townships have no water at all, but where is the institutional authority for this kind of resource allocation going to come from in a world of privatized services?

Privatization effectively depoliticizes societal decisions about resource consumption and distribution and leaves them to the rationale of the market. The state—through a regulatory agency or through legislation—can attempt to control consumption and distribution with the introduction of progressive step tariffs and minimum requirements for services, but power asymmetries between the regulator and the private company often make it difficult for the state to impose price increases that would restrict consumption at the upper end.

This is not to suggest that a centralized planning office be developed to monitor and make decisions about every aspect of urban consumption in South Africa. That is neither feasible nor desirable in a democratic society. But it is equally problematic to allow urban consumption patterns to be determined by little more than price mechanisms. The state and other non-market institutions (e.g., unions, civic organizations, environmental groups) must have significant input into how much per capita consumption of a particular service is acceptable in resource scarce or environmentally damaging situations. If there are limited supplies of key resources available, as there invariably are, and if access to these limited resources is badly skewed, as they continue to be in South Africa, there are good moral and political grounds for keeping the service in public hands.

The World Bank's position on this issue is that privatization will introduce its own conservation incentives through cost recovery (i.e., charging consumers the full costs of producing a service or removing and treating a waste rather than subsidizing these services, as governments often do). The problem with this line of argument is that even the full cost of a service may not be enough to curb consumption at the upper end. What is the likelihood, for example, that a family with a monthly income of R10,000 is going to dramatically alter its consumption of water even if the costs triple from R100/month to R300/month? As the ongoing drought concerns in Cape Town illustrate, it is only the occasional government-imposed water restriction that appear to have any significant dampening effect on water consumption in that city. Even in Hermanus, in the Western Cape, where the most progressive step tariffs for water have been instituted, price increases at the upper end have had limited success in curbing water consumption (while the gains that have been made may be attributable to other water-saving measures such as the removal of alien vegetation) (Deedat 2001).

Challenging the notion of growth is, of course, anathema to neoliberal thought and is one of the reasons that the question of overconsumption receives so little theoretical attention in the pro-privatization literature. Growth in consumption (and therefore waste) by the middle class is deemed absolutely necessary in the creation of a stronger economy in order to lift the poor out of poverty and environmental degradation. Growth is not a major environmental concern for neoliberal policymakers because it is assumed that we will always find new ways of alleviating its worst environmental side effects, either through clean technologies, better cost-benefit valuations, stronger laws, and/or market (dis)incentives. The privatization of municipal services fits nicely with this growth paradigm.

Conclusion

The environmental implications of privatizing municipal services at this point in South Africa's urban transition are potentially disastrous. Of greatest concern are the immediate environmental justice implications of privatization: companies red-lining poor neighborhoods; poor households receiving substandard services; worsening accountability and monitoring of private firms in black residential areas; and the public health and safety risks associated with environmental violations and poor working conditions. But longer-term consumption issues, and current distribution issues, are also critical, with privatization promising very little in the way of curtailing overconsumption or providing a more equitable share of resources.

What, then, are the alternatives? With national government retaining a tight grip on fiscal spending, and with a growing preference amongst politicians and bureaucrats for private sector service delivery at all levels of government, there would appear to be shrinking scope for the public sector to deal with the environmental injustices of inadequate service delivery. Despite the trends, however, the public sector remains the main provider of municipal services in South Africa and there is legislative and political space to push for continued and expanded support for the public sector option.

One of the first priorities of local governments should be full-scale audits of the human and capital resources available to them. Only then can managers and other stakeholders make informed decisions about the potential for public sector reform and/or the need for additional resources. Without this information decisions about privatization are being made in a vacuum and the potential for a more efficient and more equitable use of public resources may be lost forever. These audits should include an analysis of the resources available to cities from national government as well as the tax reform options available to local governments. If the public sector is indeed the "preferred" option for service delivery there is a need to commit resources to a better understanding of what these options are.

There is also a need for better cost-benefit evaluation techniques to assess the implications of privatization on the broader public good (health and safety, social stability, etc.). Ideally, these methods should be easily reproducible by lay persons so that governmental and non-governmental stakeholders can conduct their own methodologically sound evaluations of service delivery options. Good evaluations will depend on good information, however, which is why proper audits of public sector resources are so critical.

Finally, there is a need to engage municipal unions and civil society more fully in the planning and implementation of public services. As noted earlier, municipal workers are extremely knowledgeable about the services they deliver and about the environmental implications of service delivery, as are the residents who receive (or would like to receive) these services. But despite a strong commitment on the part of the ANC to community participation in service delivery, and its continued commitment on paper to "integrated development planning," relatively little has happened in the way of meaningful and sustained engagement with communities. Most service delivery decisions continue to be made by (apartheid-era) bureaucrats. If privatization entrenches these top down decision-making practices and makes service delivery companies less accountable to the public, as this chapter argues it does, the potential for a more democratic, equitable, and accountable environmentalism in South Africa's poorest urban neighborhoods is indeed seriously limited.

Notes

The author would like to thank Alex Loftus and Anita Kranjc for assistance with research for this chapter and Ian Ritchie for commenting on an earlier draft.

1. Johannesburg has been the most active in this regard with the introduction of its *iGoli 2002* program which lays the groundwork for the outright privatization of some services (Rand Airport, Metro Gas) as well as short- and long-term contracting out of a wide range of municipal services (e.g., water and sanitation, refuse collection). The cities of Nelspruit and Dolphin Coast have also signed long-term contracts for the management of their water systems by large multinational corporations. Cape Town has been less aggressive in promoting privatization but has outsourced a wide range of minor contracts and appears set to consider outsourcing, or at least corporatizing, a much broader set of core services like water, refuse, and sanitation (MSP 2000). Other towns that have extensively privatized

or outsourced municipal services include Stutterheim and Queenstown in the Eastern Cape and Beaufort West, in the Western Cape.

2. For a detailed account of the World Bank's role see Bond (2000b and c).

3. It is worth mentioning here that the national government approved R45 billion in expenditure on new military hardware at the same time as it was holding back on intergovernmental transfers.

4. Based on results of a survey conducted by David McDonald and Laïla Smith for the Municipal Services Project. A detailed report on this research will be published in 2001 as part of the Project's Occasional Papers series and can be found at http://www.queensu.ca/msp.

5. Personal communication with Roger Ronnie, Secretary General of SAMWU, 5 December 2000.

6. Despite these concerns the regulatory agency has been hailed as a success story by the World Bank and other pro-privatization organizations (Artana, Navajas, and Urbiztondo 1998, 1999), with the notable caveat from one group of researchers at the World Bank who criticized the regulatory agency for being "too political" and for delaying decisions because consensus must be reached amongst the competing interests of the six-member board (Alcazar, Abdala, and Shirly 2000).

References

Ahmad, J. 1995. "Funding the Metropolitan Areas of South Africa." *Finance and Development*, September.

Alcazar, L., M. A. Abdala, and M. M. Shirley. 2000. *The Buenos Aires Water Concession*. Washington, D.C.: The World Bank.

ANC (African National Congress). 1994. *The Reconstruction and Development Programme*. Johannesburg: Umyanyano Publications.

Artana, D., F. Navajas, and S. Urbiztondo. 1998. *Regulation and Contractual Adaptation in Public Utilities: The Case of Argentina*. Washington, D.C.: Inter-American Development Bank.

———. 1999. "Governance and Regulation in Argentina: A Tale of Two Concessions." In D. William, D. Savedof, and P. T. Spiller, eds. *Spilled Water: Institutional Commitment in the Provision of Water Services*. Washington, D.C.: Inter-American Development Bank.

Barchiesi, F. 2000. "The Politics of Municipal Solid Waste." Paper presented at the Urban Futures Conference, Johannesburg, 10–14 July.

Bartone, C., J. Bernstein, J. Leitman, and J Eigen.1994. *Towards Environmental Strategies for Cities: Policy Considerations for Urban Environmental Manage-*

ment in Developing Countries. Urban Management Programme Policy Paper 18. Washington, D.C.: World Bank.

Beal, J., and O. Crankshaw. 1999. "Victims, Villains and Fixers: The Urban Environment and Johannesburg's Poor." Paper presented at the conference on African Environments: Past and Present, Oxford University, 6 July.

Bond, P. 1999. "Basic Infrastructure for Socio-economic Development, Environmental Protection and Geographical Desegregation: South Africa's Unmet Challenge." *Geoforum* 30.

————. 2000a. "Municipal Privatization Debates." In P. Bond, *Cities of Gold, Townships of Coal: Essays on South Africa's New Urban Crisis.* Trenton, N.J.: Africa World Press.

————. 2000b. *Elite Transition: From Apartheid to Neoliberalism in South Africa.* London, UK, Sterling, Va., and Pietermaritzburg, South Africa: Pluto Press and University of Natal Press.

————. 2000c. "The World Bank Urban Agenda." In P. Bond, *Cities of Gold, Townships of Coal: Essays on South Africa's New Urban Crisis.* Trenton, N.J.: Africa World Press.

CISO (Criminal Intelligence Service of Ontario). 1993. *Organized Crime and the Environment.* Toronto: Criminal Intelligence Service of Ontario.

Cointreau-Levine, S. 1994. *Private Sector Participation in Municipal Solid Waste Services in Developing Countries Volume 1—The Formal Sector.* Urban Management Programme Discussion Paper 13. Washington, D.C.: World Bank.

Cook, C. 2000. "UK Environment Agency." Accessed online at http://www.environment-agency.gov.uk//modules/MOD44.1773.html

Cray, C. 1991. *Waste Management: An Encyclopedia of Crimes and other Misdeeds.* London: Greenpeace.

Crooks, H. 1993. *Giants of Garbage: The Rise of the Global Waste Industry and the Politics of Pollution Control.* Toronto: James Lorimer and Company.

CUPE (Canadian Union of Public Employees). 2000. *Who's Pushing Privatization: Annual Report on Privatization.* Ottawa: Canadian Union of Public Employees.

Deedat, H. 2001. "Hermanus: Playground of the Rich, Home to the Poor–Draft Report for the Municipal Services Project." Cape Town: Municipal Services Project.

Dumol, M. 2000. *The Manila Water Concession: A Key Government Official's Diary of the World's Largest Water Privatization.* Washington, D.C.: World Bank.

Eberhard, A., and C. van Horen. 1995. *Poverty and Power: Energy and the South African State.* London: Pluto Press.

EBIC (Environmental Background Information Center). 2000. "Corporate Profile: Waste Management Incorporated." Accessed online at http://www.ebic.org/pubs/wmx.html

Ferro, D. 2000. *El Servicio de Agua y Saneamiento en Buenos Aires: Privatización y Regulación.* Buenos Aires: CEER.

Gidman, P., with I. Blore, J. Loretzen, and P. Schuttenbelt. 1995. *Public-Private Partnerships in Urban Infrastructure Services*. UMP Working Paper Series 4. Nairobi: Urban Management Programme.

Hardoy, J.E., D. Mitlin, and D. Satterthwaite. 1993. *Environmental Problems in Third World Cities*. London: Earthscan.

Hawley, S. 2000. *Exporting Corruption: Privatisation, Multinationals and Bribery*. The Corner House Briefing, 19. London: Corner House.

Hoornweg, D., with L. Thomas. 1999. *What a Waste: Solid Waste Management in Asia*. Urban and Local Government Working Paper Series 1. Washington, D.C.: World Bank.

IDRC (International Development Research Centre). 1992. *Cities in Transition: Towards an Urban Policy for a Democratic South Africa*. Ottawa: International Development Research Centre.

———. 1995. *Building a New South Africa: Environment, Reconstruction and Development*. Ottawa: International Development Research Centre.

Khan, F. 1991. "Environmental Sanitation." In M. Ramphele and C. McDowell, eds. *Restoring the Land: Environment and Change in Post-Apartheid South Africa*. London: The Panos Institute.

Khosa, M. 2000. "'Facts, Fiction or Fabrication?' Service Delivery, 1994–1999." In M. Khosa, ed. *Empowerment Through Service Delivery*. Pretoria: Human Sciences Research Council.

Lawson, L. 1991. "The Ghetto and the Greenbelt: The Environmental Crisis in the Urban Areas." In J. Cock and E. Koch, eds. *Going Green: People, Politics and the Environment in South Africa*. Cape Town: Oxford University Press.

Leitmann, J. 1994. *Rapid Urban Environmental Assessment: Lessons from Cities in the Developing World Volume 1—Methodology and Preliminary Findings*. Urban Management Programme Discussion Paper 14. Washington, D.C.: World Bank.

Loftus, A., with D. McDonald. 2001. "Of Liquid Dreams: A Political Ecology of Water Privatization in Buenos Aires." *Environment and Urbanization* 13 (2).

Manson, J. 1994. "At the Limits: The Success and Failure of Water Privatization in Britain." *The Urban Age* 2 (2).

McDonald, D. 1994. "Black Worker, Brown Burden: Municipal Labourers and the Environment." *South African Labour Bulletin* 18 (5).

———. 1996. "The Politics of Ecology in South Africa: Urban Governance and Environmental Policy in Cape Town." Ph.D. diss., University of Toronto.

———. 1997. "Neither From Above, Nor From Below: Municipal Bureaucrats and Environmental Policy in Cape Town, South Africa." *Canadian Journal of African Studies* 30 (2).

———. 1998. "Three Steps Forward, Two Steps Back: Ideology and Urban Ecology in the New South Africa." *Review of African Political Economy* 75.

———. 2000. "E.Coli: Hard Lessons from Canada." *Services For All: The Newsletter of the Municipal Services Project* 1.

McDonald, D., and L. Smith. 2001. "Privatizing Cape Town: From Apartheid to Neoliberalism in the Mother City—Draft Report." Cape Town: Municipal Services Project.

MIIU (Municipal Infrastructure Investment Unit). 2000. Accessed online at http://www.miiu.org.za/mission.html, 10 December 2000.

Mulgan, R. 2000. "Comparing Accountability in the Public and Private Sectors." *Australian Journal of Public Administration* 59 (1): 87-97.

———. 1997a. "Contracting Out and Accountability." *Australian Journal of Public Administration* 56 (4): 106-16.

———. 1997b. "The Processes of Public Accountability." *Australian Journal of Public Administration* 56 (1): 25-36.

MSP (Municipal Services Project). 2000. "Comments on the Unicity Commissions Discussion Document: Developing the Future City of Cape Town," mimeo.

Naidoo, J. 1995. "Taking the RDP Forward: Report to Parliament." Pretoria: Government Printers.

Pape, John. 2001. *Poised to Succeed or Set Up to Fail.* Municipal Services Project Occasional Papers Series 1. Cape Town: Municipal Services Project.

PSIRU (Public Services International Research Unit). 2000. Accessed online at http://www.psiru.org/news/2910.htm

RDSN (Rural Development Services Network). 2000. "Water For All: Meeting Basic Water and Sanitation Needs." June, mimeo.

Roberts, A. S. 2000. "Less Government, More Secrecy: Reinvention and the Weakening of Freedom of Information Law." *Public Administration Review* 60 (4): 308-20.

RSA (Republic of South Africa). 1994a. "Reconstruction and Development." White Paper. Cape Town: Government Printers.

———. 1994b. Local Government Transition Act of 1993. Cape Town: Government Printers.

———. 1995. "Municipal Infrastructure Investment Framework." Pretoria: Government Printers.

———. 1998a. Draft White Paper on "Integrated Pollution and Waste Management for South Africa." Pretoria: Government Printers.

———. 1998b. National Water Act. Pretoria: Government Printers.

———. 1998c. National Environmental Management Act. Pretoria: Government Printers.

———. 2000a. "Municipal Infrastructure Investment Framework (MIIF): Draft." Department of Provincial and Local Government, February, mimeo.

———. 2000b. Local Government Property Rates Bill. Pretoria: Government Printers.

———. 2000c. White Paper on "Municipal Service Partnerships." Pretoria: Government Printers.

Sclar, E. 2000. *You Don't Always Get What You Pay For: The Economics of Privatization.* Ithaca and London: Cornell University Press.

Schuttenbelt, P., and J. Lorentzen. 1994. "Public-Private Partnerships in Municipal Infrastructure Services." *The Urban Age* 2 (4).

Serageldin, I., M. Cohen, and K. Sivaramakrishnan, eds. 1994. *The Human Face of the Urban Environment: Proceedings of the Second Annual World Bank Conference on Environmentally Sustainable Development.* Environmentally Sustainable Development Proceedings Series 6. Washington, D.C.: World Bank.

Serageldin, I., and A. Steer, eds. 1994. *Valuing the Environment: Proceedings of the First International Conference on Environmentally Sustainable Development.* Environmentally Sustainable Development Proceedings Series 2. Washington, D.C.: World Bank.

Shin, E., M. Hufschmidt, Y. Lee, J. Nickum, and C. Umetsu, with R. Gregory. 1997. *Valuating the Economic Impacts of Urban Environmental Problems: Asian Cities.* Urban Management Programme Working Paper Series 13. Washington, D.C.: World Bank.

Stren, R., E. Rodney, R. White, and J. Whitney. 1992. *Sustainable Cities: Urbanizing and the Environment in International Perspective.* Boulder, Colo.: Westview Press.

UNDP-World Bank. 1998. *Water and Sanitation Program Report 1997–98.* Washington, D.C.: United Nations Development Programme—World Bank.

Unicity Commission. 2000. "Discussion Document: Developing the Future City of Cape Town." August, mimeo.

Wilson, F., and M. Ramphele. 1989. *Uprooting Poverty: The South African Challenge.* Cape Town: David Philip.

World Bank. 1992. *World Development Report 1992: Development and the Environment.* New York: Oxford University Press.

———. 1994a. *World Development Report 1994: Infrastructure for Development.* New York: Oxford University Press.

———. 1994b. *Making Development Sustainable: The World Bank Group and the Environment Fiscal 1994.* Washington, D.C.: World Bank.

World Bank-UNCHS. 1999. *Cities Alliance for Cities Without Slums: Action Plan for Moving Slum Upgrading to Scale.* World Bank Group Annual Meetings 1999 Special Summary Edition. World Bank and United Nations Centre for Human Settlement (UNCHS-Habitat).

Contributors

PATRICK BOND is Associate Professor at the University of the Witwatersrand Graduate School of Public and Development Management in Johannesburg, where he is also Co-Director of the Municipal Services Project. Bond has served as a senior policy advisor to the South African government's Office of the President and numerous agencies, including the Department of Water Affairs and Forestry, as well as to provincial and municipal governments, trade unions, township civic associations, and environmental groups.

JACKLYN COCK is a professor of sociology at the University of the Witwatersrand in Johannesburg and has written extensively on issues relating to gender, the environment, and militarization. She is the author of *Maids and Madams* and *Colonels and Cadres*, and co-editor of *Going Green: People, Politics and the Environment in South Africa*.

BELINDA DODSON has an Honours degree in Geography from the University of Natal in Pietermaritzburg and a Ph.D. from Cambridge University. She was a lecturer in the Department of Environmental and Geographical Science at the University of Cape Town from 1990 to 1997. Her research interests include migration, gender, development, and environmental issues. Dodson is currently a research associate with the Southern African Research Centre at Queen's University in Canada.

DAVID FIG has a Ph.D. from the London School of Economics and Political Science and teaches sociology at the University of the Witwatersrand, Johannesburg. He has been Director of the Group for Environmental Monitoring in Johannesburg and from 1995 to 1999 he served on the Board of South African National Parks. He also represented NGOs on the management team of the Consultative National Environmental Policy Process, on the National Climate Committee, and on the national biodiversity policy reference group. Currently he serves on the boards of Biowatch South Africa, LEAD Southern Africa, and the Wits School of the Environment.

JAN GLAZEWSKI is Professor of Law in the Institute of Marine and Environmental Law at the University of Cape Town. He teaches, researches, and consults in the field of environmental law and is author of a leading textbook, *Environmental Law in South Africa*. He was involved in getting environmental rights incorporated in both the Namibian Constitution (1990) and the current South African Constitution (1994).

DAVID HALLOWES and **MARK BUTLER** are independent researchers based at *Critical Resource* in Pietermaritzburg where they conduct research and facilitations, mainly for civil society organizations working in the development field in South Africa. Their emphasis is on environmental justice issues.

FARIEDA KHAN is a longtime researcher in the field of South African environmental history, and a doctoral candidate in the Department of Environmental and Geographical Science at the University of Cape Town. She is also an independent consultant, specializing in social impact assessment.

PETER LUKEY is a veteran of the South African green movement. As a civil engineering technician, ecologist, and freelance environmental consultant he was involved in the founding of Earthlife Africa and has been active within the environmental justice movement since the late 1980s. From 1995 to 2000, Lukey was the Environmental Programme Coordinator for the Danish Cooperation for Environment and Development (DANCED) programme in Southern Africa.

THABO MADIHLABA is National Projects Coordinator at the Environ-mental Justice Networking Forum (EJNF), where he has worked since 1996. Actively involved in mining and environment issues with com-munities throughout South Africa, Madihlaba is a former trade unionist (NEHAWU) and a trained health professional.

DAVID A. MCDONALD is Director of Development Studies at Queen's University in Canada and is Co-Director of the Municipal Services Project. A political economist and geographer, McDonald has been working in the area of urban infrastructure and environmental justice in South Africa since the early 1990s, predominantly in Cape Town.

DUDLEY MOLOI is a freelance writer based in South Africa.

NJONGONKULU NDUNGANE is the Anglican Archbishop of Cape Town.

MPUME NYANDU is a freelance writer based in South Africa.

BOBBY PEEK is an environmental activist and Director of *groundWork* in Pietermaritzburg, a nongovernmental organization that promotes en-vironmental justice and community-driven sustainable development. From 1996 to 1999 he was the National Community Campaign Coordi-nator for the Environmental Justice Networking Forum (EJNF). His work in South Durban received recognition in 1998 when he was awarded the prestigious Goldman Environmental Prize for Africa.

GREG RUITERS is a lecturer in political studies at the University of the Witwatersrand. He is currently completing a Ph.D. at Johns Hopkins University on water privatization in the Eastern Cape and is Co-Director of the Municipal Services Project.

Index

Addo National Park, 35
African National Congress (ANC): as
ally of environmental justice movement, 2, 131, 316, 319; as part of coalition, 133; Freedom Charter of,
113; legislative reforms of, 2, 6, 8,
101, 207, 229, 252, 292–93, 300–
302. *See also* post-apartheid reconstruction; Reconstruction and Development Programme
African National Soil Conservation Association (ANSCA), 23
African Wildlife Society, 23–24
agricultural development. *See* development: agricultural
Agulhas National Park, 143
Ahwahneechee Indians, dispossession
of in United States, 136
AIDS, in Lesotho, 238
Alexandra Township: and LHWP, 227–
30, 243–53, 256–61, 266; "East
Bank" of, 109–11
Aloes, toxic waste site in, 203, 205–6,
220–22, 265
ANC. *See* African National Congress
ancestral land. *See* dispossession
Anglo American Corporation, 163, 170,
209, 233

Angola: and apartheid, 74; slaughter of
wildlife in, 24
ANSCA. *See* African National Soil Conservation Association
anthropocentricism, of environmental
justice, 3, 83, 284
anti-apartheid activists: noninvolve-
ment of in environmental debates,
1, 7; unbanning of, 2, 28, 115, 160,
277
anti-racism movement, in United
States, 114–15
apartheid: and development, 68; Betterment Planning initiative of, 67, 73;
end of, 5–6, 28; government policies
during, 1–2, 55–57, 62, 74, 136, 171,
179, 232; impact of on environment,
93–98, 102, 131–33; racial planning
of, 71
archaeological sites, in national parks,
133, 148
Argentina. *See* Buenos Aires
asbestos, dangers of, 7, 31–32, 71, 159,
199–201, 280
Asmal, Kader (Minister of Water Affairs
and Forestry), 203–4, 208, 210–13;
and LHWP, 223, 228, 233, 236, 243,
252, 255–56, 260–61